My Black Stars

From Lucy to Barack Obama

My Black Stars

From Lucy to Barack Obama

Lilian Thuram

with the collaboration of Bernard Fillaire
Translated by Laurent Dubois
Edited by David Murphy
(assisted by Charles Forsdick and Aedín Ní Loingsigh)

LIVERPOOL UNIVERSITY PRESS

Originally published in French under the title, *Mes Étoiles Noires: De Lucy à Barack Obama* (Philippe Rey, 2010).

This translation of *Mes Étoiles Noires* is published by arrangement with Fondation Lilian Thuram, copyright holder of the original edition.

The works referenced in the text are included in the bibliography at the end of the volume. Where published English-language translations of French-language texts already exist, these have been used, and are referenced in the bibliography. All other translations are by the translator.

Map on pages 280–81 © Fondation Lilian Thuram/Design: Lépac (www.lepac.org), 2015.

This translation published 2021 by
Liverpool University Press
4 Cambridge Street
Liverpool
L69 7ZU

British Library Cataloguing-in-Publication data
A British Library CIP record is available

ISBN 978-1-80085-917-3

Typeset by Carnegie Book Production, Lancaster
Printed and bound by CPI Group (UK) Ltd, Croydon CR0 4YY

To my first and greatest star, my mother, Marianna

To my sisters, Martine and Liliana

To my brothers, Gaëtan and Antonio

To my sons, Marcus and Khephren

And to all the world's children

Contents

Acknowledgements

The author would like to thank: Lucie Alves, Alain Anselin, Agnès b., Serge Bahuchet, Cécile Berger, Vincent Bessières, Pascal Blanchard, Claude Boli, Pascal Boniface, Anne Bosco, Jackie Vernon Boyd, Pascal Brice, Philippe Broussaud, Jacques Bungert, James and Laurence Burnet, the team at B. World Connection, Olivier Cachin, Juan Campmany, Martine Castro, Yves Coppens, Christine Coste, Thierry Demaizière, Paul Demougeot, Hugues Després, Rokhaya Diallo, Cheick Modibo Diarra, Doudou Diène, Cheik M'bake Diop, Louise-Marie Diop-Maes, Yandé Christiane Diop, Marcel Dorigny, Elsa Dorlin, Laurent Dubois, Rachel Dugan, François Durpaire, Patrick Estrade, Mireille Fanon-Mendès France, Charles Forsdick, Mostafa Fourar, Muriel Gauthier, Martine Geiger, Henriette Girard, Édouard Glissant, Dieudonné Gnammankou, Alfons Godall Martinez, Olivier Guilbaud, Catherine Guillebaud, Jean-Claude Guillebaud, Mary Ann Hennessey, Françoise Héritier, Stéphane Hessel, Evelyne Heyer, Ninian Hubert Van Blyenburgh, Rachel Khan, Serge Kotchounian, Richard E. Lapchick, Joan Laporta Estruch, Yannis Marian, Thierry Marszaleck, Stéphane Martin, Achille Mbembe, Elikia Mbokolo, Nathalie Mercier, Anne Meudec, Philippe Miclot, Edgar Morin, Rachel Mulot, David Murphy, Maguy Nestoret, Aedín Ní Loingsigh, Sylvie Ofranc, Josep Ortado, Sif Ourabah, Ian Peisch, Ghislaine Prévos, Pierre Raynaud, Christophe Réthoré, Carole Reynaud Paligot, Maurice Rives, Anne Roussel-Versini, Marie Santiago, Isabelle Sauvé, Marta Segú i Estruch, François Sémah, Christian Séranot-Sauron, Sylvia Serbin, Françoise Sule, Jean-Claude Tchikaya, Alban Teurlai, Jane Tiberi, Odile Tobner, Tzvetan Todorov, Dominique Valbelle, Jean-Louis Valentin, Gilles-Marie Valet, Françoise Vergès, and the team at Maison des Civilisations et de l'Unité Réunionnaise (MCUR), Paul Vergès, Anna Vicente, Rafael Vila San Juan, Marga Villoria, Michel Wieviorka, Julia Wright, Gihane Zaki.

Thanks to Bernard for his patience and for being such an attentive listener.

And a big thank you to Lionel Gauthier ... for everything.

Introduction

When was the first time you heard about black people in school? When I ask this question, most people reply that it was in connection with slavery.

I remember the first time they talked to us about slavery at school. I was the only black person in my class. I was shocked and began to wonder what my ancestors had done before they were enslaved? I didn't dare to ask the question though, as I felt stamped, branded, and all alone in the classroom. From that day on, I saw the other pupils differently. And they probably saw me differently too. At that time, slavery meant just one thing to me: 'whites enslaved blacks'.

To understand my reaction, you need to put yourself in my shoes as a child. Just imagine a young white pupil who has never once in school heard mention of a white scientist, political leader, revolutionary, philosopher, artist, or writer. Imagine that child faced with a universe in which everything beautiful, profound, moving, delicate, original, pure, good, subtle, and intelligent was uniformly black – a universe in which God, the Supreme Being, was also black. Imagine how disturbing this would be for that child. The child would wonder: was there ever a moment, in the history of the world, when a white person did something good? Then one day, as prescribed by the curriculum, the child would finally be offered this information about themselves: 'Your ancestors were slaves.' If this were all the child learned about the past, the experience of learning history in school would inevitably make them feel inferior. What a limiting model to give a child for thinking about their future! What a limited vision of history and identity!

As the years passed, the questions in my head became ever more pressing. I heard black adults around me say that whites were racist, that they would never change. In my life, however, I've been lucky enough to meet different people who, each in their own way, have given me the tools to understand history. They have taught me about many other great individuals in human history beyond those I learned about in school. In particular, they taught me about a wide range of *black stars*, heroes whose names, works, deeds, and achievements were totally unknown to me.

I came to understand that slavery was not so much a confrontation between whites and blacks, but an economic system, an ordered and organized activity, a carefully planned trade that bought and sold human beings. In fact, whites have at times been enslaved too: the proof is that the word 'slave' originally comes from the name Slavonia, a region of Eastern Europe where people were once bought and sold.

I regularly visit schools to discuss racism. I ask the children how many races there are. Sadly, they often reply: 'Four: white, black, yellow, and red'. That answer reveals to us the very basis of racism. It's shocking that children still don't know that there is only one human species, *Homo sapiens*. And then when I ask them about the characteristics of different races, they say: 'Black people are really good at sport, they're good singers and dancers...'

This is happening in the early twenty-first century. What conclusion can we draw other than that our educational system has failed? When you look at our society, you can't blame these children. These kinds of representations are still embedded in the broader social unconscious. We will only know that mindsets are changing when books and the posters on school walls show scientists and inventors of all colours, when the history of the great African, Asian, and Amerindian civilizations – like those of Mali, India, or Mexico – are taught in our schools.

If we really want to change society and fight racism, we can't depend on affirmative action or an assertion of a group identity. Only a change in our collective imagination will bring us closer together and break down cultural barriers. Only that will enable us to overcome the major obstacles hidden behind words like 'visible minority', 'diversity' – the sense of 'us' and 'them' that is determined by people's skin colour.

As long as we remain prisoners of the ideology of the nineteenth-century scientists who classified men and women as 'superior' or 'inferior', we will be unable to understand that the black soul, black people, and black thought don't actually exist any more than than there exists a white soul or white people or white thought. These are social constructs. Blackness does not exist any more than whiteness does. There is no black mission, no white man's burden, no black ethic, no white intelligence. There is neither black history nor white history. We have to tell the history of the whole world so that we can better understand humankind, and prepare for our children's future. With this book, I hope to contribute to that project.

Our African 'Grandmother'

Lucy

3,180,000 years ago

We share a common origin. In the beginning we
were all Africans, born three million years ago,
and that should inspire in us a sense of fraternity.
Yves Coppens

To open this long history of black women and men, where else
could I start but with the story of the First Man? Humanity was
born in Africa, all researchers are agreed on this. The 80 billion
Homo habilis, *erectus*, *sapiens* who have followed since then all have
the same origin. So, in a way, discussing the history of black people
involves talking about women and men of all colours. That is the
central idea of this book.

Whether we are descendants of *habilis* (the first), *erectus* (the
second), or *sapiens* (the modern), I like the idea of *Homo* because it
symbolizes the spirit of curiosity, ingenuity, and discovery. But we
actually need to go back much further, to the pre-humans, to Lucy,
born in East Africa 3,180,000 years ago, because she represents the
entire pre-historic age.

If we stick to strict scientific categorization, then Lucy certainly
wasn't a human being. But she belongs to the group of species that
formed the pool from which the ancestors of humanity emerged.
She is one of the 'flowers in the bouquet' of pre-humans. Lucy is
the mascot of humanity, our symbolic grandmother, even if her
'foundational' status has now been surpassed by the discovery of a
6-million-year-old Kenyan, a 5.7-million-year-old Ethiopian, or by
Toumaï, who lived in Chad around 7 million years ago.

To learn about Lucy, I talked to Yves Coppens, a Professor at
the Collège de France and the man who discovered her together
with Donald Johanson and Maurice Taïeb. Yves Coppens is not just
a researcher. He's also a teacher and storyteller. He defines Lucy's

history as 'the story of the history of the heroine of the story of the history of Man'. Hers is a foundational tale that teaches us a great deal about ourselves, and anchors us in time immemorial.

'In the middle of a rectangle 10 metres long by 2 metres wide, open to the sky and eroded by runoff water, dozens of little bits of bone stuck out of the ground, hinting at the presence of an almost complete skeleton.' For researchers, the discovery of this first fossil, on 24 November 1974 in the Ethiopian hills of Afar, remains unforgettable.

This remarkable witness to the birth of humanity had miraculously survived predators, erosion, and the other ravages of time. The night they discovered her, Yves Coppens and his collaborators worked under a tent to finish marking out their amazing find. Champagne corks were popped in celebration and someone put on a tape of The Beatles singing *Lucy in the Sky with Diamonds*. And that's how this gentle and familiar name was unanimously chosen to christen Lucy! The name sounds less harsh and is easier to pronounce than the catalogue number, AL 288, or the scientific name, Australopithecus Afarensis. As for the Ethiopians on the expedition, they called her *Birkinesh*: 'You are a marvel.'

How should I describe Lucy, the first black star of this book? 52 small, identifiable bones. 52 fragments that allow us to decipher and understand her existence. After adjusting them, the researchers were able to determine her age and her size. They estimated her weight. They hypothesized about how she walked, what gestures she used, how her voice sounded. They inferred what she ate, what her social life might have been like, and how she died.

Lucy was 1.2 metres tall and weighed between 20 and 25 kilograms. The curve of her spine proves that she stood upright. She was a biped: she walked! The discovery of a series of footsteps belonging to two individuals, who walked side-by-side, in northern Tanzania, a few hundred thousand years before Lucy, confirms this. And the traces she left reveal that she had a narrow heel and curved toes.

More specifically, when she walked Lucy swung her hips. Due to the instability of the articulation of her hips, she swayed as she moved. In fact, Lucy walked like a human but climbed trees like a monkey. She spent half her time hanging from branches.

Her larynx wasn't far enough down her throat to make it possible for her to speak words. She preferred using sign language and, when she had to warn her companions, she shouted. Based on the wear on her teeth, researchers have concluded that she lived in a tree-lined savannah where she ate fruit and young plants, but also roots and tubers, as well as perhaps insects and the carcasses of small creatures.

Lucy was part of a group of a dozen individuals who controlled a territory somewhere between 10 and 90 square kilometres. The terrain was often hostile. But as she was clever and inventive, she was able to escape the curved teeth of the *Machairodus* (a type of big cat) and the horns of the *Dinotherium* (a type of elephant).

Lucy is a 'woman', as the anatomy of her hip bones shows. And she is a 'black woman'. In order to protect her from the strong UV rays of the sun in tropical Africa, her body, which was perhaps hairless, secreted a high density of melanin, a pigment that is dark maroon in colour. In fact, there is no white, yellow, or black, just a single colour, maroon, that goes from lighter, when the production of melanin is lower, to darker, when it is higher. Skin is a biological umbrella that is adjusted according to the level of UV rays that might pass into the body.

In a way, there is nothing more simple or natural than this beautiful colour, which has led to the spilling of so much ink – and even more blood. It is only a problem to have extremely fair skin in a hot country, or to have very dark skin in a country without light, which can lead to a lack of Vitamin D in children as they grow up.

We can imagine that Lucy's hair was curly and dense. In hot countries, hair serves to retain the perspiration from the head, and so to limit dehydration. In colder countries, hair is straighter and spaced out more to allow for the circulation of water.

If you get rid of the corporeal envelope of a human being and delve inside the body, it is impossible to determine its origin. Whatever their colour, there will always be 639 muscles and 5 litres of blood. Each human will always be 99.9% genetically similar to other humans.

It is estimated that 80 billion humans have walked the earth since our birth as a species. With the exception of twins, none of them have ever had the same genotype: each is unique. An analysis of all of the variable characteristics of the human genotype easily shows that the number of possible different individuals is much larger than the number of atoms in the universe (10 to the power of 80)! So those who insist on talking about race today should say that we are '7 billion different human races'.

The fact that we are all relatives, that all human populations have the same distant ancestors, explains why we have the same variations in our genes, no matter what we look like. All our genes are copies of the genes of the first humans.

Having given birth to half a dozen or perhaps a dozen children, Lucy died when she was 20, at the end of a full life. 20 was a ripe old age at a time when the body reached maturity by the age of 10. Was it due to her own weakness, to a mistake, to treachery, or to an accident that she drowned in a pond? She did drown – scientists have proof of that. No scavenger scattered her bones, and pond sediment surrounded her natural resting place.

Time passed. Since Lucy's death, layers of sediment have covered other layers of sediment. From generation to generation parents have transmitted different combinations of their genetic variations to their children. The skulls of Lucy's descendants developed and, over the generations, they became *sapiens*. As time went on, they began leaving their African home in greater numbers. More and more frequently, they left their African cradle, risking journeys beyond the savannah, penetrating the forests, crossing the oceans, the deserts, and the mountains. When they reached a hill, they climbed it. When they reached the peak, they wanted to go further. This is how Lucy's descendants gave birth to the entire world, right down to modern man – this 'African immigrant'.

The Black Pharaohs

Taharqa
Reigned 690–664 BCE

What if most people were to imagine blackness differently, a blackness populated by great black historical figures, pharaohs for example? I named one of my sons Khephren, after a pharaoh from the Ancient Egyptian Empire. I wanted to give him a broader vision of history. I wanted him to know, through his name, that the history of black people is so much more than the history of slavery.

In 2003 the Egyptologist Charles Bonnet made a discovery at the Doukki Gel site, in Nubia: a grave containing seven monumental statues, including one statue of the most glorious of the black pharaohs of the 25th dynasty: Taharqa.

'Taharqa', the Egyptologist writes, 'has a body of fine-grained black granite. His hair is covered with a skullcap decorated with two cobras. One wears a white crown, the other a red crown, and they form a double knot at the top of his skull, with their tails hanging down the back of his neck...

'His face has fine and regular features, and his slightly full lips appear to be smiling. His eyes are lined with paint, his eyebrows are thick and close together, his neck is strong, his shoulders large and round. A pleated loincloth surrounds his hips. On his feet are sandals decorated with a winged beetle that holds a round disk in its front legs. He wears a belt inscribed with the words: "The perfect God, Taharqa, living eternally."'

Taharqa was crowned king of Egypt in Memphis (just a few miles from contemporary Cairo) in 690 BCE. He came from the great black kingdom of Nubia, part of a lineage that included many prestigious ancestors. Nubia, located in the north of what is today called Sudan, was then the 'land of Kush'. It is mentioned in the Bible, in the Book of Isaiah 38:9 and 2 Kings 19. The capital of Nubia was Napata.

Today, few people know about Nubian civilization. But it was one of the great civilizations of antiquity. Nubia and Egypt, like twin sisters, were always in contact. As is the case in many families, there were times of peace and times of discord. The Egyptians needed metals from Nubia, its deposits of precious gems, the products of its livestock, and its military genius. The Nubians benefited from the Egyptians' manufactured goods. The two regions saw long periods of exchange, but also periods of conflict.

Long before the existence of Taharqa, around 1560 BCE, the Egyptians colonized Nubia and remained there until 1000 BCE. This period of coexistence, over 500 years, created a new civilization based on a set of shared ideas, a mixing of cultures in which each enriched the other. The Nubian elite sent their children to be trained in the court of the pharaohs, while the Egyptians learned much from the Nubians. The arts of war, religion, and the beliefs of the two became so intertwined with one another that the powerful priests of the Karnak temple were of Nubian descent.

Both the Nubians and the Egyptians worshipped Amon, god of air and fertility. His statue stands in the great temple at the foot of the sacred mountain of Gebel Barkal, in Nubia. A needle made of rock standing 74 metres tall juts out from the mountain. It looks like a cobra, the royal symbol. Depending on the time of day, it seems to be wearing either a white crown or a red one... In 1457 BCE Thutmose III, the 6th pharaoh of the 18th dynasty, had inscribed on a tablet that Amon had appeared to him in a dream and had inhabited Gebel Barkal. So Nubia and Egypt are really two halves of one kingdom, the kingdom of Amon, united in a mythical past.

Over the millennia, Egypt went through periods of prosperity and of decline. During the difficult times, it fragmented into a myriad of antagonistic principalities, and fell into political and cultural decline. This left Egypt vulnerable to invasion by its neighbours. In 747 BCE, taking advantage of the Egyptians' weakness, the Nubian king Piyé took power in the valley of the Nile, installing a dynasty of black pharaohs who left a profound mark on Egyptian civilization.

King Piyé conquered Thebes and took over the great religious centre of Memphis. The available chronicles describe the new pharaoh as a pious and honest man, who avoided the unnecessary shedding of blood and was merciful to his enemies. Thanks to these qualities, the ancient Romans and Greeks described his career as 'stainless'. Having pacified the north, he returned to the land of Kush and installed himself at Napata, where he died in 716 BCE.

The brother of Piyé, the pharaoh Shabaka, succeeded him. He established himself at Memphis, and fought victoriously against the Assyrian and Saite chiefs, reunifying the south and the north. He covered the country with temples, reinvigorating the cult of the Egyptian gods. The Nubian black pharaohs seem to have felt a duty to maintain religious traditions.

The Nubians clearly did not see themselves as 'foreigners' in Egypt, as this desire for religious revival demonstrates. Their conquest was not simply driven by a desire for expansion. Their motivations were deeper and more religious. The Nubians both thought and felt that they were the 'inheritors and ancestors' of the Egyptian pharaohs. Their domination was part of the divine order of things, a necessary return to the golden age of the unified kingdom of Amon, which could be considered the first monotheistic religion in human history. The black pharaohs of the 25th dynasty were, as Egyptologist Timothy Kendall writes, 'God's representatives on Earth, chosen to unify and protect his ancient kingdom'. We can understand their desire to return to Egypt the splendour of its past by striving for the rebirth of the traditions of the Ancient and Middle Empires.

The successor to Shabaka was Shabataka, the nephew of Piyé, who was crowned in 702 BCE in Thebes. During his 20-year reign, he maintained peace, strengthened Egyptian beliefs, and greatly developed the arts, in the spirit of his ancestors. His brother Taharqa succeeded him.

Taharqa, the black pharaoh whose great achievements are universally recognized, was part of the great lineage of the founders of the New Empire. Even more than his predecessors, he returned to ancient traditions: the pyramids as funerary monuments, the archaic style of hieroglyphs. His construction projects are legendary. He built temples throughout the entire nation, at Kasr Ibrim, Semna, Bouhen… He renovated Thebes, notably Karnak, where he expanded the sacred lake and erected a kiosk with columns 21 metres high in the main courtyard of the temple. The structures he built are astounding in their beauty and originality.

In Nubia, where he was born, he restored the temple of Gebel Barkal, a subterranean sanctuary, and the temple of Amon, where the rooms carved from the rock of the sacred mountain had been in ruins since their completion under Ramses II. He decorated the walls with inscriptions, repaired the pylons and columns, and had giant statues of lions made of red granite brought from lands far away. He supported new forms of sculpture that respected Egyptian tradition but were Nubian in character. In Meroe, the capital of Kush (or Nubia) in the sixth century, 50 pyramids remain to this day. There are nearly 300 in Sudan.

Fair and just, Taharqa pursued a policy of balance and harmony, respecting the 'law of Maât'. The Egyptian *Book of the Dead*, which is considered the 'Bible of Ancient Egypt', recalls its principles, the primary duties of the pharaoh:

> Practise justice and you will last on this earth.
> Comfort those who cry.
> Do not oppress the widow.
> Never expel someone from the property of their father.
> Do not attack the possessions of the nobles
> Avoid unjust punishment.

Facing threats from the princes to the north and from the Assyrians, Taharqa fought back and at first was strong enough to repel the invasion, earning him a mention in the Bible. But he was finally vanquished at Memphis by the Assyrian king, Assarhaddon, in 674 BCE.

The chronicles of that ruler recount:

> At 15 days march from Memphis, his royal residence, I fought continuously without interruption in a series of bloody engagements against Taharqa, the king of Egypt and Kush, whom the Gods curse. Five times, I struck him with the heads of my arrows, inflicting mortal wounds. Then I besieged Memphis, his royal residence, and I conquered it in half a day using mines, breaches, and assault ladders. I destroyed it, I knocked down the walls, and I set it on fire. As booty, I took his Queen, the women of his Palace, Ushankhuru, his presumptive heir, his other children, his possessions, his horses, an incalculable number of his livestock both big and small.

Defeated, having lost his entire family, his army, and the capital of Egypt, Taharqa retreated to Thebes to organize the resistance. Two years later, he reconquered Memphis and a part of Lower Egypt. But the successor of Assarhaddon, the legendary Assurbanipal, decided to put an end to this resistance. 'Inspired by an oracle,' he destroyed Taharqa's army in open country.

Taharqa, forced once again to take refuge in Thebes, reflected on these terrible defeats. He concluded they had been caused by the repetition of mystical events that announced the return of the forces of chaos in the divided land.

We know little about his final years, except that he ensured that the plan for the subterranean rooms of his pyramid tomb – an edifice 60 metres tall, the highest ever built in Sudan – was an exact replica of the symbolic tomb of Osiris, the god of the dead. Shattered by the forces of chaos, he identified with this god who had been eliminated by his brother Seth, then resurrected by Isis and Nephthys. Like Osiris, he would live on. The forces of evil would be driven out, and he would re-establish the Maât and the unity of the empire.

After his death, his successors perpetuated the tradition of ancient Egypt, convinced that they were the only legitimate guardians of the Sacred Mountain. For the great figures of Antiquity who would later flood into Egypt, it was Nubia that created Egyptian culture. Gaston Maspero, professor at the Collège de France, summarized how the thinkers of Antiquity saw the Egyptians in his book *The History of the People of the Orient* (1886): 'The near-unanimous testimony of ancient historians was that they belonged to an African race – meaning Negro – who were first established in Egypt, on the middle part of the Nile, and who descended gradually towards the sea, following the course of the river.'

The story of Taharqa and of the 25th dynasty is part of the widely accepted histories of the black pharaohs. I have chosen to focus on him as an example of 'Negritude' because, among the pharaohs, he is the only one unanimously recognized by researchers as such. But the nature and origins of the heritage of ancient Egypt are still a subject of controversy. Evoking the Egypt of the black pharaohs still stirs up strident debate and a mountain of prejudice.

The pioneer of the 'African school' was Cheikh Anta Diop (1923–86), a Senegalese academic whose research contributed to the reintegration of Egypt into broader African history. His work has been controversial. His thesis, which is that Egyptian civilization is part of the 'Black African' world, and that Western imperialism 'whitened' the prestigious land of Egypt specifically in order to justify colonialism, provoked a huge debate among French academics in 1954. Cheikh Anta Diop's position regarding Black Egypt is the result of both his scientific rigour and his sense of political engagement, from his support for the struggle against apartheid in South Africa, to the struggle for democracy and secularism in Senegal. The publication of Diop's *Negro Nations and Culture* in 1954 acted as a 'banner for a cultural revolution, which black people waved before a colonial power that had difficulty accepting that it was time to let go of its overseas territories' (to quote Lilyan Kesteloot, an historian of African literature). It was received enthusiastically by the writers of the Negritude movement. Aimé Césaire called the book 'the most audacious that a Negro has written until now and which will undoubtedly contribute to the awakening of Africa'.

Until the 1950s and 1960s, Western, European, and Arab historians always perceived ancient Egypt as integral to their own societies, but not as part of Africa itself. As a result, ancient Egypt was set apart from black Africa.

The attribution of civilization's great achievements to a mythical white migration is nothing new. In the nineteenth century, the discovery of the magnificent civilization of Zimbabwe induced an impassioned response from scholars throughout the world. 'The city was not constructed by Africans', the German scholar Karl March affirmed in 1871, 'because the style of construction is too elaborate: it is the work of Phoenician or Jewish settlers.' The English archaeologist Theodore Bent concluded around 1890 that the civilization of Zimbabwe was the work of 'the descendants of white invaders who came from the North'.

It was only in the twentieth century that Egyptologists like Jean Leclant, Professor at the Collège de France, and Jean Vercoutter, at the University of Lille, began their remarkable work on ancient Nubia. At an important international conference in Cairo in 1974, they declared that Egypt was 'African in its writing, in its culture, in its way of thinking'. The arguments of Cheikh Anta Diop had finally been accepted, at least in part.

Indeed, while in the United States his work is widely cited and recognized, a certain number of European researchers continue to dub him 'Afro-Centric'. They criticize him for having an ideological and non-scientific approach; they accuse him of having 'blackened' Egypt in order to awaken the consciousness of black Africans by offering them an illusory prestigious past. Since I am not an expert, I can't establish how much of this is true. But it doesn't diminish the fact that these texts show us that the kingdoms of Kush and Egypt were connected, that their exchanges were not only commercial, and that their cultures and populations were traditionally mixed. As for the possibility of power alternating between Egypt and Nubia, this is demonstrated by the reign of the 25th dynasty.

Cheikh Anta Diop's work brought about a profound change in perspective, but the history of Egypt still remains opaque to us.

That is not only because it was so long ago, but also because of the distorting effects of Western perspectives on this history. The reigns of the black pharaohs have not yet revealed all their mysteries.

In 1783, after a journey to Egypt, Volney, a French orientalist and philosopher, wrote: 'What a subject of meditation it is to see the current barbarism of the Copts, born of the alliance between the Egyptians' profound genius and the Greeks' brilliant spirit, to think that this race of black men, today our slaves and the object of our disdain, is the same to which we owe our arts, our sciences, and even the use of language...'

A Wise Man from Ancient Greece

Aesop

Seventh–sixth centuries BCE

About 2,500 years ago, a man known as 'The Cripple' (*aisopos* in Greek) lived between Samos and Delphi. He left behind 127 fables in prose, many of which were rewritten in verse by Jean de La Fontaine in the seventeenth century. In French schools, we still learn La Fontaine's rhyming versions of these fables in a way that imprints their morals on our minds. At the time of La Fontaine, Aesop's fables played a major role in education: pupils read *The Fox and the Crow, The Wolf and the Lamb, The Ant and the Cicada, The Fox and the Rose Bush, The Hare and the Tortoise, The Two Pots*, and many others. They were deeply influential and inspired many works in verse, drawing, painting, and later in comics and film.

There are two versions of Greek history. One presents Greek culture as essentially European, emblematic of white beauty. The other, which the Greeks themselves acknowledged during the Classical period, presents a hybrid world that arose from colonization of Greece by the Egyptians and the Phoenicians around 1500 BCE.

The Congolese historian Théophile Obenga, in his study, *Egypt, Greece, and the Alexandria School*, demonstrates that no Greek scholar ever doubted the intellectual and scientific superiority of the priests of the Nile Valley. Homer, Herodotus, Socrates, Plato, all recognized their debt to Egyptian civilization, which was at the origin of many of their own myths and customs.

Herodotus, for example, insisted on the fact that the astronomical calendar, which divided the year into 12 parts, was an Egyptian invention. Homer, around 850 BCE, affirmed that Egyptian doctors were the 'most knowledgeable in the world'. Aristotle wrote that 'Egypt was the birthplace of the mathematical arts'. The British historian Martin Bernal, in his famous book *Black Athena*, convincingly made the case that the roots of ancient Greece were Afro-Asiatic.

The lessons we learn in school are shaped by the prejudices inherited from the eighteenth and nineteenth centuries. At that time, it was unthinkable for the philosophers of the Enlightenment to imagine Greece as the product of the mixing of Europeans and African colonizers, as their society lived off the profits of slavery.

But according to the most recent studies, Aesop was a Nubian and was brought to Phrygia as a slave. His fables were probably inspired by tales from the region where he was born. Slaves have always resisted not only through amazing feats such as those of Spartacus but also through daily cultural rebellion. Aesop developed a refined intellectual strategy. It started with the constant observation of his master, whom he studied carefully in order to learn his weaknesses.

Through his short tales, Aesop found a way to swap places with his master. He subverted what was imposed on him in order to preserve the humanity that his master sought to take from him. Through his fables, he stood up and affirmed his dignity. They include advice about prudence, ability, and ingenuity. A true 'book of knowledge for dealing with adversity', they present a perfect set of moral principles. In *The Lion and the Mouse*, the mouse seems to be weaker, but in the end the lion is only a 'paper lion' since he needs the mouse to gnaw through the ropes imprisoning him.

Writings from this period rarely mention the 'Negro' Aesop, but they emphasize his frighteningly ugly appearance: 'a pig-monkey', 'a pot with legs', 'a tumorous jar', 'an amulet against the evil eye', 'the day's mistake'. He was described as potbellied, with a pointy head and pug nose, stooped, dark-skinned, shortish, knock-kneed, with short arms, bowed legs, and thick lips. As if that wasn't enough, his speech was muddled and inarticulate.

Make no mistake though. The truly frightening thing about him was the scale of his intelligence. The horrible depictions of Aesop only made him greater, underlining the contrast between the way he looked on the outside and the inventive, astute spirit within. Under the 'grotesque mask' were hidden 'fascinating images'.

Over the course of his life as a slave, Aesop fought constantly against his master Xanthos, whose name means 'blond'. The story of Aesop's life, then, is that of a 'blond' master constantly humiliated by his 'black' slave. It is the story of a master forced to beg for help from his slave, who sometimes even needed him to act on his behalf.

When his master died, Aesop was emancipated. He was barely out of slavery when he found his voice. He went to see Croesus on a diplomatic mission, which he carried out successfully thanks to the strategic use of a fable. He subsequently placed himself in the service of the 'King of Babylon', who greatly enjoyed his riddles and little stories.

Driven by a desire to travel, he went to Delphi. There he became drunk on his own talent, and his ego, like the frog in his fables, began to swell. His excessive pride led him to place a statue of himself next to one of the Muses. He turned his back on his origins, deriding the inhabitants of Delphi as 'sons of slaves' because they didn't have enough land to produce the food they needed.

This irritated the Delphians so much that they decided to rid themselves of Aesop. They secretly placed a sacred goblet in his luggage. As the ex-slave departed for Phocis, he was stopped and accused of theft. Found guilty, he was condemned to death by being thrown from a huge boulder near the temple of Delphi.

'As he was being carried to his execution', writes Jean de la Fontaine, 'he found a way to escape, and went into a small chapel dedicated to Apollo. The Delphians dragged him out. "You have violated this sanctuary", they declared, "because it is only a small chapel, but a day will come where your wicked ways will find no refuge, not even in the temples. The same thing will happen to you as happened to the eagle, who, ignoring the pleas of the snail, snatched up a hare who had taken refuge with him; the descendants of the eagle were punished to the very bosom of Jupiter."'

Soon after his death, a violent epidemic ravaged the population. The Delphians asked the oracle how they could appease the wrath of the gods. The oracle responded that there was nothing for them to do but to atone for their crime and fulfil their obligation to Aesop.

All children educated in French schools know the fables of La Fontaine. Teachers should explain the link between Aesop and La Fontaine, the black and the white. Teaching students that intelligence transcends colour is a way of educating against racism with sensitivity, humour, and judgement.

'Every Life is a Life'

The Hunters of Manden

1222 CE

In 1222, 567 years before the Declaration of the Rights of Man, on the day of the coronation of Soundiata Keita as the emperor of Mali, the Charter of Manden (or Mandé) was sung in the land of the Mandinka. The empire of Mali, then at its peak, stretched from the Atlantic Ocean to Niger. The increase in trade had brought great prosperity to the empire. According to historians, this Charter guaranteed a period of exceptional peace and liberty. It is a model of humanism and tolerance:

Every life is a life.

It is true that some lives begin before others,
But no life is more 'ancient', more respectable, than another life.
The hunters declare:
Since every life is a life,
Any harm done to a life requires reparation.
Therefore,
No one should attack their neighbour without cause
Or cause harm to those around them,
Or martyr those like themselves.
The hunters declare:
Everyone should watch over those around them,
Everyone should honour their parents,
Everyone should educate their children correctly,
Everyone should 'maintain', and provide for the needs of the members of their family.
The hunters declare:
Everyone should watch over the land of their fathers.
By land or country, we mean especially and above all the people;

For any country, any land that saw its people disappear from
   its surface would soon become nostalgic.
The hunters declare:
Hunger is not a good thing,
Nor is slavery a good thing;
There is no worse calamity than these things in this bad
   world.
As long as we hold on to the quiver and the bow;
Hunger will no longer kill anyone in Manden,
If famine were to venture to strike us
War will never destroy another village
In order to take slaves;
That is to say that from now on no one will place a bit in the
   mouth of those like them in order to sell them;
From now on no one will be beaten,
Or put to death,
Because they are the son of a slave.
The hunters declare:
The essence of slavery is extinguished today,
'From one wall to another', from one border to another of
   Manden;
Starting today, raids will be banned in Manden;
Starting today, the torments born of these horrors are over in
   Manden.
What suffering these torments have brought!
Especially when the oppressed has no recourse.
The slave enjoys no consideration,
Anywhere in this world.
People used to say to us:
'Man as an individual
Made of flesh and bone,
Of marrow and nerves,
Of skin covered with hair,
Nourishes himself with food and drink;
But his soul, its spirit, lives on three things:
Seeing what he wants to see
Saying what he wants to say
Doing what he wants to do;
If one of these things was lacking in the human soul,
It would suffer.
It would surely sicken.'
Therefore, the hunters declare:

From now on everyone has control over themselves,
Everyone is free in their actions,
From now on everyone is entitled to the fruit of their labour.
That is the oath of the Manden.
Addressed to the ears of the entire world.

These major principles of respect for human life, individual liberty, and the abolition of slavery were proclaimed by a brotherhood of hunters late in 1222. Quite a surprise for those who consider Africa to be a savage land, without a real history! One of the most perverse racist theories is the belief that the history of Africa can be reduced to slavery and colonization. In other words, that the history of black people only began the day Europeans first saw them! This reductive approach erases millennia of African civilizations, like those of Nubia, Kongo, Zimbabwe, etc. It supports the idea that black peoples are inferior intellectually, culturally, morally, and politically.

That is exactly what the French president Nicolas Sarkozy declared, one day in July 2007, in Dakar. He declared that the African had not yet 'entered sufficiently into history': 'The African peasant … only knows the eternal renewal of time, regulated by the rhythm of the same gestures and the same words. In this mindset where everything always starts over again, there is no room for human adventure or for the idea of progress.'

The fact that the representative of a powerful country like France could repeat, word for word, the racist writings of the eighteenth or nineteenth century – like those of Carl Linnaeus who declared that 'the Black African is guided by fantasy; the European man is guided by custom' (*Systema Natura*, 1758), or Victor Hugo who wrote of 'Africa, this block of sand and ash, this inert and passive slab, which for 6,000 years has stood in the way of universal progress' (1879) – demonstrates how deeply ingrained these theories are. In response, I offer this treasure of humanity, the 'Oath of the Hunters of Manden'.

This oath was translated by the Malian researcher Youssouf Tata Cissé, based on the tale told to him in 1965 by Fadjimba Kanté, the patriarch of the blacksmiths of Tégué-Koro (in Mali) and leader of the brotherhood of hunters. I can imagine a few mocking smiles at the idea of 'oral sources'. In the West, transmission can only occur through writing, and oral sources are viewed with suspicion.

But in Africa, oral transmission constitutes a powerful tradition. Its credibility, its power, and its impact are based on its precision. In African societies, one of the first conditions of its truth is that not everyone can presume to transmit these words. Only the caste of the Griots is entrusted with them, and they maintain the high standards of oral transmission. Over centuries, these Griots, women and men, have been taught within their ethnic groups to conserve the memory of events, of music, of myths, of what is said and left unsaid.

African oral transmission is the work of 'professionals' who transmit knowledge to one another, with the science of language necessary to express facts, data, locations, and people. It's not possible for just anybody to walk into an African village and claim to tell some story or other about their past. 'Where do you come from?' people will ask. 'From what family? How was this event transmitted to you? By whom?'

My Senegalese friend Doudou Diène – a diplomat and a consultant to the UN on contemporary forms of racist discrimination, xenophobia, and intolerance – was the director of a UNESCO (United Nations Educational, Scientific and Cultural Organization, created in 1945) research project called 'Slave Routes'. The team he led investigated slavery in Africa in the sixteenth century, and at first turned to written sources. But these were the writings of Europeans, which only reinforced existing forms of prejudice. The UNESCO researchers thought that there had to be another unwritten memory, that of Africans, whether they were enslaved or not, and they organized a conference about this oral transmission. This knowledge had been obscured, and it was imperative to give it back its legitimacy.

In 2003 UNESCO established a Convention for the Safeguarding of Intangible Cultural Heritage. In 2009 it added the Charter of Manden to the list representing this heritage.

In the West, as the anthropologist Claude Lévi-Strauss puts it, 'you get old without becoming an elder'. In Africa, elders are venerated for their knowledge of oral tradition. Or, to quote the words of the writer Amadou Hampâté Bâ to UNESCO in 1966: 'In Africa, when an old man dies, a library burns down.'

The Pride and Courage of a Queen

Anna Zingha

c.1582–17 December 1664

It was the year 1622. Princess Zingha had departed the province of Matamba, the last bastion of Angolan resistance against the Portuguese invasion. She marched towards Luanda, where the viceroy of Portugal awaited. Luanda was one of the coastal kingdoms that over the years had fallen into the hands of the Portuguese, leaving Angola without access to the sea. The princess's mission was to negotiate a treaty, which would be no easy task, given that her brother, King Mani Ngola, had just suffered a terrible defeat.

Princess Zingha had barely entered the main room of the Governor's Palace when her gaze froze. She saw the viceroy Don Joao Correia da Souza comfortably seated in an armchair. Across from him, a simple pillow on the ground was reserved for her. Her pride was injured and she refused to accept this humiliating insult. She summoned one of her servants and ordered him to allow her to use his back as a chair. Those assembled were alarmed and dazzled at the same time. An artist immortalized the scene, and his drawing of it soon became known around the globe.

Princess Zingha stayed in this position throughout the entire negotiation. The viceroy was disconcerted and began to lose his sense of superiority. He tried to hide his discomfort by acting ever more brusquely and multiplying his demands. He began with what he hoped would be a knockout punch, demanding that his soldiers who had been captured by King Mani Ngola should be immediately freed. The impassive princess calmly responded that she saw no harm in this, as long as all the men and women of her country who were held as slaves were also freed! Having lost the first round, the viceroy pursed his lips, played for time, and then finally addressed the key issue: the drawing up of new borders.

The princess surprised the viceroy by negotiating as though they were equals. She refused any shrinking of her kingdom's borders.

In the end, she obtained the withdrawal of Portuguese forces beyond the previously recognized borders, and the recognition of her sovereign power over the kingdom of Matamba. She conceded, nevertheless, that she needed to offer something in return. To satisfy both parties, she agreed to liberate Portuguese prisoners and to cooperate in the exchange of prisoners enslaved by her own people.

The viceroy seemed ready to accept this treaty, but not without trying to obtain an additional concession: the princess was to deliver 13,000 slaves per year, in return for so-called 'protection' by the king of Portugal! The princess struck back: 'Know, sir', she responded, 'that while the Portuguese have the advantage of possessing a civilization and knowledge that is unknown to Africans, the people of Matamba have the privilege of being in their own country where they are surrounded by riches that, despite all his power, the king of Portugal will never be able to offer to his subjects!'

It was difficult for the viceroy to refute this claim. After all, when in the sixteenth century their caravels first arrived off the coast of Angola, the soldiers had been welcomed like guests, pampered and fed by a population whose autonomy and brilliant organization were obvious. 'A veritable El Dorado of eight unimaginably fertile provinces, watered by many rivers and highly conducive to self-sufficient agricultural food production combined with cattle-raising', writes Sylvia Serbin in *The Queens of Africa and the Heroines of the Black Diaspora*. 'The villages, laced with alleys of orange, pomegranate, and lemon trees, were connected by well-maintained paths.' During the time of Princess Zingha, a century later, the area was still living through its golden age. 'Nature seemed, in that place, to take pleasure in assembling all the advantages that divine hands only granted separately in other lands', wrote one European traveller. 'Although black, the inhabitants of Angola are in general quite skilled and very clever.'

The Angolans and Portuguese might have continued to live peacefully, if the colonists had not quickly discovered the immense riches of the country! The Cuanza River, which ran through the kingdom, was full of diamonds. The news spread like wildfire...

Aimé Césaire wrote in *Discourse on Colonialism*: '[T]he great historical tragedy of Africa has been not so much that it was too late in making contact with the rest of the world, as the manner in which that contact was brought about; that Europe began to "propagate" at a time when it had fallen into the hands of the most unscrupulous financiers and captains of industry; that it was our misfortune to encounter that particular Europe on our path, and that Europe is responsible before the human community for the highest heap of corpses in history.'

It was pure greed that pushed the Portuguese king to order, in 1575, the appropriation of land and goods 'as far as possible'. But small groups of soldiers, weakened by the hardships of a trying ocean crossing, were in no position to succeed in carrying out such orders. And so a new strategy was developed to weaken its African colonies: mass deportation. The goal was to take away a nation's lifeblood and to introduce war and discord between various small kingdoms. In order to do this, the Portuguese forged alliances with certain petty kings along the coast who agreed to serve them. The two groups developed a 'vicious complicity', based on corruption – the foundation for all forms of slavery, colonialism, and neocolonialism. These local feudal lords captured their neighbours without difficulty and subsequently delivered them as slaves to the Portuguese in return for weapons, glass beads, and alcohol.

The slave trade not only filled the coffers of Europeans, but also emptied Africa of its greatest riches: its youngest and strongest women and men. This dismemberment of Africa was carried out over centuries and continues today through the same mechanism: the corruption of the political elites.

The resistance of Princess Zingha is as remarkable as it is emblematic. Her memorable entry into diplomacy was not accidental. She was 40 years old when she carried out her famous negotiation with the Portuguese and already had a great deal of political experience. Her father, the eighth king of Matamba, had initiated her at a young age into the mysteries of power and turned her into a true stateswoman. The princess was no frail young girl. She also had to endure violence at the hands of her own family.

Her brother, Mani Ngola, was impulsive, spineless, and thick-headed. He so hated the natural authority of his sister that when her child was born, fearing that he would steal his seat on the throne, he had the baby thrown into boiling water. Later, men in his pay captured Zingha and shoved an iron poker into her vagina to ensure that she would never have an heir.

Mani Ngola stopped at nothing to secure power. When his father died in 1617, he assassinated the designated successor to the throne. Dreaming of launching his reign with a glorious victory against the invader, he threw himself into a ridiculous war that led to the massacre of half his army. He lost 15,000 men.

This was the context in which Zingha carried out her memorable negotiation with the viceroy of Portugal. He was so fascinated by her majestic talent that he offered to play host to her while the treaty was being ratified back in Lisbon.

The few months the princess spent in Luanda shaped her future reign. She observed the way the Western soldiers were armed, and especially how they trained. She had spies inform her about troop movements and put her in contact with soldiers from the small kingdoms that had fallen under Portuguese control. She promised these soldiers land if they deserted and thus succeeded in recruiting many men trained in Western strategies of war.

At the same time, the princess observed and absorbed the culture and language of the invaders. When invited to church, she didn't simply admire the outfits and listen to the songs. She also considered the advantages she and the other sovereigns in the region might gain by embracing the religion of the Portuguese. She believed that conversion would place them on an equal footing and that the Portuguese would henceforth have to treat them with more respect.

No sooner said than done. She was baptized in the cathedral of Luanda. She chose the viceroy Don Correia da Souza and his wife Anna, who gave the princess her Christian name, as her godfather and godmother. So she became Anna Zingha.

Soon afterwards, however, the viceroy returned to Portugal. His successor, thirsting for gold and conquest, forced King Mani Ngola into a new round of conflict. In 1624 Ngola sent his troops into battle along the banks of the Cuanza River. Poorly prepared, they were wiped out by the overwhelming firepower of the Portuguese army, fuelled by the addition of 10,000 African mercenaries recruited in the Kongo. Mani Ngola managed to escape by jumping into the river. 'After swimming to a sand bank', Sylvia Serbin recounts, 'he was saved by two servants from the court who, by chance, were on the same tiny island. They tended to his wounds and gave him something to drink … In the moments before dying, struck down by poison, it dawned on the imprudent tyrant that Zingha had exacted her revenge.' So it was that she took power over the kingdom of Matamba.

Crowned as queen, Anna Zingha played for time with the Portuguese, negotiating each time they seemed to want to shrink the borders of her kingdom. She reassured them of her peaceful intentions, all the while preparing her arms and her troops. At the same time, she quietly rallied other states. The ends justified the means, so she had no misgivings. In order to convince the Jaga warriors, known for their bravery and even more for their cruelty, to join her, she invited them to a banquet where she displayed her determination and her power.

Years passed, during which she never ceded an inch of territory. Often she led her troops into battle herself.

In 1641 the Dutch fleet attacked the Portuguese colony at Luanda. The Portuguese were defeated. Queen Anna Zingha seized the occasion and offered the Dutch a monopoly over trade with Angola if they helped her to re-establish the rights of the Angolan sovereigns over their territory. So it was that, over the course of a few short years, the fortunes of Rotterdam were built, along with the peace of the Angolans. Thanks to the gold and diamonds contained within their soil, they were able to return to their villages and their farming.

But peace, unfortunately, was short-lived. In 1648 the Treaty of Westphalia guaranteed the independence of the United Provinces (present-day Holland) in exchange for its possessions in Africa and the Americas. The rules of the political game were set outside Africa, far from the talented Queen Zingha. Ironically, it was this European treaty that allowed Portugal to regain possession of Luanda.

The wars grew more intense, and Queen Zingha, now in her seventies, criss-crossed her kingdom at the head of her troops. Given that the war seemed to be accomplishing nothing but the wearing down of the two sides, a final treaty was signed. The king of Portugal declared that he would 'condescend' to grant a few provinces of his kingdom of Angola to the queen. Refusing as always to consider herself a vassal or dependent of the Portuguese king, Anna Zingha gave this courageous response:

> What right does he have over my states? Do I have rights over his? Is it because, today, he is the strongest? But the authority of the strongest reveals nothing more than power, and never legitimises such usurpations. Therefore the king of Portugal would simply be committing an act of justice, and not of generosity, in returning to me not a few provinces but my entire kingdom, over which neither his birth nor his strength gives him any kind of title.

The treaty was ratified in Lisbon on 24 November 1657 by King Alphonse VI. It would be respected by all parties.

Anna Zingha was 78 years old. During the final years of her life, she saw her kingdom at peace. She dealt with everyday issues, presided over the court of appeals, journeyed around her lands on horseback, reorganized the administration, and put into place a law of 'parity'. For each official position held by a man, a woman was named as deputy. Each was responsible for his or her own work. She demanded that the women of the Angolan nobility learn to read and write, and also to fight.

In popular memory, Queen Anna Zingha has remained a unique figure. But pride and courage are universal values.

The Struggle for a New Kingdom

Dona Beatriz

c.1682–1706

Towards the end of the 1600s, Dona Beatriz, a young girl born in the Kongo, lay tucked up in bed shivering with fever. Everyone thought she would die. Suddenly a man dressed in monk's clothing appeared to her in a vision. It was Saint Anthony who, in his celestial voice, urged her to live piously, 'to preach and to lead the people forward'. Immediately, her fever broke and the young girl came back to life. She explained her vision to her father and mother, telling them of the importance of this divine commandment. Compelled to obey it, she gave away all her riches and renounced all worldly property.

In his great wisdom, Saint Anthony instructed her to liberate the kingdom of the Kongo from the Portuguese invaders who, with the Pope's blessing, had launched the slave trade in 1455. He also commanded her to return the exiled King Pedro IV to his throne in Sao Salvador, and to cure the people of their misery.

Dona Beatriz set out to fulfil her duty...

Dona Beatriz was born in the Kongo, a prosperous kingdom that included parts of the present-day Democratic Republic of the Congo, Angola, and Gabon. The territory totalled 300,000 square kilometres. Kongo means 'a circle, the universe, the centre of the universe'. Why did France later impose a 'C' as the 'correct' spelling of this name? Using a 'C' distorts the meaning of the country's name, misrepresents its women and men, and falsifies the ancient history of a people.

In 1482, when Diego Cao and the first Portuguese navigators set foot in the kingdom of the Kongo, 'they discovered a swarming crowd of people dressed in silk and velvet, large states that were well organized down to the smallest of details, with powerful rulers, and rich industries. Civilized down to the marrow of their bones! The idea of the barbarous negro is a European invention.' So wrote the German anthropologist Leo Frobenius in 1911.

What was once one of the most powerful nations in Central Africa thanks to its mastery of the use of iron, its fertile fields, and its land filled with gold and copper, now lives in extreme poverty. Until the arrival of the Europeans the Kongo, like societies all over the world, had practised 'slavery for internal use', for agricultural work, and for the development of the country's own economy. But after 1532, the raids between neighbouring ethnic groups multiplied in a rush to provide the Portuguese with slaves in return for weapons. These weapons were the only way for people to avoid being enslaved themselves. The infernal cycle of the slave trade had begun.

But we should not limit our use of the word 'slavery' to black people alone. It comes from the Latin word *slavus*, as most of the slaves of the late Middle Ages were Slavs from the Balkans. In Rome, the word was *servus*, and in medieval France it was 'serf'. Until the end of the Middle Ages, Europeans were sold by other Europeans and sent to Muslim countries.

Until the end of the seventeenth century, the Mani-Kongos, rulers of the Kongo, maintained good relations with the Portuguese. The Kongolese welcomed with great generosity these foreigners who arrived from the sea, and politely accepted their religion and the presence of Capuchin, Jesuit, and Dominican missionaries. The Mani-Kongo Alfonso I followed the Holy Scriptures so completely, it was said, that he forgot to eat! His son, sent to study theology in Lisbon, became the youngest ordained African bishop in 1518.

Alas, in 1500 the Portuguese Admiral Pedro Alvares Cabral 'discovered' Brazil. Of the 85 million Indigenous peoples in the Americas, five to six million were in Brazil. They were progressively exterminated by weapons, disease, and mistreatment. Between 1500 and 1900, their population fell by 85 per cent. Yet the sugar cane industry required more and more labour. Portugal therefore looked hungrily to the Kongo, which represented a fabulous reservoir of slaves!

Alfonso I would normally have done anything to help his Portuguese friends. But there was a problem: the slavery that they were proposing was in direct conflict with the very religion they had inculcated in him. He opposed the deportation of his people in any form. The Portuguese grew angry and, in 1540, tried to assassinate him. So began the first slave raids, organized from bases in Angola by nobles paid by the Portuguese. Corrupted by weapons, European clothing, alcohol, and glass beads, these princely elites delivered slaves captured in neighbouring territories. Slaves were the only currency accepted by the Portuguese.

The historian Sylvia Serbin, who told me the story of Dona Beatriz, notes: 'The immorality of slavery was not an obstacle, since even the white priests who were serving as their moral guides let themselves become corrupted by the traffic of black people!' Many of these priests, indeed, had invested in the slave trade, and it was in their interest for it to thrive. The collusion between the slaving powers and the Church was blatant in both Africa and in the islands. 'The profits of the Jesuits in Martinique are far too great', an official on the island wrote in 1717. 'They own a plantation where there are at least 130 blacks...'

There were always clerics in the first ships that reached the African or American coastlines. The merchants arrived later, once the land had been pacified by the gun and holy water. An integral part of the royal courts, the clergy Christianized the souls of the rulers and shaped their policies. As they read the Bible, they were implicitly or explicitly supporting the enslavement of Africans. Only those in remote areas were able to maintain their animist traditions.

Around 1702, when the tragic story of Dona Beatriz began, the kingdom had long been Christianized. Fragmented into several rival principalities engaged in the slave trade, the kingdom was weak. It was so weak, in fact, that Pedro IV, then the king of the Kongo, was forced to abandon his devastated city of Sao Salvador, the heart of the kingdom. He withdrew to the north, to Mont Kibangu, leaving behind him a frightened people.

Born into an aristocratic family of Mukongo, the young Kimpa Vita was baptized and given the Christian name Dona Beatriz. She received the Catholic education then provided to all Kongolese nobles. Her belief was firm and sincere. Too firm and sincere, though, because her faith in the liberating words of Christ tolerated no lies, and she turned against her confessors, who had forgotten that these same words had freed the Christian slaves of Rome. Thus, the Holy Scriptures were transformed, as they would be more than once during the era of slavery and colonization, into tools of resistance and revolt.

Dona Beatriz was 20 when she realized that black people were not treated as brothers, as the Scriptures demanded.

In 1704 she created the Antonian movement. 'Saint Anthony', she told her disciples, 'told me that a new kingdom will be born. We must rebuild the city of Sao Salvador and bring back King

Pedro IV. God wants this city to once again become the "Biblical Bethlehem".'

She mixed African traditions with Catholic teaching. The appeal she consistently made to followers, and then the wider population, was simple: we are the children of God, and our religion is equal to theirs. Take up the weapons of faith, rise up against the missionaries who are corrupting your country, who worship the money of the temple!

'You recite the Salve Regina and you don't even know why!' she told them. 'They ask you to fast during Lent when you are worn out from the scarcity of food! If you want to be washed of your sins, you need only to stand in the rain. Confession serves no purpose … Good deeds are done in vain … Only your intentions count for God … My brothers, take as many wives as you wish if that is your custom!'

She planned to create an African Church that would rid the king's entourage of Portuguese missionaries. She revitalized the traditional cultural roots of her country. The rite of the Antonians, which mixed animism and Catholicism, rapidly attracted more and more people. Dona Beatriz spread the 'good news': soon the Black Christ would deliver them from the yoke of colonialism!

She urged the people to return to Sao Salvador: 'In a repopulated Sao Salvador, the roots of felled trees will turn into gold and silver. Beneath the ruins, we will discover mines of precious gems and rare metals. In Sao Salvador, all the riches that the whites have stolen from us will be given to those who adhere to the true faith and who contribute to the rebirth of the kingdom.'

Thousands of loyal devotees followed her. People came from all around to see her. Her miracles became mythical: she healed the sick, brought the rain, made dead trees green again. It was also said that every Friday she ascended to heaven to plead the cause of her people, and the next day returned to earth to pursue her mission.

Driven by the fervour of their faith, an entire people headed towards the royal citadel, praying and singing. Among the followers was a certain Barro, whom Dona Beatriz named Saint Jean. They arrived at the citadel and clambered over the outer barricades before Dona Beatriz asked to speak to the king.

Bernando, a Capuchin father, stopped them. He feared this Antonian movement like the devil, seeing it as a threat to Catholic power in Africa. It might, if allowed to continue, create a schism over Christian dogma. He also feared the effect Dona Beatriz's charisma would have on the king. 'This woman utters dangerous absurdities', he told the monarch. 'Listen to what she says: "The Holy Land is in the Kongo ... The true founders of the Catholic religion belong to the black race ... Jesus Christ was born in Sao Salvador ... He was baptized in Sundi, which we call Nazareth ... Jesus Christ, the Madonna and Saint Francis are Kongolese!"'

Allow me a brief digression here. One day, while talking with my son, I asked him to describe God to me.

'A man with a white beard.'
'What colour is he?'
'He's white.'
'That's strange ... They say God, the Supreme Being, made man in his image. So you, who are dark brown, how can you imagine him as white?'
'It's true. I never thought of that.'

In any case, the cult of the 'Black Virgin', in whose name several hundred churches were consecrated between 1170 and 1270, posed more than a few problems for the Catholic authorities, who were obliged to cite the smoke from candles or the sins of believers to explain the blackness of these statues of the Madonna! I've actually always asked myself why God is even represented in churches.

The monk Bernando admonished the king: 'Refuse this heresy. Make your kingdom Christian and your power will grow. Put down the Antonian movement.' Despite these warnings, King Pedro received this strange woman. He listened, charmed by her faith and her message. She proposed the unification of the kingdom, its regeneration...

But he hesitated. To lead the great rebirth that Dona Beatriz proposed, and to return to Sao Salvador, carried with it great dangers. The king was a coward. His heart was torn between his Catholic advisors and the 'Virgin of the Kongo'. He hesitated for two long years, during which time Dona Beatriz successfully built up her church. The 'Little Anthonys' travelled around the country and converted the nobles to their cause. Her followers were now numbered in their thousands.

For the missionaries, the situation had become intolerable. Dona Beatriz's prestige increasingly threatened business interests, a greater sacrilege even than that of offending God! How might they successfully convince the weak Pedro IV of the threat posed by Beatriz? No one knew. But the repression that followed was ferocious and bloody, reflecting the fear felt by these little monks.

Then, Dona Beatriz suddenly disappeared. Some believed she had fled, others that she had left for heaven to join Saint Anthony and that she would soon come back to life. In fact, the 'Virgin of the Kongo', the 'Maid of Sao Salvador', was still a mortal woman. She was hiding her belly, in which was growing the fruit of her love for Barro, known as 'Saint Jean'.

The Portuguese troops eventually found her in the bush with Barro and their newborn child. The missionaries rejoiced. The child was proof that she was an impostor! Two hundred years earlier Joan of Arc had called herself a 'Virgin Maid' to prove that she was sent by God and was not a witch. Her virginity symbolized her physical and religious purity. The priests saw Dona Beatriz's child as a godsend. Did its existence not prove that she was 'impure, the daughter of the snake'? They called her a liar, physically abused her and demanded that she publicly renounce the error of her ways. Dona Beatriz refused. Speaking of her child, she declared: 'I cannot deny that he is mine. But I do not know how I had him. I can say only that he came to me from the heavens and will be the saviour of our people.'

She was brought in chains, her child in her arms, before Father Bernardo, head of the Capuchins, who interrogated her:

'Who are you?' he asked.
'I am Saint Anthony', she replied. 'I come from heaven.'
'And what news do you bring from up there', he asked sardonically? 'Can you tell me if there are black peoples from the Kongo in heaven, and if they still have their black colour up there?'
'In heaven, there are baptized black children, as well as adults. But they don't have a colour, black or white, for in heaven there is no colour!'

Father Bernardo was scandalized by this response. Her revolt, her claim that she performed miracles, her attacks on the practice of slave trading, and her reply to his questions – all this was enough to convict her of heresy. 'We declare that under the false name of Saint Anthony she has tricked the people with her heresies and her falsehoods. In consequence, the king his lordship and the Royal Council sentence her to die at the stake, along with her companion who calls himself Saint Jean.'

The execution was planned for 2 July 1706. 'After the order was given, they were brought to the pyre', Father Laurent de Lucques recounted. 'She carried her child in her arms. The sight provoked such a great tumult in the distressed crowd that there was no way for us to offer any assistance to the condemned couple. A great pile of wood had been gathered, on to which they were thrown. They were covered with other pieces of wood and burnt alive. Not yet satisfied, some men came the next morning to burn again a few bones that were left, reducing everything to fine ash.'

Dona Beatriz, like Joan of Arc more than two centuries earlier, died 'with the name of Jesus on her lips'. As for the newborn, he was saved from the flames at the last moment by Father Laurent de Lucques, who pleaded with the king to show him mercy.

Raised by the public to the rank of martyr despite an unfair trial, Dona Beatriz is often considered the 'Joan of Arc of the Kongo' or the 'Black Joan of Arc'. Of course, it is Westerners who have given her these names. But this comparison between Joan and Beatriz reminds us that the missionary church has, for a long time and on many continents, often sided with the powerful.

General-in-Chief
of the Russian Imperial Army
Abraham Petrovich Hannibal
1696–14 May 1781

In order to learn about Hannibal, I went to speak to my friend Dieudonné Gnammankou. He became interested in this great man while at high school when his father gave him a general history of Africa. In the fourth volume, devoted to the slave trade, he learned that some deported Africans had ended up in Europe, where they had pursued prestigious careers. Among them was was the figure of Hannibal, whose great-grandson was none other than Alexander Pushkin, one of the most famous Russian poets.

Such a fascinating individual! What an extraordinary life!

At the dawn of the eighteenth century, in Cameroon, a 7-year-old African boy was captured in an Arabo-Ottoman raid and taken to the court of Sultan Ahmed III in Istanbul. The sultan made him a squire, converted him to Islam, and called him Ibrahim.

A year later, in 1704, another unexpected turn of events saw the child secretly taken to the court of Tsar Peter I, better known as Peter the Great, emperor of all the territories of Russia. Having taken a liking to the child, the tsar adopted him and freed him from slavery. He gave him a new religion and a new name. Baptized in the church of Saint-Paraskeva of Vilnius, he was henceforth called Abraham Petrovich.

He was educated in the court alongside grand dukes and grand duchesses who considered him their brother. Wasn't he, after all, the protégé of the emperor? The child had a lively intelligence and was exceptionally gifted in mathematics. The best teachers in Europe were brought to the palace for him.

Such care and attention on the part of the tsar towards a black child might seem surprising. But Russian society at the time was not yet tainted by the racial prejudices that were to appear in the nineteenth century. Furthermore, Peter the Great planned to modernize Russia and to introduce Enlightenment values. To hell with colours and nationalities! To build his society, he introduced to his country expertise of all kinds and of all origins, and he recruited the greatest specialists from all over Europe: the British for his naval fleet, Frenchmen for his artillery...

When he was 15, the young Abraham became the tsar's confidant and aide-de-camp, accompanying him into battle. Then, he was put in charge of his private library. When Peter travelled to France, it was Abraham who bought his books. The tsar placed him in the care of the Duke of Maine so that he might learn geometry, artillery, and the art of fortifications. The relationship between the tsar and Abraham had become so strong that the studies the tsar had him pursue in Prussia were the same ones he had intended for his own son, Tsarevich Alexei – who instead ultimately opted for theology! Abraham thus became the first modern Russian military engineer.

He studied the fortifications of Vauban and then, in 1717, joined the army of Louis XV. He showed himself to be so audacious, and such a great strategist, that he was promoted to the rank of captain in the French army. It was there that he earned the nickname Hannibal.

Abraham alias Hannibal returned to Russia in 1722. In addition to his rank of captain, he now had a diploma in engineering. He taught the art of fortification and artillery in engineering schools. In 1725 he drew up a treatise on geometry, the first written in Russia. The following year there was a treatise on fortifications. He carried out a series of major building projects, notably the construction of the famous Peter-and-Paul fortress in St Petersburg and the Kronstadt canal. By the time Peter the Great died, Hannibal was the General-in-Chief of the Russian Imperial Army, the General Director of Fortifications, a diplomat, and the military governor of Estonia. He was the fourth highest-ranking official of the Russian state.

This makes clear how much, independent of colour, the social class in which a person is raised, and their access to education, determine the course of their lives. Had he remained a slave, Hannibal would never have been able to develop his skills and talents.

He still needed to marry, and he tried twice. The first time, he fell madly in love with the daughter of a Greek officer, Evdokia Dioper. They were married, but she loved him far less than he loved her. Indeed, she was secretly engaged to another man and she gave birth to a blond girl with blue eyes… Then, Evdokia tried to poison Hannibal with the help of her lover. Divorce was inevitable. Soon afterwards, Hannibal met a Swedish aristocrat, Christine-Régine of Schoëburg. Their love was mutual. They married and were happy. Like all the nobles of this period, they had many children.

Despite all he had achieved, Hannibal never forgot his origins. He felt such great nostalgia for them, in fact, that in 1742, when he was dubbed a knight, he asked the empress to have a special decoration inscribed on the top right-hand corner of his coat of arms: an elephant and the word 'FVMMO', which means 'homeland' in the Kotoko language. (The Kotokos are still found today in Cameroon, Chad, and Nigeria.)

By the time he died at the age of 85, Abraham Hannibal had founded a black dynasty in Russia. And his blood, mixed with that of foreign families, now runs through the veins of princes in Greece and Britain.

Among his seven children, the third, Joseph was not only a great officer, but also the ancestor of the line of the Pushkins who would earn a permanent place in history. Joseph married a daughter of the Pushkin family with whom he had a girl, Nadine. She was known as the 'beautiful Creole', and she fell in love with one of her cousins, Serguëi Pushkin. They were to become the happy parents of the illustrious poet Alexander Pushkin.

A Philosopher from Ghana

Anton Wilhelm Amo

c.1703–c.1759

> And one could say that if their intelligence is not of another species than ours, then it is greatly inferior. They are not capable of paying much attention; they mingle very little, and they do not appear to be made either for the advantages or the abuses of our philosophy.
>
> Voltaire, *An Essay on universal history, the manners, and spirit of nations* (1755)

This statement, made by one of the most brilliant and tolerant minds of his time, is astonishing.

At the dawn of the eighteenth century, Amo, a small child from Ghana, was offered as a gift to two nobles living in Amsterdam: Duke Anton Ulrich of Brunswick-Wolfenbüttel and his son, August Wilhelm. The generous donor was the Dutch West India Company, which specialized in the buying and selling of slaves.

It was common in that period for Africans to be offered in this way to the European nobility. Amo's brother had left for Amsterdam before him, but he did not please his masters and was deported to Suriname as a slave.

It was 1707. Amo was four years old. He was treated well while on board because he needed to arrive safe and sound. A year later, he received a Christian baptism and, from then on, was called Anton Wilhelm Amo, each of the dukes having graced him with one of their names. But most importantly, his 'benefactors', guided by the teachings of the early Enlightenment, set him free. We also know that they provided Amo with a very high-level education. Soon Amo was plunged into the fields of astronomy, logic, theology, law, physiology, and political theory. He learned to speak Latin, Greek, Hebrew, French, Dutch, and German! This knowledge allowed him to rapidly reach the heights of the academic world of that era.

In 1727 he matriculated in philosophy at the University of Halle, 'the centre of the German Enlightenment'. Two years later, he defended his thesis *De Jure Maurorum in Europe* (*Law and Africans in Europe*). Clearly, this 'exceptionally gifted' man had forgotten nothing of his African origins. Rather than labouring over a traditional, uncontroversial thesis, he developed the idea that the African kings, as a result of having been subjugated by the Roman Empire, now possessed certain rights to liberty. Therefore, their enslavement by Christian Europeans was illegal! Well before the African Americans W. E. B. DuBois, Thurgood Marshall, Rosa Parks, or Martin Luther King, Jr, Amo used the law to shift people's ways of thinking.

Through his writing, Amo also showed that black people never doubted their own humanity, even in the face of terrible constraints.

His work incited an outburst of racism, for he not only attacked common assumptions but also business interests. After all, the European slave trade was not just a confrontation between whites and blacks, but an economic system founded on the exploitation of human beings by other human beings.

In 1730 Amo left the University of Halle and began studying medicine at the Saxon University in Wittenberg, which had a reputation as one of the most avant-garde institutions of the time. He distinguished himself so much from his peers that, as the great abolitionist Abbé Grégoire wrote, 'the rector and the University Council thought it necessary, in 1733, to pay tribute to him publicly with an epistle of commendations in which they recalled that "Terence, too, was from Africa, and that many martyrs, doctors, and fathers of the Church were born in this same land, where the arts and humanities were flourishing".'

In 1734 Amo defended his second thesis. Once again, he developed groundbreaking ideas. Against the dominant schools of thought, particularly that of the Church, he aligned himself with the 'materialist' currents beginning to appear in the early eighteenth century. He argued that the soul is not the principal motor of the body, and that instead 'the vital forces of the human body are based in mechanical forces'. Today these ideas seem banal, and it is difficult to understand how 'revolutionary' they were in the eighteenth century, when they were part of the anti-clerical currents of the 1750s. During this period, those who articulated such arguments risked excommunication or worse. Julien Offray de La Mettrie, a doctor and philosopher, lost his position as the doctor of the French guard in 1745 for having defended a thesis exploring similar ideas.

We don't know precisely what Amo did over the following years. It seems that the court of Berlin conferred on him the title of Councillor of State, and that he wrote poetry and several novels. After the death of the prince of Brunswick, Amo supposedly fell into a deep melancholy and resolved to leave Europe, where he had lived for more than forty years, in order to return to the land of his birth. But this is only guesswork.

We do know for sure that he returned to his homeland. Amo, then about 50 years old, led a solitary life. His father and his sister were there too, but his brother was still a slave in Suriname. Amo died at an unknown date, probably around 1759.

Over the following years and up until our own time, Amo's ideas and writings were taken up by others. The abolitionists of the nineteenth century drew on his works to defend the argument that Africans have the same intellectual capacities as whites. Diplomats in the twentieth century referred to Amo to underline the extent to which 'for a long time, relations have been amicable between Europe and Africa'. Even communist East Germany used the fact that Amo had been welcomed 200 years earlier in a university there, that was then a socialist institution, to evoke the 'historical traces of the assistance that communist countries have always given to African countries pursuing socialist development'.

Finally, intellectuals of African origin have paid homage to his legacy. The pro-independence activist and pan-Africanist thinker Kwame Nkrumah (1909–72), who led an independent Ghana as its first prime minister and then president from 1960 to 1966, claimed to have been inspired by Amo, the dispossessed, an intellectual who now belongs to Africa, or simply to the entire world.

When will men have the intelligence to draw on all the philosophies of the world – those of the Bantu, the Chinese, the Dogon, the Amerindians – to build a new humanity?

The Musician of the Enlightenment

Chevalier de Saint-Georges
24 December 1745–10 June 1799

During the eighteenth century there were about 5,000 black people in metropolitan France compared to about 20 million whites. When black people went about in public, their appearance drew crowds, attracted attention, and generally caused a degree of shock. The hero of this tale hated putting a few layers of white powder on his face each morning in order to avoid the insulting remarks. But he understood that he would have to climb very high in his society in order to escape criticism. He would have to stand out and earn admiration.

So he swam with one arm tied behind his back, skated on the frozen Seine, rode on horseback, learned to wield a sword with such skill that he came to be considered the greatest fencer in the entire kingdom of France, and he handled a pistol expertly (like a god, it was said). Better still, he was a virtuoso on the violin, having studied with the most famous French violinist of the time, Jean-Marie Leclair. He became an expert harpsichord player, composer, and orchestral conductor.

To return to the beginning of this story, around 1744, it is important to focus on Count Georges de Bologne, owner of a 50-hectare plantation in Guadeloupe, which was 'furnished' with 60 slaves. It was a comfortable position that allowed him to live well. As was the wont of many slave-owners, he satisfied his sexual desires with one of his slaves, Anne Nanon, a young woman of Senegalese origin. Out of this relationship was born, on Christmas Day, a son whom the count named Joseph.

According to article 13 of the 1685 Code Noir (the Black Code), this child of a slave mother could not be emancipated. Nevertheless, it is clear that the count felt a certain affection for his son, as little Joseph received a good education. When he was 8, he was sent to Paris to pursue his studies. His mother and father joined him there two years later. Joseph henceforth lived in the wealthy neighbourhood of Saint-Germain, and he was 'free' since all servitude was outlawed in the capital.

At the age of 11, Joseph was accepted into the academy of Nicolas Texier de la Boëssière, where he was to prepare for a career as a military officer. The curriculum included mathematics, history, philosophy, Latin, foreign languages, music, art, fencing, swimming, horse riding... The classic, humanist education of all young boys from well-off families.

Finally, when he turned 17, his father procured him a position as a 'squire' – that is, a gentleman who carries a knight's shield. He also acted as 'Advisor to the King and General War Inspector'. This paternal gift provided him with a title and a new name: from then on he was known as the Chevalier de Saint-Georges (Knight of Saint George). Why not 'de Bologne'? Because the Code Noir prohibited 'free people of colour', whether of mixed race or black, from bearing the names of their masters.

My own name, Thuram, seems likely to be an incomplete anagram of Mathurin, registered number 3037 at the time of abolition, which became Thramin; or else of Mathurine, number 1273, which became Thurma and then Thuram. 'When slavery was abolished in 1848', the genealogist Michel Roger told me, 'a former slave master was chosen and placed in charge of the civil registry, with the task of giving a name to each former slave.'

The underlying idea was to prevent those who were of mixed ethnicity from ultimately becoming 'more white than many Spanish' as a result of interracial relationships. The concern was that, having taken names similar to those of whites, they would usurp titles that would open the doors to careers in law, to civil service positions, and to the higher ranks of the army. In addition, there was a fear that through marriage these 'negroes' would bring degeneration, disease, and cholera to white society. These prejudices were anchored in a collective mentality that endures to this day. Didn't people claim at the end of the twentieth century that AIDS had been transmitted from the green monkey to black people? And then from Black Africa to white countries...

In the eighteenth century, a slave's name was intended to draw a line that he was forbidden to cross. Moreau de Saint-Méry, a theorist of racial hierarchy, wrote in 1797 that 'a line projected into infinity will always separate the white lineage from the other'. Furthermore, in his *Topographical, Physical, Civil, Political, and Historical Description of the French Portion of Saint-Domingue*, we also find the famous pages where he describes 128 different shades of racial mixing! He launches himself into complicated mathematical calculations: 'If a white man mixes with a mulatta, who has a maximum of 70 white parts, the quadroon who results will be 99 parts white, while the same white man mixed with a mulatta who is 56 parts white minimum, will produce a quadroon with only 92 parts white.' And on he went. Today, the arguments of this 'Enlightenment man' are seen as a kind of paranoid delusion. They were once, however, the expression of the dominant way of thinking, at a time when the laws of genetics were barely known.

Nor was this an example of some atavistic, crude form of racism. The majority of cultivated colonists knew that the 'free people of colour' were their equals. The proof is that they sent them to Rome to paint (Lethière), to Paris to study music (Saint-Georges), and to Germany to study philosophy (Amo). But these colonists also understood that the equilibrium and especially the economy of the colonies could only be maintained through an imaginary hierarchy of the races.

Starting in 1769, Saint-Georges excelled at what we call classical music. He was the lead violinist in the 'Concert des Amateurs' directed by Gossec, who had taught him musical composition. In 1773 he took over as director of this orchestra, which featured over 80 musicians and which two years later was lauded as the 'best symphonic orchestra of Paris, indeed of all Europe'.

From 1773 to 1775 he conducted and played his own violin concertos, which received 'great applause as much for the merits of his performance as for his composition'. Of course, there remained some stubborn individuals, such as the Baron Melchoir who, influenced by Voltaire's negrophobic ideas, questioned his creative talent. He certainly recognized that the Chevalier de Saint-Georges played the violin extremely well, but he argued that a black man could never do anything more than imitate, skilfully copying the art of whites. 'While nature may have served the mulattoes in a particular way', the Baron Melchoir said, 'by giving them a marvellous aptitude in the exercise of all arts of imitation, she seems however to have refused them that surge of feeling and genius that is necessary for the creation of new ideas and original conceptions.'

Nevertheless the aura surrounding the Chevalier de Saint-Georges grew. In admiration and recognition of his talent, King Louis XVI offered him the position of director of the Royal Academy of Music, a post previously occupied by Lully and Rameau. This time, his colour became an obstacle. The singers Sophie Arnould and Rosalie Levasseur, and the lead dancer of the Opera, Marie-Madeleine

Guimard, presented a petition to the queen: their honour and the delicacy of their consciences made it impossible for them to 'submit to the orders of a mulatto'.

A recurring racist fantasy claims that African men have a dangerous sexual temperament. Saint-Georges was inevitably deemed to be a 'Black Don Juan'. A weak and powerless Louis XVI didn't dare to impose his will to bring this debate to a close.

Even so, Saint-Georges stubbornly pursued his career. In 1776, he published his Concert Symphonies No. 1 in C Major and No. 2 in A Major, followed in 1777 by three concertos for violin and six quartets for strings. At the peak of his career, he was more famous and acclaimed in Paris than even the divine Mozart himself, whose famed Concerto for the Clarinet in A Major was inspired by Saint-Georges' Concerto for the Clarinet.

Ten years later, on 9 April 1787, Saint-Georges was in London. In the presence of the Prince of Wales and his entire court, he duelled with the scandalous Knight of Eon, a transvestite, diplomat, and captain in the Dragoon Guards. A white man dressed as a woman fighting a black man in a duel! The spectacle was titillating, libertine … but also pathetic, for the knight was over 60 years old. Saint-Georges, out of pure gallantry, allowed himself to be defeated.

But Saint-Georges did more than entertain audiences. He was also concerned with the fate of slaves, and he met with abolitionists.

Back in Paris, he directed the six Parisian Symphonies, Nos. 82 to 87, by the great Joseph Haydn! The next year, in 1788, he joined the Society of the Friends of the Blacks, which was fighting for the abolition of slavery and for equality between 'free people of colour' and whites.

Then the Revolution broke out. Saint-Georges thought it might bring about a miracle and he threw himself, body and soul, into the struggle. When, on 2 September 1791, the National Assembly approved the formation of a corps of black troops, Saint-Georges became its leader. At the head of 800 infantrymen and 200 cavalry, he was the first black colonel in the history of France! His 13th Regiment of Chasseurs, a precursor of the future regiments of *tirailleurs* from Senegal, was nicknamed 'the Black Legion' and the 'Legion of Saint-Georges'. Commanding one of his squadrons was Thomas Alexandre Dumas, Haitian in origin and nicknamed the 'Black Devil'. Dumas was a future revolutionary general and the father of the author of *The Three Musketeers* and *The Count of Monte-Cristo*. He was, later, brutally dismissed by Napoleon for daring to stand up to him.

When the royalist Austrians besieged Lille, Saint-Georges' Legion was the first to fight back. Its mission was simple: to charge and break through the enemy lines. The Austrians were forced to retreat. In this battle, Saint-Georges saved the Republic by thwarting the treasonous General Dumouriez, who had led the French to victory at the famous battle of Valmy before going over to the enemy.

Saint-Georges was hailed as a hero, but not for long. The harpsichord lessons he had once given to Queen Marie-Antoinette and his friendship with the Duke of Orléans made him suspect in the eyes of the revolutionaries. He was arrested on 4 November 1793 at Château-Thierry. Fouquier-Tinville accused him of being linked to other traitors whom he had already ordered to be arrested. He was imprisoned at Chantilly, and then at the castle of Hondainville where he remained for a year. In the end, though, it was his accusers who ended up on the guillotine.

In the spring of 1797 Saint-Georges led a new orchestra, the Circle of Harmony, all the while continuing to compose. He died of natural causes on 10 June 1799. Three years later, through the law of 30 Floréal Year X (aka 20 May 1802), Napoleon Bonaparte re-established slavery. Consequently, the work of Saint-Georges was banished from music repertoires.

During this same period, a man of African descent, the son of a Caribbean man and a Polish woman, lived in England. His name was George Augustus Polgreen Bridgetower (1780–1860). This violin prodigy also helped to change the perception of black people. His association with Ludwig von Beethoven remains famous and is seen almost as miraculous. In 1803 Beethoven composed for (and with) Bridgetower his famous Violin Sonata No. 9, which he dedicated to his collaborator: 'Sonata mulattica composta per il mulatto', or 'A mulatto Sonata composed for the mulatto'. Following a quarrel between the two men, he changed his mind and in 1805 dedicated it to the violinist Rodolphe Kreutzer, who was never interested in playing it anyway. And, when it premiered on 24 May 1803, it was Bridgetower who played it at the Auergarten Hall in Vienna, with Beethoven on the piano!

'Uproot the Tree of Slavery with Me'

Toussaint Louverture

20 May 1743–7 April 1803

> In overthrowing me, you have cut down in
> Saint-Domingue only the trunk of the tree of
> liberty of the Blacks; it will grow back from the
> roots, because they are deep and numerous.
>
> Toussaint Louverture

Over the centuries, Toussaint Louverture has become the emblematic figure of the struggle against slavery and for independence from colonialism. In order to better understand his life, I talked to the historian Marcel Dorigny, who is a specialist on the Ancien Régime colonies, as well as on slavery and abolition.

Toussaint was called 'Louverture' because he always created an 'opening' leading his troops into battle. To understand him, we have to get a sense of life in Saint-Domingue during that period. Situated in the Antilles, off the coast of the United States, it had served as a pirate den in the 1620s. Shared between the two monarchies of France and Spain, the island was gradually occupied by a large number of colonists. They developed a strong economy by exploiting the black slaves, who had replaced Amerindians and white indentured labourers. The French part of the island prospered and, at the time of the Revolution, it was producing a third of French imports. This part of the island would, in 1804, become Haiti, the first independent black republic.

François-Dominique Toussaint was born on 20 May 1743 in the north of Saint-Domingue, the part of the island where the culture of resistance to the colonists was forged. He was still a child when the great revolt led by Makandal took place at the end of the 1750s. Makandal was the famous 'maroon' who, for eighteen years, opposed the white colonists. He was so feared that whites themselves attributed magic powers to him, particularly that of being a 'poisoner'. They had to find some explanation for his charismatic influence over other slaves. The pro-slavery lawyer Moreau de Saint-Méry wrote of Makandal: 'The school in which he taught his dark arts was open to all, he had agents in all parts of the colony, and death would follow at the slightest signal ... He predicted the future, had revelations and such an eloquence ... and on top of that, the greatest courage and the greatest firmness of spirit, which he was able to conserve in the midst of the cruellest tortures and ordeals.'

Makandal said that God had sent him to Saint-Domingue to kill the whites and liberate the blacks. It is said that one day, in front of a gathering of slaves, he pulled three handkerchiefs out of a vase: one yellow, one white, and one black. He held up the yellow one and said: 'These are the first inhabitants of Saint-Domingue.' He held up the white handkerchief: 'Here are the colonists.' And finally the black handkerchief: 'Here are the future masters of the island!'

His 'powers' did not prevent Makandal from being captured and sentenced to death on 20 January 1758. However, even though he was tied to a post, surrounded by the rising flames, he freed himself and escaped! He was recaptured and would not escape the flames a second time. But in the minds of the enslaved population of the northern plain, Makandal lived on, a hero who periodically reappeared. Every time a revolt broke out in Haiti, it was Makandal. Every time trouble arose, it was Makandal. Even today, he fosters hope.

It was in this place, on this island, between a life of oppression and a dream of liberty, that Toussaint Louverture was born of a father 'imported' from Africa who was of royal stock. His great-grandfather Gaou-Guinou was the king of Allada, in Benin. Born a slave on a plantation owned by Count Breda, Toussaint benefited from the protection of the count's legal representative, Monsieur Baillon de Libertat. Baillon played a very important role in Toussaint's life, teaching him to read and write as well as about the medical properties of plants, knowledge that earned him the nickname 'leaf doctor' and contributed to his prestige. At that time, medicine and magic were closely associated and conflated in people's minds.

Toussaint's early life is more or less unknown to us. How could anyone have guessed the destiny of this slave? We know only that he worked as a coachman, then as an overseer of other slaves.

Tradition tells us that he was emancipated at the age of 33. The same age as Christ when he was crucified… It is a suspicious number, especially given that the Code Noir described manumission, the liberation of a slave, as a kind of birth. The slave had no civil existence. The act of manumission replaced his birth certificate and made him a subject of the king, as if he had not lived prior to that time.

Toussaint followed the classic path of free blacks in the colony. He married Suzanne, a free black woman who owned several fine properties. They had two children: Isaac and Placide. Toussaint was now living comfortably, a landowner who possessed at least one slave.

There are no traces of him or his statements at the time of the French Revolution. He was certainly listening, and very well informed, but he doesn't appear in the records. It is true that, at the beginning of the Revolution, the main problem in Saint-Domingue was the question of the free people of colour, those who had succeeded in acquiring land and sometimes slaves and who wanted equality with whites. Toussaint himself was not a mulatto. He was black. Nothing on the surface appeared to have destined him for revolt.

In France, however, there were violent confrontations over the question of rights for 'free people of colour'. Two representatives of these 'free people of colour' were in Paris at the beginning of the Revolution: Vincent Ogé and Julien Raimond, both mulattoes and slave owners. They demanded the same rights as whites. The revolutionaries, whose notions of equality often shifted according to the circumstances, categorically rejected this demand. Colour prejudice was the keystone of the economic system, particularly in Saint-Domingue, a colony with massive commercial potential. Barnave called this a 'moral principle': the black must be persuaded that he is inferior to the mulatto, the mulatto that he is inferior to the white. As for the abolition of slavery, it was simply unthinkable.

It is always hard to admit that the Declaration of the Rights of Man of 1789 fails to make explicit mention of the abolition of slavery. Yet Article 1 is unambiguous: 'Men are born and live free and equal in rights.' One could legitimately deduce from this that slavery had been abolished. Indeed, on 20 August 1789, Mirabeau, the most important member of the Society of the Friends of the Blacks, wrote to the deputies of Saint-Domingue, who had signed the Declaration of the Rights of Man: 'Gentlemen deputies from Saint-Domingue, today you have abolished slavery on your plantations … Unless you dare tell us that your slaves are not men. *Or that this article applies only to white men…*' But Mirabeau also well understood that the Declaration was intended for internal use only. The new Constitution would contain an article stipulating that the 'French colonies … though part of the French empire, are not included in the present Constitution'. After December 1799, Bonaparte would cite this article in order to declare that the colonies would henceforth be governed by 'special laws', and to re-establish slavery.

Scandalized by their exclusion from these fundamental rights, the representatives of the mulatto population, Vincent Ogé and Julien Raimond, recalled that Parisians had asked no one's permission before storming the Bastille. Although Raimond was obliged to remain in France on account of his age, Ogé returned to Saint-Domingue and prepared a revolt. Sadly, his troops were too few. On 25 February 1791, 13 of his companions were sentenced to the galleys and 22 to be hanged. Ogé and his brother-in-law Chavannes, accused of having planned a revolt of people of colour, were sentenced on 9 May 1791 to 'have their arms, legs, thighs and loins broken on the wheel, their face turned to the sky … and to stay there for as long as it pleases God to leave them alive'. The white provincial assembly stayed on and witnessed the torture until the very end. As Victor Schoelcher, the French abolitionist, would write subsequently, the assembly 'expressed satisfaction in noting that the scaffold where the two martyrs perished was not placed in the spot reserved for criminals of the privileged race'. In France, however, many were deeply shocked to learn the details of this form of torture, breaking men on the wheel, which had been abolished at the beginning of the Revolution. Many children born in the spring and summer of 1791 were given the name Ogé.

The revolt of Ogé and Chavannes created an irreversible division between the whites and the mulattoes. The possibility of reconciliation was gone. The slaves took advantage of the split. The blacks and the mulattoes now rallied around their common interests. A few months later, there was a great insurrection. It started during the night of 22 August 1791.

Around 30,000 slaves revolted at the same time! How was such a feat possible? When I spoke to my friend Doudou Diène about slavery, he explained that it was a commonplace idea in the eighteenth century that the black man was so inferior that he didn't even understand his own suffering. As he did not have the capacity to understand his own suffering, he was incapable of resistance, or so the argument went. And so the reality of black resistance was concealed. Blacks were confined to their image as victims, as inferior people, when in fact many of them actively resisted. They often resisted in great numbers, sometimes in isolation, but were always violently repressed.

The Saint-Domingue insurrection, however, showed the extent to which the blindness of the whites and the power of their colour prejudices could actually help the slaves liberate themselves. The massive revolt that took place on the night of 22 August had been organized for months in advance by slaves, who gathered every night that God gave them. They did so right under the noses of the whites, who saw nothing because they considered them to be simply 'chattels'. In their minds, the slaves were incapable of thought. So, when the blacks got together at night, when they played drums and danced, the whites saw only the expression of their 'savage' nature and believed they were simply 'letting off steam'. However, in their gatherings, the enslaved were in fact imagining the possibility of a new political order.

The slaves understood that the whites considered them to be objects, and didn't even notice them. They took refuge in the places whites weren't looking: their gods, their myths, Vodou. They organized the revolt under their masters' unseeing eyes, creating networks that made it possible for their plans to spread immediately throughout the island. There were no cell phones, but the music of the drums transmitted the signal.

The slave insurrection was preceded by a gathering in the middle of a wooded area, Bois-Caïman. This magico-religious ceremony was to become a myth in Haiti, as Saint-Domingue would come to be known, a nation born, it is said, that night in Bois-Caïman. Under the watchful eye of the priestess Cécile Fatiman, 'a mulatto woman with green eyes and long, silky black hair', everyone sat together in a large circle. After a long, meditative silence, one of the men recounted the inhumane treatment they had endured at the hands of their masters, then finished with the story of the torture of General Ogé.

'They all took an oath to avenge his death and to perish rather than return to slavery', wrote Civique de Gastine. 'They renounced the religion of their masters, and sacrificed a black ram to the memory of Ogé. The man who carried out the sacrifice, having examined the intestines of the victim, declared to the assembly that the gods would always be in their favour [...] They were about to retire when a bird the size of a pigeon fell from the treetops into the middle of the assembly, stone dead. The one who performed the sacrifice interpreted this event as a good omen, and after their priest had purified the bird, he gave everyone a feather, assuring each of them that they would be invulnerable as long as they carried it on them...'

Officiating at the heart of the ceremony was Boukman, the leader of the revolt. In Anglophone Africa, Boukman means 'the man of the Book', the wise man who knows the Holy Scriptures. Hérard Dumesle, a deputy to the Haitian parliament, recorded a declaration that Boukman was said to have made at Bois-Caïman:

> God who makes the sun that illuminates us from above, Who embroils the seas, who makes the storm rage, God is there, do you hear?, hidden in a cloud, And there he watches us, he sees everything the whites are doing! The God of the whites orders crime, and wants nothing good for us, But the God there who is so good, orders us to take vengeance; He will guide our arms, he will give us assistance; Cast down the portrait of the god of the whites, who thirsts for tears in our eyes; Listen to liberty, it speaks in all of our hearts.

Not a lot is known about Boukman: he was shot early in the insurrection, decapitated, and his head paraded through the streets of the town of Le Cap with a banner that read: 'The head of Boukman, leader of the rebels.'

Contrary to what the whites believed, what had started was not a revolt but a war. In the first week, hundreds of plantations were burnt down. Within four days, a third of the northern plain was nothing but a pile of ashes. The whites responded with appalling violence: an unending succession of decapitations and firing squads. Along every road in the north of the island, the heads of black people were exhibited on wooden spikes. This repression served only to increase the number of rebels. A fire had been lit that nothing could stop...

With Boukman gone, the two leaders of the revolt were Jean-François and Georges Biassou. Toussaint was the latter's aide-de-camp. This was the moment that Toussaint Louverture 'officially' appeared in the history of Saint-Domingue.

The revolt spread. At the outset the rebels mostly fought with pikes, sticks, iron staves prised from barrels, and knives. But the Spanish on the other half of the island soon began supplying them with rifles and ammunition. Spain, it should be remembered, was acting in royalist solidarity against the newly revolutionary France. The revolt served its aim of destabilizing the edifice of the revolutionary government.

In October 1791, when news of the rebellion arrived in France, the movement to abolish slavery was weaker than ever. The insurgents – Biassou, Jean-François, and Toussaint – fought victoriously against the French troops sent as reinforcements. From then on, Toussaint was known as Toussaint Louverture, and was promoted to the rank of Lieutenant-General of the Armies of the King of Spain.

After 20 April 1792, the war waged by the slaves benefited from the other wars that France was fighting simultaneously in Europe (in Austria, Prussia, Spain, Holland), especially when Britain joined the fray in February 1793. The slaves took advantage of the stranglehold in which France found itself. Their revolt spread even further.

Within a few months, the entire colony was in a state of insurrection. As a result, those in power in France approved a decree granting equality to the free people of colour, hoping to maintain French rule by dividing the population. They sent three 'civil commissioners' to apply this decree: Sonthonax, Polverel, and Ailhaud. They arrived on 17 September 1792 with 6,000 troops, and tried desperately to put this law of equality into practice over the course of the following year, convinced that this was the only way to make the slaves obey once again. They had forgotten the engrained racial prejudice that ran through the white population in the colonies: for them, equality with free people of colour was unthinkable. As for the slaves, they had nothing to lose and continued to fight ferociously. By June 1793 the colony had been ruined by this civil war. On 20 June Sonthonax made a radical proposal. He offered liberty and citizenship to the slaves who would fight for the Republic. Some of the troops camped above Le Cap accepted, and assured the victory of Sonthonax. Ten thousand colonists fled with their women and children, taking refuge in Cuba, in Jamaica, and then in the United States.

The British threatened the coasts, while on the island itself, the Spanish controlled the border area. It was absolutely imperative that the situation be calmed and that additional troops be immediately raised to hold back the British. Sonthonax could see no way out. To save the colony, he decided to proclaim the general abolition of slavery, and called for the support of the 'Republic's new citizens' against the royalist British invader!

On 29 August 1793 Sonthonax announced the end of slavery in France's most important colony. That same day, Toussaint

Louverture, Lieutenant-General of the Armies of the King of Spain, issued the proclamation in which he presented himself as the leader of the blacks:

'Brothers and friends, I am Toussaint Louverture; perhaps my name has made itself known to you. I have sought vengeance for my race. I want Liberty and Equality to reign in Saint-Domingue. I am working to make that happen. Unite with us, brothers, and we will all fight for the same cause. Uproot the tree of slavery with me.'

Sonthonax distributed weapons to the emancipated ex-slaves. 'The Republic has given you freedom', they were told, 'defend it! If the English win, you know what awaits you!' It was as free men that they fought fiercely to defend their territory, which they had conquered at great cost, against the British and the Spanish. The decision to abolish slavery was certainly driven in part by sincerity, but it was also a political and strategic choice. If France had been unable to call on the services of the newly freed slaves, the British would have conquered the colony.

Sonthonax had neither the right nor the mandate to proclaim abolition. It may have been illegal, but it was no less real for that. It was now difficult to backtrack.

Sonthonax sent three deputies to Paris to represent the new population of Saint-Domingue: a mulatto, Mills; a black man born in Africa, Jean-Baptiste Belley; and a white man, Dufay. These three deputies were immediately thrown into prison, as representatives of a rebellious colony. However, four days later, after an intense debate in the National Convention, they were freed. 'Citizens, your Committee on Decrees has verified the powers of the deputies of Saint-Domingue to act as national representatives', the spokesman declared on 3 February 1794, 'and finds them to be in order. I propose that we admit them into the Convention.'

Thus, they entered the National Convention on 4 February 1794. The three deputies explained that the slaves turned citizens and soldiers had saved Saint-Domingue, that thanks to them France still held the colony. The Convention abolished slavery, basing its vote on the report made by Dufay, and in the presence of Belley, who made a deep impression.

The legalization of the abolition of slavery persuaded Toussaint Louverture to return to the French-held part of the island. He wanted to transform a law that was still only a declaration into a reality. Aimé Césaire analysed the process in his essay *Toussaint Louverture, the French Revolution, and the Colonial Problem*: 'Toussaint Louverture appeared on the grand stage of history with the aim of taking the Declaration of the Rights of Man literally ... He personified the principles of the Revolution and declared them relevant to black people. These laws had been decreed in the abstract, but they had to be brought to the people, to all peoples ... (when, in fact, the rights of man have often been reduced to those of European men alone).' On horseback in front of roughly 5,000 men, Toussaint solemnly rallied to the cause of the abolitionist Republic. Biassou and Jean-François remained loyal to Spain. And so the 'old' Toussaint, then 50, began his great military and political career late in life. He was promoted by the Directorate to the rank of brigadier general, then general, then general-in-chief, and finally governor of the island.

Sonthonax was sent on a second mission to Saint-Domingue, this time to reorganize the colony within the framework of liberty for all. He assumed joint control of the island alongside Toussaint. But their ambitions and their political projects diverged. Sonthonax conceived of the territory as a French colony, while Toussaint envisaged it as largely autonomous and governed by the black population. Although Sonthonax represented the political power of metropolitan France, he was constantly confronted with the real power of General Toussaint Louverture.

In his struggle against the British and the Spanish, Toussaint demonstrated an indisputable strategic genius combined with a very sharp political instinct. He knew only too well that he had to change society from within. Progressively, he replaced the dominant white caste with a new black elite who exercised power and made political decisions. He distributed plantations abandoned by the colonists to his officers, creating a class of black property-owners who took control of the colony's economy. His vision of wealth for the island was to maintain the plantation system, minus slavery, in order to ensure its economic prosperity and continuing wealth. But he also knew that, in the wake of the uprising, the colony was in ruins. As a realist, he didn't aim to eliminate the former white elite entirely. In the 1801 Constitution that he promulgated by his own authority, he offered an amnesty to any white colonists who would return to the island and he guaranteed their protection. As the incarnation of a new kind of power, a black power, he felt an immense sense of pride. But he used this power with moderation, insisting on the need to return to work, an ordered society, the protection of the colonists, security, and confidence in the future.

It is a historical irony that his Constitution was based on Bonaparte's Article 91 which called for 'special laws' to deprive the colonies of their legal equality with the metropole. The need for distinct laws for the colonies was justified through the invocation of 'the nature of things, the difference in climate and customs'. In the letter that he sent to Bonaparte, Toussaint Louverture told him: 'Citizen General, in your great wisdom you have provided for the existence of special laws for the colonies, which are very far from the metropole ... we have made special laws for Saint-Domingue.'

From 1798, after Sonthonax had returned to France, Toussaint governed the colony alone, having rid himself of all representatives of metropolitan power. He negotiated trade treaties with the United States and Britain, which infuriated Napoleon.

One must not forget the relationship Toussaint maintained with the Spanish portion of the island, in what is today the Dominican Republic. For a long time, the white French colonists had their sights set on the Spanish half. The two colonies, though they were on the same island, had experienced very different types of development. The French part of the island was home to about 500,000 slaves, the highest concentration of slaves in the Americas, and was the most important producer of sugar in the world. The Spanish part had 40,000 slaves and no sugar. The French felt a little cramped in their Pearl of the Antilles, to the point that some began dreaming of expansion. The Spanish side, which was twice as big and which produced absolutely nothing, would have been a perfect acquisition!

Spain went to war with the French Republic, and was defeated. On 22 July 1795 Spain signed the Treaty of Basel. One of its many clauses ceded the Spanish part of Saint-Domingue to the French. Finally, the entire island was French! Except that France didn't enforce the treaty. Why? Because slavery was abolished in the French part, but not in the Spanish part. Unifying the two halves would mean applying the abolition of slavery on the entire island!

The Treaty of Basel included another clause in which France promised not to have black troops enter the Spanish zone. But Toussaint Louverture didn't take this restriction seriously. In 1801 he crossed the border with his army, expanding the abolition of slavery to the entire island. For the First Consul Bonaparte, this was a coup d'état! He felt that Toussaint had betrayed him. On 29 October he decreed: 'The occupation of the Spanish portion by Toussaint is null and void...' He then sent his brother-in-law, the Captain-in-Chief Leclerc, to re-establish slavery in Saint-Domingue, tear up Toussaint's Constitution, and evacuate French troops from the Spanish part of the island.

Bonaparte sent Toussaint a long letter on 18 November 1801. It is a gem of deviousness. 'It is with great pleasure that we acknowledge and proclaim the great services you have completed on behalf of the French people. If the French flag still flies over Saint-Domingue, it is thanks to you and the brave black population.' A black population that he was preparing to return to the condition of slavery!

Leclerc left for this new war with 23,000 troops. He disembarked on the island on 1 February 1802 and entered Le Cap on 5 February. The town was, once again, engulfed by fire and blood. Toussaint Louverture proclaimed: 'If the whites of Europe come as enemies, set fire to the towns where you are unable to resist them, and take to the hills.' Following his orders Christophe, one of his generals, set fire to Le Cap. Another, Dessalines, set fire to the town of Saint-Marc. He led by example, first setting fire to his own house.

Leclerc rapidly gained control of the main towns, or of their ruins, in the north and the west. But he still had to fight against Toussaint's black guerilla troops, against the mulatto troops and the maroon troops, all united in opposition to a new invasion that threatened once again to deprive them of their liberty.

After two months of war, Leclerc had lost 12,000 men! So he accepted proposals for peace. The adversaries negotiated and came to an agreement: 'Sacrosanct liberty for all the citizens of Saint-Domingue, the maintenance of rank and function for all the indigenous military officers and civilian officials. Toussaint is to keep his general staff and to move about where he wishes within the territory of the colony.'

An error on Leclerc's part? It was a lie, in any case. Despite the promise of the captain-in-chief, on 7 June 1802 Toussaint Louverture was arrested in an act of treachery and immediately brought to a ship called *The Hero*. It was there that, addressing himself to the divisional chief, he pronounced his famous words: 'In overthrowing me, you have cut down in Saint-Domingue only the trunk of the tree of liberty of the black people; it will grow back from the roots, because they are deep and numerous.'

Upon arrival in France, he was imprisoned in the Fort de Joux in the Jura Mountains. The next day, he was stripped of all his titles. For France, he was nothing more, than the *negro*, Toussaint.

He spent the entire winter in prison, completely isolated in a cell whose only opening was mostly walled over. A small band of light was all that remained. The only people who visited were under orders from Bonaparte to 'treat him with the greatest contempt'. He saw a doctor, the director of the prison, his jailor, and on two or three occasions General Cafarelli. Bonaparte had sent him not to negotiate but to find out the location of the supposed 'treasure of Toussaint', which some claimed he had buried on his plantation in Ennery... But this was simply a myth.

He died of an attack of apoplexy on 7 April 1803.

In the folds of the handkerchief that covered his head, they found a letter written in Creole. A cry from the heart against the intolerable injustice that had been done to him:

> Arbitrarily arresting me, without listening to me, without telling me why, taking away all my property, pillaging my entire family, taking my papers, loading me on a ship, sending me as naked as an earthworm, spreading the most calumnious of lies about me, and after all that throwing me into the depths of a cell: Is it not to cut off someone's legs and order him to walk? Is it not to cut out his tongue and tell him to talk? Is it not to bury a man alive?

But is he really dead? We find incarnations of Toussaint Louverture throughout world history, because justice is never simply granted. It must be earned.

The Liberator of Haiti

Jean-Jacques Dessalines
20 September 1758–17 October 1806

In July 1802, barely a month after the deportation of Toussaint Louverture to the Fort de Joux in France, General Richepanse re-established slavery in Guadeloupe. This would cost the lives of 10,000 people.

The news quickly spread to Saint-Domingue. Guadeloupe was only a few days away by boat. It struck like a thunderbolt in a colony that had almost been pacified.

With Toussaint Louverture out of the way, some were quick to believe that the revolution of Saint-Domingue was finally over. The French colonists who remained on the island indulged in shockingly brutal repression, organized in collaboration with General Leclerc's troops. They confiscated the weapons that Toussaint and Sonthonax had given to the black plantation workers. Everyone remembered the words once pronounced by Toussaint: 'Here is your liberty. The person who tries to take this rifle away from you will want to make you a slave once again.' No one had forgotten how, as he was reviewing his gathered troops, he would grab a rifle and cry 'This is our liberty!'

Those who refused to surrender fled into the hills, these ancient volcanoes. The executions multiplied.

The news of the re-establishment of slavery was a catastrophe for the black population. But, strangely, it was equally catastrophic for Leclerc, who sensed that this measure was a monumental blunder. The plan had been kept secret: why unveil it now? On 6 August Leclerc wrote an astonishing letter to the First Consul Napoleon Bonaparte:

> I had begged of you not to do anything that would make them fear for their liberty until the time when I was in the right position, and I was marching steadily towards that

moment. Suddenly there arrived in the colony the law that authorized the slave trade in the colonies, along with letters from the merchant houses of Nantes and Le Havre asking *if we can send blacks here.* Even worse, General Richepanse has just re-established slavery in Guadeloupe. Now *our plans for the colonies are perfectly well known.* If you want to keep Saint-Domingue, send a new army. As disagreeable as my position is, *I am using terrible violence to set an example.* Since I have nothing left but the use of this *terror* that is what I am resorting to. On [the island of] Tortuga, out of 450 rebels, I had 60 hanged…

Troops composed primarily of slaves recently arrived from Africa regrouped in the mountains, and they fought relentlessly. Their leaders, too, were African-born. Many of the fighters had been warriors in Africa before being enslaved, and they used the combat techniques they had learned there against the French.

All those who felt threatened by the re-establishment of slavery increasingly stood together. The black plantation labourers left the fields for the woods and the hills, preparing a guerrilla war. The spirit of resistance spread. Leclerc resorted to 'a war of extermination and the destruction of a large portion of the plantation labourers', but every day he lost some of his troops, composed in part of local recruits, who deserted and joined the insurgents. The guerilla warfare was carried out by small groups of fighters who fought desperately, and who were mobile and flexible. Faced with constant skirmishes and harassment, a regular army had no chance of winning.

The ignominious General Rochambeau, son of the famous general who with Lafayette had contributed to victory in the US War of Independence, helped Leclerc in his work of extermination by sending him dogs from Cuba who were specially trained to 'feast on the Negro':

I am sending you, my dear commander, a detachment of 150 men from the National Guard of Le Cap, commanded by Monsieur Bari, as well as 28 bulldogs. These reinforcements will put you in a position to complete your operations. I must inform you that neither rations nor money for the dogs' food is included.
You must give them Negroes to eat.
I salute you affectionately.

But the 'Negro' held firm. Leclerc panicked. He demanded that Bonaparte send 10,000 men. Leclerc's troops perished in ambushes, deserted, or died of yellow fever. Leclerc himself succumbed to the disease on 2 November 1802. It changed nothing, however, as his successor Rochambeau used brutal violence with even more relish.

The second part of the war for Saint-Domingue began. This time, all of the mulatto and black forces, together with the maroons, rallied under the command of Jean-Jacques Dessalines, Toussaint Louverture's successor.

Dessalines was a former slave born in Saint-Domingue, not far from Le Cap. He had a rebellious childhood, running away so frequently that his body was covered with scars. Victor Schoelcher recounted that he used to shout with fury: 'As long as these marks appear on my flesh, I will make war against all the whites!' He refused to have anything to do with white people, and even pretended that he spoke only Creole.

He followed the same path as the 'old' Toussaint Louverture, except that he was 15 years younger. In 1791 he was one of the insurgents alongside Boukman. He then joined the bands of rebel slaves based on the Spanish side of the island, where he became a high-ranking officer. He returned to the French side to reunite with Toussaint once slavery had been abolished in 1794. He showed himself to be 'bursting with fire and courage' in the war against the British, to the point that Toussaint more than once had to call him back to order: 'I said to prune the tree, not to uproot it!'

In October 1803, with 20,000 men, he laid siege to Port-au-Prince. The city fell, and its French commander took refuge in Le Cap, where he joined forces with the remainder of the expedition led by General Rochambeau.

Le Cap was protected by advance fortifications. Rochambeau was convinced that Dessalines' troops would never dare attack the town. But he failed to take account of General Capoix, of whom Victor Schoelcher offers this picture, at once terrible and lyrical:

This Negro, nicknamed Capoix la Mort, charged with a half-brigade that retreated after being horribly mutilated by fire from the fort. He led them back again; the hail of bullets drove them back to the base of the hill. Boiling with rage, he went to get new troops, mounted his horse, and for the third time rushed forward; but once again the thousand deaths vomited out from the fortress pushed him and his brigade back. Never have any soldiers had less consideration of death than did his. They were ablaze with a Homeric zeal. A few words were enough for him to rally them for a fourth time. Forward! Forward! A bullet killed his horse and he fell, but quickly, freed from the tangle of corpses piled up around him, he hurried to take up his place again at the head of the blacks. Forward! Forward! His hat, decorated with feathers, was picked off by grapeshot. He responded to the insult of having his hat forced off by raising his sword as though he was showing his fist, and throwing himself into the attack...

After eight days of siege and fierce resistance, Rochambeau, his troops worn down by famine and yellow fever, surrendered. Allowed to leave, he embarked for France. Sometimes, however, there is justice after all. On the way to France, he was captured by the British Navy, who threw him in prison, where he wallowed for more than eight years.

On 1 January 1804 Dessalines proclaimed independence and announced that the new state would be called Ayiti, the Amerindian name of Haiti. In so doing he returned the island to its origins and paid homage to an indigenous population that had been virtually exterminated upon the whites' arrival.

The new flag was blue and red: history has it that, a year earlier, on 18 May 1803, an enraged Dessalines ripped the white out of the French flag, then handed the two remaining parts to Catherine Flon, who sewed them together using her long hair as thread! He apparently opted, in 1804, for a darker blue. In any case, since then 18 May has been celebrated as Flag Day

The country was recognized by France in 1825 in return for the payment of an 'indemnity' of 150 million francs (more than 21 billion in today's dollars) and a 50 per cent reduction in import taxes! A true act of piracy.

This debt added to the difficulties of a country already faced with an impossible economic situation and ongoing internal conflicts. The political 'dream' of Dessalines, of a free and autonomous nation, remains unfulfilled to this day.

The Poet of Paradise Lost

Phillis Wheatley
1753–5 December 1784

I, young in life, by seeming cruel fate
Was snatched from Afric's fancy'd happy seat:
What pangs excruciating must molest,
What sorrows labour in my parents' breast?
Steel'd was that soul and by no misery mov'd
That from a father seiz'd his babe belov'd:
Such, such was my case. And can I then but pray
Others may never feel tyrannic sway?
Phillis Wheatley, *Poems on Various
Subjects, Religious and Moral*

In school, I remember learning the poems of Victor Hugo, Lamartine, Baudelaire, but never those of black men and even less of black women. I couldn't even imagine that a female black poet existed. Neither, I expect, could my teachers. However, at the end of the eighteenth century in America there lived a great poet named Phillis Wheatley.

She was born in 1753, in Senegal. We still don't know this young girl's real name. As she had to hide this name, she may well have forgotten it herself. Her father would no doubt have murmured it quietly in her ear after her birth, for tradition had it that she must be the first to hear it. And then, like a character from Alex Haley's *Roots*, her father would have shown her the sky and said: 'Look! This is all that is greater than you!'

I know nothing about her first years, but I imagine that she was carried on her mother's back as she worked in the fields, until she was big enough to stand on her own two feet. And then I see her walking, playing, learning traditional practices like all the other little girls of the village, up until the day she turned seven years old when she was kidnapped in a raid.

'Raid', 'kidnapped'. It is essential to understand the reality to which these terms refer. It is a village in flames in the middle of the night, white or black slave traders loaded down with weapons, killing those who resist or who are too weak to endure the journey: the old, the crippled, the newborn. It is a procession of terrified women, men, and children, tied to each other with leather straps, driven onwards by the cracking whip; they reach a large ship where, trembling, they expect to be 'devoured', for, according to the elders, they were to be carried off to a country to be sold to enormous cannibals.

The little girl was taken to America and unloaded in Boston, the capital of Massachusetts. There, she was auctioned off. The auctioneer advertised her: 'Seven years old! Ready to be trained! Will make an excellent brood mare!' Stripped of her clothes, she was felt by the hands of the buyers. A rich merchant acquired her. He gave her the first name Phillis, after the boat that had transported her to the United States. And, as was the custom, he gave her his own last name: Wheatley.

Mr John Wheatley didn't want for slaves, but he had promised his wife Suzanne a young housemaid to serve her and, he hoped, to distract her. As they had nothing to do, the wives of plantation owners and merchants were practically dying of boredom.

But something strange and incredible happened. Rather than withdrawing into her sadness, the young girl came to life, her spirits rose, she radiated energy. She was so animated and curious about everything around her that Mr Wheatley's sister-in-law Mary took a particular interest in her. She taught Phillis to read the Bible and the basics of Latin and Greek. She loaned her books about history, geography, astronomy, and the works of ancient poets like Horace, Virgil, Ovid, and Homer. Between her domestic tasks, Phillis absorbed this education and soon surpassed the children of the planters in her knowledge.

At the age of 13, she began to compose short poems full of charm. Her proud masters presented her to their social circle. Obviously, her poems were not yet of great originality. But the fact that they existed was already a kind of miracle. Imagine that the French literary giant, Victor Hugo, had, at the age of 7, been kidnapped in a raid and then forced into slavery in a far-off country. Is it likely that he would have been writing better poetry than Phillis Wheatley in a language he had not fully mastered and at such a young age?

The young slave had a passion for the literature of her time. We know that she was particularly fond of *Paradise Lost* by John Milton.

What a symbolic title for her! But then everything changed. In 1772 Phillis attempted to publish a collection of 39 poems modestly titled *Poems on Various Subjects, Religious and Moral*. For a slave to have the gall to publish something at all was inadmissible! The fact that her poems were also of rare depth and intelligence made this truly intolerable. A black person could never have written something so beautiful. There must have been deceit involved. Everyone was certain that some practical joker had dictated the verses to her.

Phillis was called before a tribunal of experts. Imagine her sitting straight up in her chair, confronted by 18 wigged interrogators. They asked her questions about the Greek gods and characters from the Bible. They subjected her to the torture of a spelling test, and questioned her knowledge of Greek and Latin conjugation. They asked her to translate texts by Virgil and to recite passages from *Paradise Lost*, and even from her own poems!

The young Phillis held strong in front of the judges. And so, after having gathered testimonies from her master, the governor and lieutenant-governor, and from 15 other prominent citizens, the judges certified that the 'little negro slave' was indeed the 'author of her text'.

At the end of this incredible literary trial, Phillis Wheatley 'legally' became the first female black poet in literary history … in the minds of Westerners, that is! I say this specifically because, for many of our contemporaries, black history only begins with slavery. But there is no doubt that there were thousands of female black poets before Phillis Wheatley, from the dawn of time, who composed marvellous poems in their own country, their own land, and their own language.

Phillis Wheatley's texts were published in London and caught the attention of the literary establishment. In addition, the abolitionist movement seized upon them. In the year of their publication the Abbé de Feller wrote in his *Historical and Literary Review* that these poems were 'remarkable for the quality of their author, and for the argument they make against the extravagant philosophers who have sought to place Negroes in the class of savages, and to turn them into a different species from our own'.

She was sent to Britain, where she captivated London's high society with her personality. King George III himself asked that she be presented to him.

I wish I could end the story of Phillis Wheatley's life there. It would be a little bit like a fairy tale, and we'd find a certain justice in it. But I must go on. Just when Phillis was about to be presented to King George III, she learned that her mistress was gravely ill. Summoned to return as quickly as possible, she hurried to the bedside of Mrs Wheatley, who died within moments of her arrival.

Three months later, after having granted Phillis her freedom, Mr Wheatley too died. There was nothing left for Phillis to do except leave this house where, in the end, she had been nothing more than another piece of property. Phillis was free! But to do what? Liberty came to her too late. How was she to take advantage of it when she owned nothing?

She would eventually find work, but it was the most menial and most difficult type of work. Such was the destiny reserved for black people.

We know little about her final years, except that in April 1778 she married a free black man named John Peters, a handyman. We also know she had three children with him. Poverty, exclusion... We do know that she continued to write and to send and receive letters.

When I wrote the French edition of this book, I wanted to cite some of her letters and other poems, but to this day no major re-edition of her work has been published, nor has it been translated into French. What a shame! If children in France and other Western countries were to learn the poems of Phillis Wheatley, or other black poets, don't you think that they would leave school with fewer prejudices?

The Oath of the Ancestors

Guillaume Guillon Lethière
10 January 1760–22 April 1832

Monsieur Pierre Guillon, the king's agent in Guadeloupe, was a man of his time. He did not recognize the child he conceived with a slave named Marie-Françoise, for such a gesture would have violated the Code Noir. He didn't give the child his name, instead calling him 'Letiers', that is to say 'the Third', because he was the third child by this slave. You might think that a man who assigns his child a serial number is a monster, but the situation was more complicated than it seemed. In that unfortunate era, Monsieur Guillon was practically a saint. He took care of his number 3 as though he were a legitimate son. He made sure that he received an excellent education and, since the child showed real talent for drawing and painting, he sent him to France in 1774 to study art.

At the School of Fine Arts in Rouen, Letiers sought to remove the humiliating connotation attached to his name by writing it 'Lethière'. And he lost himself in his passion for art. Although he encountered racial discrimination, he stuck it out and continued his apprenticeship with Doyen, the king's painter. Racial prejudices were so strong at the time that between the seventeenth century and the end of the eighteenth century the use of the colour black declined. Michel Pastoureau, who researches the history of colour, describes how black disappeared from clothes, furniture, painting, and theatres, where, like the colour green, it had the reputation of bringing bad luck. Mourning was done in purple. Pigs, until then predominantly black, became pink through deliberate crossbreeding. The colour black was used in 27 per cent of coats of arms in the Middle Ages, but this dropped to 20 per cent in the seventeenth century and 14 per cent in the eighteenth century!

Lethière proved so gifted that he was offered a residency at the French Academy in Rome, in the famous Mancini Palace. It was a rare honour, as many applied to study there but few were successful. For example, Jacques-Louis David, the future First Painter to the

Emperor of France, tried to commit suicide after being rejected for the second time. Some applied seven times before succeeding.

Having won second place in the Grand Prix de Rome in 1784, Lethière was accepted as an official boarder for four years. Inspired by the ruins of the Forum and the Capitol, he drew the first sketches for his *Brutus Condemning His Sons to Death*, as well as other historical subjects. His career developed as he gained more and more prestige: he was the director of the French Academy in Rome for ten years, a member of the Academy of Fine Arts, professor at the School of Fine Arts in 1819.

Nevertheless, Lethière was not satisfied. He was in search of his life's masterpiece, his definitive work... Until the day he realized that the great subject that obsessed him was literally inscribed on his skin. So Lethière 'dared to be black'.

He had prudently chosen never to evoke his origins in his work, and had made people 'forget his colour'. In 1822, during the last years of his life, he started painting *The Oath of the Ancestors*, with which he would truly make his mark. This large canvas (333 by 225 cm) is an allegorical representation of the November 1802 reconciliation between Alexandre Pétion, the leader of the mulattoes of Saint-Domingue, and the black general Jean-Jacques Dessalines, Toussaint Louverture's lieutenant and leader of the black troops. This union had made the French defeat inevitable, and it asserted Haiti's right to independence.

In 1822 there were very few partisans of Haitian independence in France. Either people said nothing, or else they supported the reconquest of the island. The abolitionist, Abbé Grégoire, in a letter to one of his American correspondents, wrote: 'Free Haiti is a lighthouse that illuminates the Caribbean Sea. The terror of oppressors, the hope of the oppressed.'

For the first time in his life, Lethière added a reference following his signature, as a kind of protest: 'Born in Guadeloupe. Year 1760.'

This painting, rediscovered in very bad shape in the Port-au-Prince cathedral in Haiti, was restored in the Louvre Museum in Paris and returned to the Haitian people, to whom the painter had gifted it. It was exhibited for many years in the National Palace, the official residence of the Haitian president, where it was damaged in the terrible earthquake of February 2010.

'A Fist Shot Up to Shatter the Fog'

Louis Delgrès   Solitude
2 August 1766–28 May 1802   1772–19 November 1802

> Resisting oppression is a natural right.
> Louis Delgrès

On 10 May 1802 Louis Delgrès ordered that a proclamation be posted on the trees and walls of the neighbourhoods of Basse-Terre, in Guadeloupe. It was more than just a tract, or a call to resist the troops sent by the French Consul Napoleon Bonaparte under the command of General Richepanse. It was a declaration of universal rights and a call for equality between all races:

TO THE ENTIRE UNIVERSE, THE LAST CRY OF INNOCENCE AND DESPAIR.

These are the greatest days of a century that will forever be known for the triumph of enlightenment and philosophy. And yet in this same period, there exists a class of unfortunates who are threatened with destruction, and find themselves forced to raise their voices so that posterity will know, once they have disappeared, of their innocence and misery.

This cry of revolt came on the heels of the tragic re-establishment of slavery on the island of Guadeloupe. After the abolition of slavery in 1794, liberty lasted only for a short while. Eight years later, on 17 May 1802, Bonaparte decided to re-establish slavery in order to restore the sugar economy. 'We must disarm all the *Negroes*, of whatever their political party, and put them back to work in the fields', he had declared six months earlier in October 1801. 'And you, ferocious African, who for a moment stands triumphant over the graves of the masters you cowardly slaughtered', exclaimed one Baudry Deslozières, a contemporary of Napoleon, 'you must now return to the political nothingness to which nature herself destined you. Your atrocious vanity only proves beyond a shadow of doubt that servitude is your lot in life. Return to your duty and rely only on the generosity of your masters. They are white and French.'

In the context of war against Britain, the French economy could not survive without colonial commerce, which depended on strategic and economic control. The Code Noir had to be re-established. For this task Bonaparte chose a man of character, or rather a man of a disturbing character, Rear-Admiral Lacrosse. Having just arrived on the island in May 1801, Lacrosse not only had several well-respected officers 'of colour' arrested and deported, but he also levied onerous taxes with which he generously lined his own pockets. When General Béthencourt died, the next in line was Colonel Pélage. But he was a mulatto, so Lacrosse blocked his appointment. And he continued the deportations. It was a frenzy that eventually triggered a revolt among the soldiers, which he bloodily repressed. However, when he tried to arrest one of the most popular officers on the island, Joseph Ignace, it was too much. This time, the entire population was outraged. They rose up and threw him into prison.

The citizens of Guadeloupe could only wait for Bonaparte to send them a new governor, hoping he would prove himself a better Republican than his predecessor. They created a Provisional Council to govern the island, under the command of Magloire Pélage, assisted by two white men and a mulatto. Pélage was nothing like Toussaint Louverture. An individual who always played by the rules, he never stopped proclaiming his loyalty to France and to Bonaparte, which didn't make him very popular with the people of Guadeloupe. Without Pélage, the history of the Antilles would have been different. But Pélage was a coward. He hedged his bets and ultimately became a Judas and an executioner.

He did make one good decision, however, by naming his comrade Louis Delgrès commander of Basse-Terre. There was no citizen more valiant or battle-hardened.

Louis Delgrès was the son of a white planter from Martinique and a mixed-race woman. Born in Saint-Pierre in Martinique, he was a child of the islands, though not Guadeloupean. He was a 'free person of colour'. He was made a sergeant at the age of just 17. In 1791, after royalists had taken power in Martinique, he went into exile in Dominica, halfway between Guadeloupe and Martinique.

In December 1792 he rejoined the Republican ranks. In 1794 he was an officer in the Battalion of the Antilles. In 1795 he participated in a battle that took St Lucia back from the British. Gravely wounded during this campaign, he was promoted to captain as a reward for his valour. And Louis Delgrès continued fighting in the service of the Republic.

Bonaparte, meanwhile, having learned about the situation in Guadeloupe and the forced exile of Lacrosse, ignored the proclamations of loyalty coming from Colonel Pélage. For him, the revolt against Lacrosse was nothing but a mutiny. On 25 March 1802 France signed the Treaty of Amiens with Britain. The period of calm that ensued allowed Bonaparte to launch a punitive expedition against the island. He put General Antoine Richepanse in command, and his ultimate mission was to re-establish slavery.

Richepanse set sail with 4,000 men travelling on ten frigates. On 4 May 1802 he entered Pointe-à-Pitre, cheered on by a section of the population, naively convinced of France's good intentions. But the troops were unmoved by this welcome and took up positions at strategic points on the island. Then, without any further explanation, the proud soldiers of the colonial army were ordered to put down their weapons. Those who hesitated were immediately cast into chains in the holds of General Richepanse's fleet. Colonel Pélage submitted to the general's authority without resistance. In return, he remained free.

As for Louis Delgrès and Joseph Ignace, they deserted and tried to organize local resistance. In May Delgrès published this very eloquent proclamation, known as the 'Proclamation of 10 May, 1802'. The officer Monnereau, who collaborated in writing it, would pay with his life for this brave act:

> What are these demonstrations of authority with which we have been threatened? Are the bayonets of those brave soldiers, whose arrival we have been awaiting, and which previously were only directed against enemies of the Republic, to be turned against us? Ah! But if we consider the demonstrations of authority already revealed in Pointe-à-Pitre, it would seem that they are instead killing people slowly in prisons. Well! We choose to die more quickly. Let us dare say it. The maxims of even the most atrocious tyranny have been surpassed today. Our old tyrants allowed a master to emancipate his slave. But it seems that, in this century of philosophy, there exist men, grown powerful thanks to the distance that separates them

from those who appointed them, who only want to see men who are black or take their origins from this colour in the chains of slavery. From you, First Consul of the Republic, warrior-philosopher, we expected the justice we deserved. Is it just that we are left to deplore our distance from the home from which the sublime ideas which we have so often admired emanate? Ah! Without a doubt one day you will acknowledge our innocence. Then it will be too late. Perverse men will already have used the slander they pour on us to consummate our ruin.

Citizens of Guadeloupe, you for whom a difference in the colour of the epidermis is enough of a reason for you not to fear the vengeance with which we have been threatened – unless they make it a crime to not carry arms against us – you have heard the motivations that excite our indignation. Resisting oppression is a natural right. The divinity itself cannot be offended that we are defending our cause, which is that of humanity and justice. We will not soil it with even the shadow of a criminal act. Yes, we are resolved to defend ourselves, but we will not become aggressors. Stay in your homes, and fear nothing from us. We swear solemnly to respect your wives, your children, your properties, and to use all our power to make sure they are respected by others.

And you, posterity! Shed a tear for our sorrows, and we will die satisfied.

Signed, the commander in chief of the Armed Forces of Basse-Terre,

Louis Delgrès

The words printed in this proclamation spread like wildfire. Immediately, hundreds of men, women, and adolescents rushed to join Delgrès' troops. Life had changed for them in the previous eight years since slavery had been abolished. Even if there was a great deal of progress still to be made, they had forged new lives for themselves. Some had become teachers, artisans, and merchants. And now were they to be chained up once again on the plantations, under the orders of white masters? Were they to be transformed back into beasts of burden?

Aimé Césaire evokes the beliefs underpinning this revolt in a moving poem, 'Memorial to Louis Delgrès':

a mist arose
the same that has obsessed me always
tissues of noises of fetters of chains lacking keys
of scraping of tongs
of a splashing of spittle

the mist solidifies and a fist goes up
to shatter the mist
the fist that has obsessed me always

The tragedy lasted 18 long days.

The very same night of the 10 May declaration, 600 of Richepanse's soldiers were pushed back at the Morne Soldat, in the town of Trois-Rivières. Four days later, on 14 May 1802, Richepanse besieged Fort Saint-Charles, to which Delgrès and his troops had withdrawn. There were only 14 days left before the end. Fighting raged. Pélage, described by Aimé Césaire as a 'colonialist dog', led the assaults against Delgrès, his former comrade in arms.

A large number of women participated in the resistance: Marthe-Rose, Delgrès' own wife, and, among many others, the mixed-race woman, Solitude. She was there, pistol in hand. Her partner, who was, like her, a maroon, stood by her side. She was four months pregnant with his child.

We must acknowledge the role of women in these struggles against the institution of slavery, and honour them. The conditions of enslavement placed women in a pivotal position. In the Antilles as in the United States they played a critical role in these resistance efforts. In Haiti, the warrior Défilée, 'the Madwoman', carried Dessalines' body to the cemetery. In Jamaica, in 1773, Nanny led the maroons against the British. In the United States, Harriet Tubman and many other women took part in the struggle. One need only look back a few years and recall the huge strikes of 2009 in Guadeloupe, which saw many female leaders. Gender parity was respected!

Solitude is one of those women who left their mark on history. She didn't believe in the 1794 proclamation granting 'liberty' to black people. She had seen too much and knew the white masters too well to have any confidence in their humanity or their sincerity. Could a simple decree transform people's minds and spirits? Since her birth, in 1772, she had been sold and resold. Raped and beaten. She had witnessed horrors. So she decided to escape and join a community of maroons in Goyave.

Beyond the daily exploitation suffered by all slaves, women were mistreated in particular ways. When they were sold, they were separated from their men and their children. Yes, Solitude had been right to run away, for liberty was far from won. Moreover, the choice offered to the 'freed slaves' was a very limited one: either they could join the 'army of the black sans-culottes' to fight a war that wasn't their own, essentially spilling their blood on behalf of the French in their fight against the British; or they could return to lives of forced labour on their former plantations. One form of bondage or another.

From the moment slavery had been abolished, the French authorities had worried about those women and men who, in the name of 'liberty, equality, and fraternity', had fled the plantations. They hunted the fugitives down and destroyed their camps.

By the time of the 1802 siege of Fort Saint-Charles, Solitude had been playing cat and mouse with the French authorities for four years. She was glad to finally come out of hiding and join the fight. The siege raged around her...

And I sing of Delgrès on the ramparts ensconced
for three days surveying the blue heights of a dream
projected beyond the sleep of the people
for three days sustaining sustaining with the frail woof of
   his hands
our sky of squashed pollen

Delgrès' troops were short of food, supplies, and ammunition. Richepanse was just as exhausted. He called for reinforcements from Pointe-à-Pitre.

During the night of 22 May, Louis Delgrès and Joseph Ignace managed to escape the fort and vanish into the thick vegetation of the island with their troops. Ignace headed in the direction of Pointe-à-Pitre with about a thousand men in order to incite the population to revolt. However, he fell into a trap laid for him at Baimbridge, on the outskirts of Pointe-à-Pitre. Pélage had lost no time: he had assembled all the men of the city who had sold themselves to the colonists. On 25 May, at 3 a.m., he ordered cannon fire against the insurgent troops. Afterwards, they counted 665 corpses of women, men, and teenagers, including Ignace and two of his sons. Ignace's head was later impaled and exhibited on a spike. The survivors were executed by firing squad. Their memory lives on in Césaire's poem.

But when at Baimbridge Ignace was killed
when the vulture the colonialist hurrah
had hovered in its triumph over the shuddering islands

then History hoisted on its highest flagpole
the drop of blood of which I speak
wherein was mirrored as in deepest degree
that unwonted breach of fate

Louis Delgrès found refuge, along with 500 exhausted women and men, at the foot of the Soufrière volcano, on the d'Anglemont estate. It was in the village of Matouba, in the commune of Saint-Claude. Even as they ingeniously fortified the manor house, Delgrès knew it would be their tomb. What could they do against 1,800 men armed with rifles and cannon? Delgrès told all those who wished to leave that they were free to do so. Three hundred rebels gathered around him, and set off to confront Richepanse's troops in order to delay their advance. Solitude advanced with them. The father of her child had just died in the fighting.

It was 28 May 1802. The final day.

Morne Matouba
Abrupt place. Abrupt name. Godforsaken. Below
in Constantine Pass where the two rivers
peel off their hiccoughing snakeskins
there lay Richepanse in ambush
(Richepanse colonialistic bear with violet gums
fond of the sun's honey gathered from logwood)

Delgrès was wounded, his troops partly surrounded. They retreated and took refuge in the fort. Honour and dignity gave their lives meaning in these final hours.

They had placed barrels of gunpowder under the terrace. They were camouflaged so that Richepanse's troops would not see them. Both Delgrès and his aide-de-camp were ready to light the fuse.

They say that the 300 women, men, and children in the fortified manor held hands in silence. Then, at 3.30 p.m. in the afternoon, as the French advance guard broke through the entrance of the house, their bayonets fixed, they cried out 'Live Free or Die!' There followed a silence. Then a terrible explosion.

and this bordered on the exode of the drama
everything trembled but Delgrès

Richepanse and his men searched the rubble for any wounded who they could finish off or hang. Among them they found Solitude. Since she was pregnant, they decided to put her in prison. She had a future slave in her belly. It would be a waste of money to kill her!

In all, they killed 10,000 rebels. They were shot, hanged, or burned alive.

On 11 June Delgrès' wife was carried on a stretcher to her execution.

On 16 June Richepanse issued a decree re-establishing slavery in Guadeloupe: 'Until otherwise ordered, the title of French citizen will be carried throughout this colony and its dependencies only by whites. No other individual will be allowed to take on this title or to exercise any of the functions attached to it.'

On 18 November Solitude gave birth to her child.

On 19 November she was led to the gallows.

A few days later, the baby would be sold on the slave market. But if he lived long enough, resisted for long enough, if he reached the age of 46, then he eventually would have experienced the liberty for which all those Guadeloupeans had given their lives.

'Ain't I a Woman?'

Sojourner Truth
November 1797–26 November 1883

Sojourner Truth's face was craggy, her hands as large as wooden paddles, her gnarled arms like rope. Her voice was deep and her gait awkward. Her body had been shaped by physical labour. In the time of slavery, there was no 'sexual division of labour'. On the plantation, men and women were equal, both treated as beasts of burden. A mare was as good a stallion at pulling a plough. Women did the same work as men; they received the same food rations and just as many lashes of the whip. In fact, when slaves were sold at market, buyers chose the strongest looking bodies without differentiating by sex. The only important difference was skin colour. Lighter-skinned women, often born from the rape of their mothers, had the 'good fortune' to be taken as domestics, or 'favourites'. The sexual exploitation of these women was one of the most common social practices of the slave system: their bodies did not belong to them.

The women moulded by this forced labour were considered, according to the ideology of the slave system, to be virile and incapable of empathy. They were said not to possess a 'maternal instinct', let alone a sense of morality. 'Look at the infant mortality rates on our plantations!' the planters would say. In reality, the children's deaths were due to a lack of hygiene and care, but also to the resistance of mothers who refused to let their children live through the same ordeal as them. According to 'the law of the womb', the child of a slave belonged to the slave's master and would remain a slave for life. A slave woman transmitted her servile condition to her children, and this was a source of immense suffering for her.

'The specificity of their struggle on the plantations can be seen in the widespread practice of infanticide', the philosopher Elsa Dorlin tells me. 'It was a practice that lasted until the abolition of slavery in France, in 1848, and in the United States in 1865.'

Most contemporary stereotypes still deploy deeply caricatured images of the black woman. Either she is 'hyper-eroticized', endowed with a predatory eroticism, contrary to the gentle and passive image of 'femininity'; or she is represented as a 'de-eroticized' mama, frightening and overpowering.

Since the child belonged entirely to the white master, the role of the father was reduced to that of being the simple progenitor. This image of the woman who has to take care of all her own needs persists to this day in the Antilles. My mother had five children by five different men and raised us by herself. The absence of a father was neither shocking nor troubling for us. Mothers took on this solitude with dignity. That is still the structure of many families in the Antilles today.

Having refused her slave name, she chose another, more beautiful one. Sojourner, that is 'she who sojourns', or remains, and 'Truth'. She was born Isabella Baumfree, in the Dutch colony of the Count of Ulster, in the state of New York. When she was sold at the age of 11, she spoke only Dutch.

When she was 20, she was married against her will to a slave named Thomas. In 1827 she ran away from her master's farm with her youngest daughter, her other children having been sold to other plantations. She took refuge in Canada. Then, in 1828, slavery was abolished in New York. She worked for around ten years in religious communities.

In 1843 she experienced a revelation that changed the course of her life. God called upon her to liberate her people from slavery. How many of the great female figures of resistance, from Dona Beatriz in the eighteenth century to Alice Lenshina in the twentieth, have found unparalleled strength in faith! Celestial voices encouraged her to preach her cause tirelessly. And preach she did, in Connecticut, Massachusetts, Ohio, Indiana, and Kansas.

Sojourner Truth was the first black woman in the United States to speak out publicly against slavery. Through her eloquence and the strength of her faith, she touched thousands of people. 'I feel such a powerful force within me, as though the power of a nation was behind me.' Across her breast she wore a banner bearing the words: 'Proclaim Liberty throughout all the land unto all the inhabitants thereof.' In 1850, to assist her in the task of liberating souls and to support her work as a pilgrim, she published *The Narrative of Sojourner Truth: A Northern Slave*.

If we still remember Sojourner Truth today, then it is above all because of her militant activism on behalf of black women. Sixty years earlier during the French Revolution, the white activist Marie-Olympe de Gouges, disgusted by the misogyny of the Declaration of the Rights of Man and the Citizen, wrote a Declaration of the Rights of Woman and the Female Citizen, which includes these two articles:

> Article 1: Woman is born free and lives equal to man in her rights. Social distinctions can be based only on the common utility.
> Article 13: For the support of the public force and the expenses of administration, the contributions of woman and man are equal; she shares all the duties and all the painful tasks; therefore, we must have the same share in the distribution of positions, employment, offices, honours, and jobs.

Marie-Olympe de Gouges also wrote a play entitled *Black Slavery*. She intelligently observed the extent to which the condition of women could be compared to that of slaves. She knew that to be a woman meant always being considered inferior to men, always having to demand one's rights and justify oneself. She also knew how much it cost to resist. She was sentenced to death. The prosecutor of the Commune of Paris, celebrating her execution, described her as 'that woman-man, the impudent Olympe de Gouges who was the first to create female clubs, who abandoned the care of her household to get mixed up in politics...'

But Marie-Olympe de Gouges was limited by the thinking of her era and never dealt with the question of female slaves. For her, women were white and slaves were male. It was only with Sojourner Truth that the plight of black women was truly discussed – and she spoke in their name.

In 1851 Sojourner was a delegate to the first National Women's Rights Convention, in Akron, Ohio. Hearing a man in the room protest a woman's claim to equality, Sojourner stood up, walked to the stage, and gave a short speech that has become famous under the title 'Ain't I a Woman?'

> That man over there says that women need to be helped into carriages, and lifted over ditches, and to have the best place everywhere. Nobody ever helps me into carriages, or over mud-puddles, or gives me any best place! And ain't I a

woman? Look at me! Look at my arms! I have ploughed and planted, and gathered into barns, and no man could head me! And ain't I a woman? I could work as much and eat as much as a man – when I could get it – and bear the lash as well! And ain't I a woman? I have borne 13 children, and seen most all sold off to slavery, and when I cried out with my mother's grief, none but Jesus heard me! And ain't I a woman?'

During the Civil War (1861–65), Sojourner organized collections of food and supplies for the soldiers of the regiments of black troops in the Union army. In 1864 President Abraham Lincoln received her at the White House. In the wake of the Emancipation Proclamation, she helped black refugees find work. At the same time, she pursued a far more ambitious, long-term political project. At numerous public appearances, she proposed the idea of the creation of a black state in the west of the United States.

A woman resolutely ahead of her time, she campaigned for the abolition of the death penalty, for the rights of the poor, for prison reform, for the right of ex-slaves to own land.

She died on 26 November 1883 in Battle Creek, Michigan, in a community of Quakers – those 'Friends of Human Progress' – who had welcomed her with open arms.

Since her death, Sojourner Truth's influence has only grown. Here are two examples:

'The robot we are sending to Mars is called Sojourner Truth', my friend Cheick Modibo Diarra of NASA told me, because it is 'travelling' to tell the 'Truth'.

At the April 2009 unveiling of a bust of Sojourner Truth at the Visitor Centre of the US Capitol, Michelle Obama declared: 'I hope that Sojourner Truth would be proud to see me, a descendant of slaves, serving as the first lady of the United States of America.' It is no small matter that Michelle Obama, a free woman and an activist, testified to how much this other woman – free, courageous, independent, always struggling for justice – played an important role in the construction of her own personal identity.

The Greatest Russian Poet

Alexander Pushkin

6 June 1799–10 February 1837

Will freedom come – and cut my tether?
It's time, it's time! I bid her hail;
I roam the shore, await fair weather,
And beckon to each passing sail.
O when, my soul, with waves contesting,
And caped in storms, shall I go questing
Upon the crossroads of the sea?
It's time to quit this dreary lee
And land of harsh, forbidding places;
And there, where southern waves break high,
Beneath my Africa's warm sky,
To sigh for somber Russia's spaces,
Where first I loved, where first I wept,
And where my buried heart is kept.

Alexander Pushkin, Eugene Onegin

Pushkin is a Russian icon. No political regime has ever dared tamper with his image. When communism ended, his bust replaced that of Lenin. Many Russians can recite entire passages of his work. Each year on 6 June there are public readings of his poems near the Ielokhovski Cathedral in Moscow, where he was baptized. Which proves that one can be the 'sun that lights up the Russian conception of the world' (Dostoyevsky), the 'original model for Russian identity' (Grigoriev), 'the first Russian poet-artist' (Bélinski), while having what Mongo Beti calls 'the swarthy skin of quadroons and octoroons…'

The story of Pushkin's African origins is more than a curious anecdote. For his African origins had moulded him, and he knew where he came from.

It's true that Pushkin was born to a Russian mother with white, not black, skin, who was a descendant of General Abraham Petrovich Hannibal (see pp. 34–36 above), and to a Russian father of mixed Italian and German descent. He might never have claimed any attachment to his blackness. He might even have forgotten his distant filiation to an African ancestor who he had never known, had he not heard himself called a 'piccaninny' and a 'monkey'.

The world had changed. It was the nineteenth century, and the young Pushkin endured a kind of prejudice that his great-grandfather had escaped in eighteenth-century Russia. At the beginning of the nineteenth century, the stereotypes of modern 'science', which classified the so-called races according to their colour and their physical shape, had begun to seep into Russia.

Pushkin himself was caught in this trap and at the age of 15 described himself thus:

A genie's mini-mutiny,
A monkey's mouth and chin...

If he constructed his own identity as half-Russian, half-African, it was because public scrutiny forced him to. He grew up thinking of himself as Russian and African. Later, he would say that he had a double identity and he would write about it in his work. 'I am the only figure in Russian literature who counts among his ancestors a Negro', he wrote.

When, in 1820, he was exiled to Odessa because of some seditious poems he had written, he made friends with another African, a privateer named Morali (i.e. the Moor Ali). 'Maybe Ali and I have a common ancestor', he mused.

This claim to a double culture marks out Pushkin as a 'modern' writer, one who raised questions about 'cultural diversity' that simply did not arise for other Russian writers of the period.

In his correspondence, he wrote about his 'negro brothers', described slavery in the United States as 'intolerable', and denounced 'the disgusting cynicism, cruel prejudice, and intolerable tyranny' of American society. A descendant of slaves like millions of blacks in the Americas, Pushkin was very sensitive about his genealogy as is often the case for blacks of the diaspora. In *Eugene Onegin*, he informs his readers of a project very close to his heart: 'In Russia, where, due to a lack of historical memoirs, great men are quickly forgotten, the singularity of Hannibal's life is known only through family legend. In time, I hope to publish his complete biography.' He was speaking of his great-grandfather, Abraham Petrovich Hannibal.

To write this text, which would become the short story 'Peter the Great's Negro', Pushkin carried out numerous tiring journeys to the countryside where he met with the only living son of this great-grandfather, a retired general. A letter written in August 1825 attests to the frequency of their visits: 'I'm planning once again to go and see my old Negro Great-Uncle who, I suppose, will die one of these days, and there are still some of his memories of my ancestor that I need him to pass on to me.'

Pushkin was also modern in his style. His language combined the legacy of the great writers with forms of popular expression. He met with peasants, studied folklore and tradition, listened to popular tales. He even gave his heroes peasant names. It was a literary revolution in Russia. Elitism was finished. Russian popular culture entered into literature. The people found in him a narrator who gave them a voice.

Pushkin was a rebel in all things. He challenged the autocratic imperial system and never hesitated to give literary form to this challenge. Rather than using his pen in the name of conventional values, he composed verses that were vitriolic, audacious, and sensual, revealing a dangerous freedom of thought. He threw the authorities into a panic and put the clergy on edge. Consequently, he was exiled, censored, constantly harassed. Finally, his enemies rid themselves of this rebel by means of a duel.

The official reason for this duel was the mundane jealously of a bloodthirsty man. Indeed, Pushkin was often compared to the black Othello who stabbed his own wife! Supposedly, his adversary, an officer of the tsar's guard named Baron Dantès (a French dandy whom every woman wanted for a lover), had the audacity to court the poet's wife, the very beautiful Natalia Goncharova.

In reality, this was a conspiracy devised by those at the very highest levels of power, for whom Dantès was just a puppet. Pushkin's African heritage was used in the fabricated accusations that led to his death. It was well known that Pushkin didn't mess around when it came to his honour, and he had repeatedly talked about a duel. But it was also known that he fought only when he felt truly humiliated, not for trifling matters. In 1832, when a colonel whom he had accused of cheating at cards challenged him to a duel by pistol, Pushkin arrived bearing a handful of cherries!

Pushkin had no chance against Dantès, and he knew it. So why did he fight an officer of the guard who was reputed to be invincible? Because the week before, at a ball in the royal court, Dantès had once again come to woo Natalia and, this time, one 'detail' pushed him over the edge: he pointedly wore a massive ring with the image of a monkey imprinted on it.

A fight to the death over a ring? Pushkin – so intelligent, so cultured – gave into the prevailing racist discourse. Why didn't he just mock Dantès by pointing to his monkey ring and saying: 'Is that your family's coat of arms?' He could also have arrived at the scene of the duel with flowers, or simply shown a disdainful compassion towards the man.

On the morning of 27 January 1837, Pushkin rose early without telling his wife. He wrote a response to a young writer regarding a translation, and then went out. He met his witness Danzas, whom he had tasked with buying the pistols, and then went to a park in St Petersburg, on the banks of the Tchernaïa (the 'Black' River). The witnesses had to pack down the snow that covered the ground.

The duel began.

> … Advancing coldly,
> With quiet, firm, and measured tread,
> Not aiming yet, the foes took boldly
> The first four steps that lay ahead –
> Four fateful steps. The space decreasing

Dantès shot first. Pushkin was hit in the stomach but he had just enough time to shoot back, wounding his adversary in the arm. Then he fainted.

When his death was announced two days later, the entire population mourned. Russia had been widowed. Thousands came to bow before his dead body, to the point that they had to knock down one of the walls of his house to accommodate the crowd.

Pushkin's case is interesting. Here was a man with an eighth of 'black blood', who became entirely black in the eyes of his contemporaries, and who ended up seeing himself as black.

Talking with my son Khephren one day, I asked him:

'Are you the only black student in your class?'
'But Dad … I'm not black!'
'Oh really? What colour are you?'
'Well, I'm brown.'

He was right. When you think about it, there is no such thing as black or white. As the Congolese painter Cheri Samba has said: 'Why don't we rid ourselves of these misleading terms?'

The First Black American Presidential Candidate

Frederick Douglass
1817/1818–20 February 1895

Frederick Douglass was born in 1817 or 1818 – as a slave, his birth was not officially recorded, and he never knew for sure when it happened – in Tuckahoe, on a plantation in the state of Maryland. His childhood was scarred by the violence and ignorance that surrounded him. Douglass recounted a conversation between his master and his wife: 'If you teach that nigger (speaking of myself) how to read', his master told his wife one day, 'there would be no keeping him. It would forever unfit him to be a slave. He will at once become unmanageable, and of no value to his master.' The young Frederick never forgot these words. As a result, he poured his efforts into learning to read and write in order to gain his liberty. His head, like a compass, was henceforth turned towards the North, the states where liberty reigned. And eventually he made it there, in 1838, having used his prodigious ingenuity to overcome thousands of obstacles. Only 20 years old at the time, Douglass found work, established himself, married, and became a highly regarded abolitionist. In 1845 he published his famous autobiography, *Narrative of the Life of Frederick Douglass*.

Let's begin with the scandal caused by this *Narrative*. It enraged the anti-abolitionists. That was because Douglass told the truth.

> Mr Gore once undertook to whip one of Colonel Lloyd's slaves, by the name of Demby. He had given Demby but few stripes, when, to get rid of the scourging, he ran and plunged himself into a creek, and stood there at the depth of his shoulders, refusing to come out. Mr Gore told him that he would give him three calls, and that, if he did not come

out at the third call, he would shoot him. The first call was given. Demby made no response, but stood his ground. The second and third calls were given with the same result. Mr Gore then, without consultation or deliberation with any one, not even giving Demby an additional call, raised his musket to his face, taking deadly aim at his standing victim, and in an instant poor Demby was no more. His mangled body sank out of sight, and blood and brains marked the water where he had stood.

Thrown into a panic by these texts, plantation owners orchestrated a campaign of defamation. A certain A. C. C. Thompson testified that he had known Frederick Douglass well and affirmed that he was a brute incapable of stringing two words together. But Douglass had the support of one of the most powerful abolitionist organizations of the North, the Massachusetts Anti-Slavery Society. William Lloyd Garrison, the leader of this group, had noticed Douglass four years earlier when he was speaking in a lecture hall. Enraptured by his eloquence, his elevated thinking, and the justice apparent in his reflections, Garrison immediately asked him to act as as ambassador for the slaves' cause.

As a fugitive black slave who knew how to defend his beliefs, Douglass became a clear target. The property-owners incriminated in his book put a price on his head. Consequently, he was forced to flee and spend a few months in Britain, where he gave lectures. He then returned to Massachusetts to once again preach abolitionism.

His speeches were marked by a profound knowledge of the Bible and of religion. By the time he was 12, he had secretly read (thanks to a small sum he had saved up from shining shoes) a collection of essays, poems, and political dialogues called *The Columbian Orator*. Each day he pored over the text as though reading from a prayer book. Among the many revelations it contained that helped him understand the bleakness of his everyday life, there was a conversation between a slave and his master. The master lays out all of the arguments used to justify slavery. But the slave refutes them all so successfully that his master frees him! The book also included a speech by the writer Richard Brinsley Sheridan devoted to Catholic emancipation, which helped to trigger Douglass's religious conversion.

'The light broke in upon me by degrees', he liked to tell his audiences. He recounted the story of how he became conscious of the injustice that had befallen his black sisters and brothers, of why and how reading became a sacred act for him. He described the difficulties that studded his 'intellectual marronage'. He said that the discoveries he made through reading didn't always bring him joy, but that instead they sometimes opened up an abyss inciting fear, worry, anger, and hatred. Of his access to reading, he later wrote with candid retrospection: 'It had given me a clear view of my wretched condition, without providing the remedy of escape.'

Standing before delighted crowds in lecture halls, he described the tricks he had used to learn to read without attracting the wrath of masters who, had they discovered him, would immediately have condemned him to a whipping. Or worse, if they had caught him at it again.

Better fed than many of the poor white children in the neighbourhood, he traded his bread for 'that more valuable bread of knowledge'. Sometimes he stole the notebooks of one of his master's sons. But the strategy that worked best for him was to form friendships with the white boys of his age and make them his teachers.

It was during this decisive period of self-discovery that the young Douglass had an encounter that changed his life. When he told this story during his speeches, the audience was so silent, you could hear a pin drop in the lecture hall.

> I went one day down on the wharf of Mr Waters; and seeing two Irishmen unloading a scow of stone, I went, unasked, and helped them. When we had finished, one of them came to me and asked me if I were a slave. I told him I was. He asked, 'Are ye a slave for life?' I told him that I was. The good Irishman seemed to be deeply affected by the statement ... They both advised me to run away to the north; that I should find friends there, and that I should be free. I pretended not to be interested in what they said, and treated them as if I did not understand them; for I feared they might be treacherous. White men have been known to encourage slaves to escape, and then, to get the reward, catch them and return them to their masters. I was afraid that these seemingly good men might use me so; but I nevertheless remembered their advice, and from that time I resolved to run away.

Frederick Douglass was determined to escape, but to do that he needed to be able to 'write' on his own passport, to create a forgery. At that time, slaves carried notebooks in which their masters would write down where they were supposed to be travelling. Any white person at any time could demand to see a slave's passport.

But writing is more difficult than reading. Douglass resolved the problem of finding notebooks in which to practise by making use of wooden fences, brick walls, black cobblestones... In place of a pen, he used a piece of chalk. But in order to achieve his aim he also needed models to imitate, teachers, and a method.

Douglass proceeded strategically. He found his method in the Durgin & Bailey shipyard. He observed how the carpenters, after having prepared a piece of wood, would jot down the part of the boat where it was to be used. He learned how to organize letters: for the larboard side, the letter L, for the starboard side, the letter S; the combination L.F. meant larboard side forward, and so forth. He also learned by heart all the names that corresponded to these letters and immediately transcribed them, copying and recopying them endlessly. In addition, whenever he ran into a boy who could read and write, he would pretend he could write better than they could. When they asked him for proof, he would write the letters he had learned and (would) challenge them to do better. 'In this way I got a good many lessons in writing, which it is quite possible I should never have gotten in any other way', concluded Douglass.

Frederick Douglass repeated these anecdotes in all of his lectures, sowing in the minds of those who were listening the idea that there are no limits on this earth, that every barrier can be overcome. Each time, Douglass insisted on the importance of possessing knowledge and culture as fundamental to the understanding of one's situation and the era in which one lived. The weapon of knowledge makes it possible to progress, to disarm the negative forces one confronts in life.

Understanding these forces means that one is no longer a victim of them. Knowledge also increases courage. But the struggle remained, and still remains today, to bring knowledge and culture to places where they are absent, to people who would gain confidence from them.

Unfortunately, even as the consciousness of the people was being awakened to the plight of slaves in the North, the slaves' situation in the South was deteriorating. During the first years of his involvement in the Massachusetts Anti-Slavery Society, Frederick Douglass adopted a strategy of non-violence. But history forced him to change his approach. He increasingly embraced the notion of direct action. In 1850 the US Congress adopted the Fugitive Slave Act, which allowed for the capture of fugitive slaves. In exchange for California's entry into the Union as a 'Free State', the northern states agreed to return any runaway slaves to the South. From that point on, Douglass viewed insurrection as the only way to obtain emancipation.

From 1854 to 1856 he firmly and publicly supported the right of slaves and those who came to their defence to respond violently to slave-owners. He practised what he preached, lodging the famous abolitionist John Brown in his own home in 1858. Douglass had first met Brown a few years earlier, and remarked that although Brown was 'a white gentleman', he was 'a black man in sympathies, and as deeply invested in our cause as though his own soul had been pierced with the iron of slavery'. On 24 and 25 May 1856, accompanied by his sons and three other men, John Brown had taken up his sword and slain five slave-owners at Pottawatomie Creek in Kansas.

But in 1859, Douglass was forced to flee after Brown carried out a new attack, attempting to seize an arms depot in Harper's Ferry as a prelude to an invasion of the southern Appalachians. The operation failed, and Brown was arrested and sentenced by the state of Virginia to death by hanging. The events spurred Victor Hugo to write a magnificent letter to the US government, demanding clemency for Brown: 'Yes, America should know and consider this: that there is something more frightening than Cain killing Abel, and that is Washington killing Spartacus.'

This same Victor Hugo, however, was also taken in by the colonial ideologies of his time. Twenty years later on 18 May 1879, at a banquet commemorating the abolition of slavery, he sat next to Victor Schoelcher, author of the 1848 abolition decree, and Emmanuel Arago, the son of the great Republican thinker François Arago who had signed this decree as minister. 'Go forth, people!' Hugo cried. 'Take this land. Take it! From whom? No one. God gives the land to the people. God gives Africa to Europe. Take it … In the nineteenth century, the white man made the black into a man. In the twentieth century, Europe will lead Africa into the world.'

How many people, still today in the twenty-first century, are unaware of their own racism because their racial prejudices are so deeply inscribed within them? How many of those who claim to be anti-racists actually oppose the pillage of Africa's riches?

In 1860, after six months of exile in Britain, Douglass returned and took up his position once again. The next year was to be crucial. The presidential campaign had begun. Douglass called upon voters to support Abraham Lincoln, the Republican candidate. Naturally, in 1862, a year after the beginning of the Civil War, he supported the enlistment of blacks in the Union forces. He was rewarded for these efforts in 1865 when emancipation was finally proclaimed.

During the war, in 1863, Douglass recruited one hundred soldiers for a black regiment being formed to fight in the South. Among those soldiers recruited were his two sons, Lewis and Charles. At the same time, he fought vehemently against the discrimination that the black troops suffered in the Union army. The year 1865, though, saw the loss of the greatest supporter of the Union's cause with the assassination of President Lincoln on 15 April.

Eight months later, on 18 December 1865, the abolition of slavery was voted into law with the Thirteenth Amendment to the Constitution. But Douglass didn't stop there. He demanded that blacks be granted the right to vote. He fought for this through his support for the next Republican candidate for president, Ulysses S. Grant, and his message was heard. Not only did Grant win the election, but the passing of the Fifteenth Amendment on 26 February 1869 granted civil rights to 'people of colour'.

During this period, the former slave from Maryland was widely honoured. But Douglass's recognition did not slow his political activism, for the question of racial discrimination had never before been posed so incisively. The loss of Lincoln left the country with a deep wound. The Union was in desperate need of his political sense and pragmatism to rebuild itself in the wake of the war. In response to a northern decree banning Confederates from all political activity and administrative positions, southerners resorted to extreme violence. In 1865 a group of former Confederates created the Ku Klux Klan, an organization promoting the supremacy of the white 'race'.

As part of the newly founded Equal Rights Party's platform, Frederick Douglass became the first black presidential candidate in 1872. One of his fellow candidates was Victoria Woodhull, a leader in the movement for women's right to vote in the US and the first woman to be a presidential candidate. This candidacy was no insignificant matter. Men like Douglass paved the way that would eventually lead to the election of Barack Obama as president.

In 1883 the Supreme Court abrogated the law on civil rights. Seven million blacks were essentially ordered to become invisible. They were theoretically 'free' but they could have no civil existence and they must refrain from mixing with whites. This constraint didn't prevent Frederick Douglass from marrying Helen Pitts, his white former secretary, as his second wife in 1884. (His first wife, Anna Murray died in 1882.) On 9 January 1894, shortly before his death, he gave one last speech in Washington, entitled *The Lessons of the Hour*, in which he denounced lynching and discussed 'various aspects of the so-called, but mis-called, Negro problem'. After all, hasn't the real 'problem' of the black man always been the burden of white prejudice?

Smuggling in the Name of Liberty

Harriet Tubman

February/March 1821–10 March 1913

> I freed thousands of slaves. I could have freed
> thousands more, if they had known they were
> slaves.
>
> Harriet Tubman

Harriet Tubman was born Araminta Ross in Maryland, at the time
a slave state on the eastern coast of the United States. From the age
of 6 she was rented out to other slave owners by her master, Edward
Brodess: he needed to turn a profit from her. After all, slavery and
the slave trade existed, above all else, as a socio-economic system
that reduced black men and women to the rank of beasts of burden,
'human tools' that could be bought, sold, rented.

Thus, from an early age, she was put to work in the fields, tasked
with picking up rocks that might blunt the ploughshares. She also
helped sow corn and cotton. While we know little about Harriet's
individual slave life, we know a great deal about the thousands of
other Harriets who, as a group, worked and died on the plantations.
From a young age, their lives were defined by violence, injustice,
and humiliation.

Judging by her later life as a free black woman, a powerful sense
of revolt must have been building within Harriet Tubman during
her years as a slave. She carried the marks of plantation violence in
her spirit and on her body. On one notable occasion, an overseer
on the plantation threw a rock at her head after she had refused
to betray another slave who was planning to run away. As a result,
Harriet suffered serious epilepsy for the rest of her life.

In 1844, Harriet married John Tubman, a freed slave. Was it
a good or a bad marriage? No one really knows. In any case, the
marriage had no effect on her legal status as a slave.

Her master died in 1849. At that time, a death often entailed the sale of 'property', notably a plantation's slaves, by the heirs. Mr Brodess's widow was no exception and decided to sell a part of her 'estate' in order to pay off some debts.

Fearing that she would end up somewhere in the Deep South, where the conditions for slaves were even worse than those she had experienced in Maryland, Harriet began to seriously consider running away. One night in the autumn of 1849, a Saturday to be precise – as notices concerning runaway slaves would not be published until Monday morning – she fled north, leaving her husband behind. As a free man, or at least a man who thought he was free, he didn't want to risk following her. She crossed forests, eating berries, sleeping in thickets, until she met a group of Quakers. The members of this group, founded in 1640 and known as the 'Society of Friends', were the first to fight for equal rights for women and to oppose slavery. On her journey, she also crossed paths with abolitionists of all races and religions who were active in the Underground Railroad, a secret network formed to help fleeing slaves.

They all supported her. Harriet's flight continued, hidden in a bag or in an old cart. One group helped her to cross the Mason-Dixon Line, the border between the abolitionist states of the North and the slave states of the South. Another group brought her to Philadelphia where she quickly found work as a domestic servant.

Struck by this extraordinary network of solidarity, she began to pour her energies into the abolitionist movement, determined to join the struggle. It was William Still (1821–1902), an activist on the Underground Railroad, who first introduced her to the techniques of clandestine flight. He showed her how to cover her tracks and taught her the network's code language made up of railroad terminology (e.g. lines, guards, station chiefs, rails, terminals, and stations). He also explained to her the various passwords and encrypted messages (for example, the 'conductor' was the coordinator who laid out an itinerary, the 'shareholders' were the networks' sympathizers, and 'potatoes' were fugitive slaves hidden under farm produce). Harriet committed to memory all types of signals, contact points, go-betweens, staging posts (in barns, haystacks, caves, chimneys, basements…), flight and disguise strategies, and the psychology necessary to command troops.

Among the now legendary 'employees' of the Underground Railroad was the Canadian Alexander Ross, who travelled around the plantations of the South pretending to be an ornithologist!

For her part, Harriet, having amassed some money, devoted her first journey to saving the members of her family. She had four brothers and a sister enslaved in Maryland and wanted to help them. Relying on the tight-knit quality of the black slave community, she sent messages to her family telling them where to meet. Her initiation into the clandestine world of saving slaves involved successfully leading her four brothers to freedom. Sadly, she was unable to save her sister or her two children.

Harriet departed again immediately to assist other slaves, this time disguised as a farmer. She was carrying two live chickens with her. Shortly after arriving in Maryland, she found herself face to face with one of her former masters, who had placed a bounty on her head after her escape. (The state of Maryland offered up to 12,000 dollars for her capture!) Out of fright, she released her grasp on the chickens. Then she started running after them, putting distance between herself and her former master. It was an involuntary and panicked reaction, but it was an effective one as it saved her life. Quickly regaining her composure, Harriet remembered her task and retraced her steps, eventually guiding her stowaways to Philadelphia.

On 18 September 1850 a truly shameful law, the Fugitive Slave Act, was passed through a compromise between the southern slave states and the free states of the North. The Act was politically and economically expedient for the industrial North, which relied heavily on the agrarian South and realistically could refuse it nothing. The rights of man took a back seat! The Act stipulated that police in the North were to stop those individuals they suspected of being fugitive slaves and to deliver them to the authorities so that they could be returned to their owners. Anyone who assisted a runaway slave could be sentenced to six months in prison and heavily fined. The current laws in France that prohibit and criminalize assistance offered to undocumented immigrants (*sans-papiers*) are thus nothing new...

As is shown by the Oscar-winning film *Twelve Years a Slave* (2013), directed by Steve McQueen, free blacks in the northern states already ran the risk of being sold into slavery in the South by unscrupulous whites. But the Fugitive Slave Act legally created an entire new profession: 'slave chaser'. Out of pure greed, many people in the North hastened to capture free blacks and to sell them to southerners, claiming they were runaway slaves.

The northern states of the US became unlivable for runaway slaves. The network of the Underground Railroad reacted promptly and started sending escaped slaves to Canada, since the abolition of slavery in the British Empire also applied to its North American colonies. There was nothing particularly humanitarian about this decision. It was simply that advances in British industrialization had rendered slavery unnecessary. By putting pressure on other empires to follow suit and abolish slavery, the British Empire consolidated its power. 'Canada is not merely a neighbor to the Negroes', Martin Luther King, Jr declared in a 1967 speech. 'Deep in our history of struggle for freedom, Canada was the North Star.' Between 1840 and 1860, more than 30,000 African-American slaves found liberty in Canada!

The Negro spiritual 'Follow the Drinking Gourd' is one among many that hid a message to slaves telling them which path to take. The lyrics constituted a 'musical itinerary', offering them precise directions on how to escape the South.

> When the sun comes back
> and the first quail calls [migratory birds that pass the winter in the South]
>
> Follow the drinking gourd. [The Big Dipper]
>
> For the old man is waiting [someone]
> for to carry you to freedom,
>
> If you follow the drinking gourd. [...]
>
> The riverbank [the Tombigbee river in Alabama] makes a mighty fine road,
> Dead trees to show you the way
>
> And it's left foot, peg foot, travelling on
> Follow the drinking gourd.

Over the course of a decade, Harriet Tubman completed 19 journeys throughout the South and escorted more than 300 slaves to the Free States and to Canada. She did it – as she liked to repeat – without ever losing a single passenger!

She owed her success not to luck but to her strict adherence to one rule: after making the choice to risk the perilous journey north, no one could change their mind on the way, under penalty of death! Giving up or turning back was not an option. Harriet knew how to ensure respect for this rule.

She never once used the gun she carried, but she kept it at the ready when lives were on the line. As one article about Harriet recounted in 1863: 'Would you really do that?' she was asked. 'Yes', she replied, 'if he was weak enough to give out, he'd be weak enough to betray us all, and all who had helped us; and do you think I'd let so many die just for one coward man.' 'Did you ever have to shoot any one?' she was asked. 'One time', she said, 'a man gave out on the second night; his feet were sore and swollen, he couldn't go any further; he'd rather go back and die, if he must.' They tried all arguments in vain, bathed his feet, tried to strengthen him, but it was of no use, he would go back. Then she said, 'I told the boys to get their guns ready, and shoot him. They'd have done it in a minute; but when he heard that, he jumped right up and went on as well as any body…'

Harriet Tubman carried so many to freedom that the slaves, who called the South 'Egypt', nicknamed her 'Moses'.

In Canada in 1857 she met the famous abolitionist John Brown, who was advocating armed insurrection. It is said that Brown so marvelled at Harriet's intelligence and moral strength that he spoke tirelessly of his admiration, calling her 'General Tubman, General Tubman, General Tubman'.

The financial world viewed the Civil War as a confrontation between two economic doctrines, one based on protectionism and the other on free trade. For Harriet, it was a war of liberation. She joined the Union army and served as a scout, drawing on her knowledge of the terrain. She also organized a network of spies who gathered information about slaves wanting to escape to the Union.

After the war, this woman actively campaigned for the rights of blacks and of women with the bravery of a thousand men. In 1869 she married Nelson Davis, whom she had met during the Civil War and who was 22 years younger than her.

Harriet returned to Auburn, New York in 1873 where she purchased a piece of land. Much later, the US government paid her a small military pension, which she used to build a 'Home for Poor and Elderly African-Americans'. Harriet died at the age of 93.

Against the Invention of the Races

Joseph Anténor Firmin

18 October 1850–19 September 1911

Born in Le Cap Haïtien, Joseph Anténor Firmin belonged to the third generation of independent Haitians. After finishing his studies, he worked in a merchant house and then taught in a private school. Progressive and concerned with the 'question of colour', he founded a newspaper, *The Messenger of the North*. After failing in a bid for political office in 1879 and refusing the offer of a government position, Firmin left for Paris in 1884. Thanks to the support of his friend Louis-Joseph Janvier, a doctor, politician, and writer, he became a member of the Society of Anthropology of Paris, founded in 1859 by Paul Broca, an institution where 'scientific' racism held sway.

As soon as slavery was abolished in France in 1848, a new kind of colonial system was put in place. The country couldn't do without the products of its overseas territories. Ideologues, philosophers, and scientists supported and justified the 'civilizing' work of Westerners. Their arguments reassured everyone, from the exploiters to the respectable middle classes to the common people. Paul Broca affirmed, from his position as University Chair of Clinical Surgery at the Medical School in Paris: 'Never has a people with black skin, woolly hair, and a flat face spontaneously elevated themselves to civilization.' As a classic product of nineteenth-century scientific thought, he considered it his duty to speak the 'truth' about the races: 'No individual interest, however legitimate it may be, can refuse to accommodate itself to the progress of human knowledge or to bend before the truth.' Broca's rigour earned the admiration of his colleagues. He accumulated data, checked and rechecked, never considering the extent to which interpretation of the results was powerfully shaped by the social prejudices of his time. He worked to reach findings upon which society had already agreed. This was not a genuine scientific debate, for the answer had been formulated before the question: the white man stood at the top of the human hierarchy.

These developments took place in a context in which the needs of poorly paid workers and the development of an industrialized society were increasingly pressing. The dominant discourse had profoundly shifted since Montaigne, who had declared in the sixteenth century: 'They are more reasonable than us.' Starting with Descartes, in the seventeenth century, the proposition became more nuanced: 'They are as reasonable as us.' At the end of the eighteenth century, Kant reversed the proposition: 'We are more reasonable than them.' Finally, with Broca and other nineteenth-century scholars, there is no longer any doubt: 'We are the only ones who are reasonable.' During this period, no leader in the Western world questioned the legitimacy of racial classification.

The debate – still relevant today! – always focused on the possibility of education and progress for blacks. Some believed that education could raise them to the level of whites. The most progressive claimed that blacks could catch up if there were a more level playing field. For others, however, such ideas were entirely out of the question, it was a hopeless task... Georges Cuvier, a reputed French naturalist, concluded that the 'African race' was far too degraded for its intelligence to ever develop. Charles Darwin, though a committed abolitionist, nevertheless classified the Hottentots, a people who live in the south of Namibia and in the north-west of South Africa, as falling somewhere between white men and gorillas.

Anthropologists were divided into two clans. The 'monogenesists' were devout Christians, enemies of Darwin and of his theory of natural selection, who stated, Bibles in their hands, that Adam and Eve were the one, true origin of humankind. So why did these two original ancestors and their two children have descendants of different colours? It's very simple, came the response. The expulsion from paradise led certain men (the blacks) to a dramatic degeneration, while others (the whites) were largely unharmed. Original sin had struck down blacks more than it had whites.

The other current of thought was that of the 'polygenesists', who were free thinkers and 'progressives'. They defended 'true' Republican values. They had no truck with biblical interpretations or the reactionary and aristocratic vision developed by Gobineau in the four volumes of his *On the Inequality of the Human Races*. Their approach was modernist, Republican, and democratic. They made up the avant-garde of scientific research and theorization, and dared to defy the Bible by affirming that whites and blacks were of different races.

Their theories radically contradicted the established beliefs of a time when Sunday mass was an unavoidable institution. They won over the elites, but not the wider public. Christians could not accept the thesis of separate races. For them, biblical arguments had, since ancient times, provided all the proof they needed. The curse of Ham, who was punished by his father Noah for having seen him drunk and naked, weighed so heavily on his son Canaan and on Canaan's descendants that slavery, and by extension colonization, were fully justified.

> When Noah awoke from his wine, he knew what his youngest son had done to him.
> So he said, 'Cursed be Canaan; A slave of slaves he shall be to his brothers!'
> He also said, 'Blessed be the LORD, the God of Shem; And let Canaan be his slave!'
> 'May God enlarge Japheth, and let him dwell in the tents of Shem; And let Canaan be his slave!' (Genesis 9:24–27)

At the Society of Anthropology in Paris, however, everyone was broadly in agreement. Sometimes there was almost a consensus. They agreed that there were differences between the black and white races, and came to the conclusion – one that would not shock the colonists in the overseas territories – that it was better to encourage each group to develop its own strengths. In other words, there would be an implicit division in the colonies. Blacks would do manual labour; whites would do the intellectual work.

Some scholars, such as Louis Agassiz, a Swiss naturalist who had emigrated to the United States and was a great promoter of polygenesis, believed that blacks needed to be 'protected from themselves'. The best and most 'humane' way to do this was to encourage the strict separation of the races, while still granting them equal rights. That way, each group could have access to its rightful place. Even though other thinkers began to criticize his ideas towards the end of his life, Agassiz nonetheless contributed to legitimizing the de jure racial segregation that persisted in the United States until the end of the 1960s.

While Agassiz was unable to produce any empirical evidence to support his theories, he was succeeded by George Morton, who collected skulls in support of his racial theories. He had over a thousand at the time of his death, though how he obtained them is unclear. By measuring the size of the skulls, he believed he could determine which were more human than others. He filled the crania with white mustard seeds which he then poured into a graduated cylinder. His methods earned him general admiration in his era. '[A] patchwork of fudging and finagling in the clear interest of controlling a priori convictions', concluded Stephen Jay Gould about these studies in his 1981 book *The Mismeasure of Man*. But, at the time, it was Morton who wielded the numbers – and numbers, because they are susceptible to all kinds of interpretation, have the power to bewitch and to fascinate. The common people and the bourgeoisie applauded his research, especially since his results supported certain business interests. Francis Galton, another scholar, became a true celebrity when he installed his anthropometric laboratory of cranial measurement, along with various other gadgets, at the International Health Exhibition of 1884 and 1885 in London. For a few coins, a visitor could get a certain number of tests and then receive a sheet of paper with the results.

It was within this particular scientific environment, one obsessed with classifications, that Anténor Firmin was admitted into the ranks of the Society of Anthropology of Paris. Firmin bit his lip while listening to the others, barely able to believe his ears. As a Haitian who was proud of his Republic and its heroic history, how could he not be profoundly shocked, mortified even, to hear people affirm the inequality of the human races and the inferiority of the black race? Rather than interrupt the discussions and provoke a violent debate, which he suspected would lead nowhere, given how deeply so many of the figures present were imbued with racist ideas, he instead published a 662-page book entitled *The Equality of Human Races: Positivist Anthropology*.

Firmin possessed an encyclopaedic knowledge. He was an enlightened man, a positivist, and an adept of the 'objective' vision of science outlined by Auguste Comte – an approach founded on facts rather than speculation. Comte argued that an empirical study of humanity, carried out through the meticulous collection of facts, could disprove speculative theories about the inequality of the human races.

Thus, Firmin returned to the research and measurements of anthropometry and craniology, using the data collected by his adversaries to construct his own refutation of their claims. His approach was extremely intelligent, unaggressive, simple, and even humorous at times. Criticizing the fashionable racial mythology, he argued that the notion that there was such a thing as a 'pure' race was debatable given how intensely human groups had mixed over time, and he emphasized that the concept of race primarily served to divide humanity. He discussed the effect of climatic and geographical factors on skin colour and on other physical traits. He was interested in the biochemical substances within the skin, a field that had been little explored until then.

Firmin's work was executed so brilliantly that it reduced the arguments of the anthropologists to a collection of fantasies. As the historian Carole Reynaud Paligot writes in her book *The Racial Republic*: 'It was with no little irony that he compared the scholarly measures taken by Broca and his colleagues to "puerile games", and joked about a series of numbers that in fact showed "the human races, arm in arm, in beautiful proximity", all the while seeming to "laugh in the face of these scholars of classification". Firmin correctly predicted that ultimately, "the critics of the twentieth century would discredit their science".'

His refutation focused not so much on 'common sense', which could so easily be twisted, but on 'good sense', maintaining an ethics devoted to living in unity, rather than to the dividing force of hate. 'There is one easy way to determine how much truth is to be found in certain propositions and their concomitant theories', he wrote. 'One need only follow the development of the ideas on which they are based to find out what principles they lead to and what consequences they entail for scientific and social laws in general. It is from this perspective, then, that we must examine the conclusions reached by the proponents of the thesis of the inequality of the human races. If these conclusions are obviously in contradiction with every idea of progress and justice, or even with common sense; if they can be considered possible only by our overthrowing all the ideas generally considered most correct, the most favourable to stability and harmony among people and things, and the most consistent with humanity's highest aspirations; we should then have every reason to discard as false the theory on which they are based.' Firmin wondered: 'Do the scientists and philosophers who argue that races are not equal want a regime based on distinctions, the establishment of real castes, in their own nations?'

The work was very much ahead of its time and therefore largely ignored. Firmin was isolated, struggling alone against a community of anthropologists whose ideas served the aims of political and colonial powers. To offer an approach that diverged too much from the dominant one was to invite automatic exclusion. Besides, he was black. How could a black man claim to know the truth?

But Firmin never lost his sense of humour. Even as he wrote his book, he knew it would be met with silence. In response to someone who declared to him one day, 'The moral inequality of the races is a proven fact!' he replied laconically, 'So it is.' And he noted in his book his hope that mentalities might have evolved by the twenty-fifth century!

Less amusing, however, were the very real and serious consequences that nineteenth-century anthropological theories had on the world. We can still see their destructive effects today. Pseudo-scientific ideas long justified the maintenance of a substandard education for natives of the colonies. Empires contented themselves with educating colonial auxiliaries rather than men who could actually put their knowledge to good use. Authority had to remain in white hands.

The alliances between certain scientists and the economic, political, literary, and artistic elites led to the widespread diffusion of their theories in the press, in scientific books published for general audiences, and in dictionaries. In the nineteenth-century Larousse dictionary, you can find this observation: 'In the Negro species, the brain is less developed than in the white species, and the cerebral gyrus is less deep'! Human zoos attracted millions of visitors (see pp. 112–16). Textbooks and novels for young adults became receptacles for racial theories. Until the Second World War, students learned not only that there were races, but that these races were not equal.

The radioactivity of this racist thinking spurred eugenicists in the US at the beginning of the twentieth century to use intelligence tests, particularly the famous Intelligence Quotient (or 'IQ') test, to 'scientifically' prove the inferiority not only of black populations but also of Jewish and Eastern European ones. From the results of these tests, immigration restrictions were judged to be absolutely essential.

The beast is far from dead: in 1994 two Americans co-authored a book called *The Bell Curve*, in which they claimed to demonstrate, using statistics, that intelligence is hereditary and that the intelligence of white people is greater than that of black people. The roots of this type of thinking are deep and are still thriving.

Drawing their conclusions from advances made in the field of genetics, scientists today are unanimous in stating that there is only one human race. Nevertheless, the 1948 Universal Declaration of the Rights of Man has yet to be amended to this effect and still contains the word 'race': 'Everyone is entitled to all the rights and freedoms set forth in this Declaration, without distinction of any kind, such as race, colour, sex, language...'

The First Black 'Nègre' at the École Polytechnique of France

Camille Mortenol

29 November 1859–22 December 1930

According to legend, Marshall MacMahon, looking over the new student officers at France's prestigious École Polytechnique (located in Palaiseau, near Paris), stopped in front of the young Camille Mortenol, who was standing to attention in his black tunic adorned with two rows of buttons, and exclaimed: 'Ah! So, you're the *Nègre*? Very well, my friend … As you were!' Before you get offended, dear reader, you need to know that, traditionally, the most brilliant student in each year group was known as the '*Nègre*'. In this particular case, though, this term had a double meaning.

Camille Mortenol was born on 29 November 1859 in Pointe-à-Pitre, on the French Caribbean island of Guadeloupe. The son of André Mortenol and Julienne Toussaint, both former slaves, Camille quickly proved his exceptional intelligence in school. He was the top student in his year and received a scholarship to attend high school in Bordeaux, a city in metropolitan France that had amassed a significant portion of its wealth through participation in the slave trade. Until 1848, 33 years before Mortenol's arrival, the city had been the second most important slave trading port in France. Between 1672 and 1826, its ship-owners deported thousands of Africans to the Caribbean. Strangely, even though the slave trade has been considered a crime against humanity in France since 10 May 2001, there are 25 streets in the city, including the Rue Saige – named after a former mayor – that still carry the names of these slave traders. In Le Havre and La Rochelle, there are still six such streets; in Nantes there are 11. The city of Bordeaux finally acknowledged this aspect of its history in 2009 when it opened two rooms devoted to the history of the slave trade at the Musée d'Acquitaine. But Bordeaux still lags far behind Liverpool, another former slave trading port, where the International Slavery Museum was established in 2007. The goal of the Liverpool museum is 'to address ignorance and misunderstanding by looking at the deep and permanent impact of slavery and the slave trade on Africa, South America, the USA, the Caribbean and Western Europe'.

After several years of high school in Bordeaux, Camille Mortenol felt confident enough to prepare for highly competitive entrance exams to not one but two of France's elite educational institutions: one for admission into the military school of St Cyr, the other for admission to the École Polytechnique. In 1880 he was successful in both exams but decided to enter the Polytechnique, where he became the first black 'Nègre' in the school's history.

But he never forgot where he came from. Slavery had been abolished in Guadeloupe only eleven years before his birth, and his parents had suffered terribly. It is not surprising that his first choice was the École Polytechnique. In 1794, the same year that it abolished slavery, France's National Convention created the school through Article 18 of the Declaration of Rights of the Constitution.

At the time Mortenol entered the École Polytechnique, Guadeloupeans worshipped the heroic figures who had fought for the abolition of slavery: not least, Delgrès, Toussaint Louverture, Abbé Grégoire, as well as Victor Schoelcher, whom Mortenol had met and befriended. When the renowned Schoelcher was buried in 1893, it was Mortenol who led the funeral cortege alongside members of the family.

Mortenol was so successful in his studies at the École Polytechnique that, upon completion of the course, he could freely choose the branch of the military in which he wished to serve. He chose the navy. The decision was shaped by a passion passed on to him by his father who, in 1847, having purchased his own freedom, had become a master sailmaker. The wind of the open seas, the wind of liberty.

Faithfully pursuing his chosen path, the young Mortenol embarked on a prestigious naval career, one that didn't do justice to the truly exceptional nature of the man. His time in the navy began on 16 January 1883, when he boarded the frigate *Alceste* as a midshipman. But he was a victim of 'colour prejudice' and his career ended in 1902 without him ever climbing higher than the rank of ship's captain. Indeed, he had not picked an easy path to follow when he opted for the navy, an aristocratic corps with well-established codes. 'What was the scale of the prejudice encountered by the young Antillean, given the archaic mindset of the period?' wonders Mongo Beti in his *Dictionary of Negritude*.

All the same, Mortenol's career had started well. The president of the committee charged with examining the four midshipmen on the *Alceste* wrote, on 10 October 1883, 'I note with pleasure the presence of the remarkable Mr Mortenol, who has proven himself far superior to his comrades in every way.'

The confidential notes in Mortenol's dossier, conserved in the navy archives at Vincennes in Paris, reveal the reasons for the various 'roadblocks' in his career. In 1892 a vice-admiral noted: 'The officer Mr Mortenol has beautiful black skin and woolly hair. However, no matter how intelligent he is and whatever his apparent qualities, I will always consider it very dangerous to introduce officers of this race into the navy. This branch of the military has often greatly suffered from their presence ... That said, I declare that I have no prejudice against the black race, and my words are guided solely by the language of reason.'

Four years later, on 15 August 1896, more pearls of wisdom were offered by another 'well-intentioned' officer, a certain Forestier, the captain of a frigate: 'The only problem is his race, and I fear it is incompatible with a high-level position in the navy, which his merit and education would perhaps otherwise allow him to occupy ... My opinion is that the best course of action is to keep him as long as possible in the lower ranks.'

In 1894, after twelve years of naval campaigns, Mortenol was sent to Madagascar where he was frequently involved in combat. He forged a reputation as a brilliant superior officer not only because of his actions in battle but also because, over the following years, he was even-handed in his role in establishing the French colony in Madagascar, to the great benefit of the French Republic.

Between 1900 and 1902, he was in charge of a local naval station in the French Congo, and then of a ship headed to Gabon. Finally, he commanded a flotilla of French torpedo boats patrolling the South China Sea.

In the colonies, Mortenol had impressed the military commander Joseph Gallieni, one of France's most celebrated colonial administrators. Years later, when Gallieni was serving as the military governor of Paris and later as minister for war, he recalled Mortenol's organizational brilliance. And in 1914, Gallieni placed him in command of the capital's aerial defences. Mortenol improved the system of telegraphic communication, and he deployed enormous, powerful light projectors, some of which were installed on Fort Mont-Valérien, to surround Paris and blind German aeroplanes during night attacks. These innovative techniques effectively brought all such attacks to a halt.

In the end, it was on land and not on sea that Mortenol truly achieved recognition. For having defended the skies above Paris, he received the title of commander of the Legion of Honour and the rank of colonel in the Land Artillery Reserve.

Pushed into retirement after the war, he remained in Paris until his death. The people of Guadeloupe have erected a monument to him on the docks of Pointe-à-Pitre, and Parisians have given his name to a street in the 10th *arrondissement*.

Have things changed today? How many blacks are there at the École Polytechnique? In key state posts? In the higher levels of the French civil service? Today, people talk about 'positive discrimination'. While 'positive discrimination' – as the French refer to 'affirmative action' – is something I understand in moral terms, it seems like a false solution to me. It is simply a way of pushing two or three black people into the spotlight while injustice continues behind the scenes. Culture and education must be made accessible to everyone, so that all groups in society can have the opportunity and the freedom to flourish. We need to develop an anti-racist pedagogy that gets to the root of the problem. We need to change the way people think. We need to do this in order to bring an end to the superiority complex of those whites who doubt the intellectual capacities of blacks. And we need to do this so that certain blacks will permanently rid themselves of their inferiority complex.

The First Man to Reach the North Pole

Matthew Henson
8 August 1866–8 March 1955

One day, I opened a dictionary of proper names and I found the following, under the entry for 'Peary': 'American explorer. He was the first to reach the North Pole, on 6 April 1909.'

No mention of a certain Matthew Henson. As there is no statute of limitations when it comes to dealing with an encyclopaedic error or an act of deception, I'll take out my compass and set off towards the North Pole and the Arctic Ocean...

Matthew Henson was born in Charles County, Maryland, on 8 August 1866, shortly after the end of the Civil War. He was the child of farmers. To escape the violence of the Ku Klux Klan, which was founded before his birth, his family moved to Washington, DC. His mother died when he was 7, his father a year later. Now an orphan, Matthew was taken in by an uncle. He went to school for a time, then worked as a dishwasher in a restaurant. The years went by, and he looked to the skies, imagined the ocean, and dreamed of adventure. Finally, unable to bear it any longer, he packed his bundle of clothes and set off for Baltimore, 40 miles away. He was only 12. An old captain took pity on him and engaged him on his boat, the *Katie Hines*, a three-masted schooner in the Merchant Marine. Henson began work on the ship as a cabin boy and sailor.

Under the captain's command, Henson travelled to China, Japan, the Philippines, North Africa, Spain, and France He sometimes endured hunger, and sometimes cold. He awoke drenched in sweat on stifling nights in the tropics, crossed oceans where frosty ships resembled icebergs, he fought storms, lack of sleep, disease, and fever. The child learned first-hand the brutality of the world. But he also learned to read and count and quickly became interested in cartography and maritime astronomy.

When the captain died, Henson couldn't find work as a sailor, even though he had a lot of experience. He resigned himself to a job in a clothes store near Washington. It was there that, one day in 1887, his life changed. A client of the shop, an officer in the US Navy named Robert E. Peary, came to buy a sun hat. He was, he told the shop-owner, leaving to make a map of the jungle of Nicaragua in the hopes of building a canal, and was looking for a domestic servant to accompany him. As the client tried on his hat, Henson put himself forward for the job. He was 20 years old and bored with his life on land. Peary hired him.

In the course of their explorations, Henson demonstrated such excellence that Peary decided to take him on his future expeditions. Peary had a dream, an obsession, a mad desire: to be the first man to reach the North Pole. Of course, Henson accepted the invitation to join him. What he desired more than anything was to escape a life of misery.

In 1891 they crossed Greenland for the first time. Their objective was to use this mass of floating ice and icebergs as a base where they could learn how to navigate the Arctic waters, for their survival would depend on precise knowledge of the conditions. Sometimes the group split into two. While Peary left on scouting missions, Henson stayed behind at the base camp hunting, tinkering, and learning how to make igloos. The Inuit they encountered taught him their language and their customs. But he gained much more than that from them: Henson married an Inuit woman, Akratanguak, and a few years later he adopted the name Mattipaluk.

From 1893 to 1906, Henson and Peary criss-crossed the south-west of the glacial ocean, the north of Greenland, Ellesmere... Peary came back from one of these expeditions with severely frostbitten feet. Seven of his toes had to be amputated. But these journeys had allowed them to create a map of countless unknown territories.

Back in New York between 1906 and 1908, Henson worked at the Museum of Natural History as a specialist on polar territories and their populations. In order to finance his expeditions, meanwhile, Peary gave talks and organized exhibitions of Inuit wearing sealskins and carrying harpoons. 'Human zoos' were the height of fashion. In Seattle, the Inuit were lodged in a cold room in order to allow them to adapt to the region's climate! Sadly, two of them died a few months later from a deadly attack of tuberculosis.

On 6 July 1908 Peary and Henson set off aboard the *Roosevelt*, a three-masted steam schooner specially constructed for Arctic waters. It was their ninth and last expedition. On board were Peary,

Henson, and seven white Americans (who, though poorly skilled, were nevertheless paid twice as much as Henson). They skirted the coast of Greenland in August, and then spent the winter there, waiting for the beginning of spring. In Etah, they took on board 18 Inuit, along with their families and 33 dogs.

Finally, on 18 February 1909, Henson and a small group of Inuit began the push towards the North Pole. Travelling through that sea of ice was more difficult than travelling across frozen tundra. One needed to be on the constant lookout for chunks of ice that would break off suddenly, opening up huge crevasses impossible to cross. Over the course of 40 days, Henson's group and Peary's group functioned in rotation: while one rested, the other advanced.

On 6 April weather conditions were favourable. The winter storms were over. The sky was pale, colourless, the ice a spectral white. From an average of −40 degrees Celsius, the temperature had risen to a relatively mild −15 degrees, making it easier to drive the sleds.

Six men threw themselves into the race for the Pole. In front were Henson with Ootah and Ooqueah; behind, Seegloo and Eghingwah assisted Peary, who had been physically depleted by the amputation of his toes years earlier. The tension was unbearable. The Inuit worried about getting home, since they were almost out of food. It would soon become necessary to eat the dogs.

Henson, partly through skill and partly through luck, moved ahead of Peary's group and became the first man in the world to reach the North Pole – that geographic spot where 'all the time zones meet'. His Inuit friends looked around, confused. Nothing differentiated this spot from the rest, immaculate and glacial. 'Is this it?' his Inuit friends asked. 'The whites have been fighting over this?' Questions to which Henson had no response. In any case, all of them were exhausted and soon fell asleep there.

Some 45 minutes later, when Henson awoke, he saw in front of him an irritated, sick, half-blind Peary who could barely stand. His face was covered in ice and frost, his skin burned by the sun. Then Henson remembered that he was at the North Pole and called out to Peary, who turned his blind eyes to him and said, 'I'm taking Eghingway and Seegloo with me to go make some observations!' For all adventurers of the early twentieth century justified their expeditions by invoking their desire to advance science and 'civilization'.

Their success was undeniable, but the return home was gloomy. Peary didn't speak to Henson all the way back to Cap Columbia, where they arrived on 23 April after 13 miserable days. Peary was gravely offended that he had been deprived of his victory by a servant, and a 'Negro' to boot.

After a brief controversy – a competitor of Peary's, Frederick Cook, claimed to have reached the Pole on 21 April 1908, but had also earlier falsely claimed that he had ascended Mount McKinley – a committee of the US Congress declared Peary the winner, by four votes to three.

Later, Peary insisted on reading the proofs of Henson's autobiography, *A Negro Explorer at the North Pole*, and confiscated one hundred pictures he had taken. Meanwhile Peary's own account of the journey, *The North Pole, its Discovery in 1909 Under the Auspices of the Peary Arctic Club*, is an example of true condescension and prejudice: 'While faithful to me, and when *with me* more effective in covering distance with a sledge than any of the others, he had not, as a racial inheritance, the daring and initiative of Bartlett, or Marvin, MacMillan, or Borup, other members of the expedition.'

So, despite his accomplishments, Henson's only recognition was as a simple porter for his master. With no diploma, and having endured too much physical suffering to continue travelling, he found a modest job as a porter in Brooklyn, making 16 dollars a week, and then as a courier at the New York customs house. Peary never sought him out, no more than he did the Inuit who had travelled with him, though he was well aware of their extreme destitution.

It was only in 1937 that Matthew Henson was finally accepted as a member of the elite Explorers' Club. In 1944 Congress finally granted him official recognition as the discoverer of the North Pole.

That said, we should put this all in perspective. It is quite possible that the Inuit, centuries before, had discovered the North Pole 'in passing', long before Henson and Peary... Let us give credit where it's due to the native peoples, whose homelands and discoveries have so often been stolen.

A Whirlwind on Two Wheels

Major Taylor
26 November 1878–21 June 1932

In the long list of those who have fought for justice and against racism, athletes are well represented. They have paved the way more than others because the media is obsessed with their achievements. They have fought to challenge stereotypes, and they have denounced the social ghettos to which they were condemned because of their colour. They have paved the way for others.

The first black athlete to achieve fame was not – as most people assume – a footballer or a boxer, but rather a cyclist: the famous Marshall Walter Taylor. Learning his story rid me of some of my own prejudices. If you had told me, when I was younger, that a black man had once been the world cycling champion, I wouldn't have believed you.

Marshall Taylor was born in Indiana. His father was a coachman lucky enough to find work with a family in Indianapolis who displayed few of the racial prejudices of the time. The day this family offered Taylor a bicycle was the day his life truly began...

His passion for cycling was all-consuming, and he spent all his time in the saddle. He did all kinds of acrobatics on his bike, what we today would call 'free-style riding' or 'street biking', and was so good that, in 1892, a bike salesman asked him to perform in front of his shop to attract customers. The teenager was delighted: not only could he show off his skills, but he could earn a little money too. He agreed to wear a soldier's outfit for the occasion, and he quickly came to be known as 'Major Taylor', a nickname that would stick throughout his career. He also threw himself into competition and won several races.

In 1895 he settled down in Middletown, Connecticut, and found work as a mechanic at the Worcester Cycle Manufacturing Company. His boss, Birdie Munger, invited him to ride for the company team. His talent immediately shone out. By 1896, at the age of 18, Taylor already held the record for the fastest mile, surpassing all the professionals, and had won four prizes. He became a professional himself in 1897, and during his first season won eight grand prix and became the second-best mile racer in the US. He was dubbed the 'Worcester Whirlwind'.

At the same time as he was achieving these victories, he was also encountering the racism that would continue to poison his entire career. He may have been beating records as a cyclist, but he was also experiencing great injustice: he was not allowed to enter certain competitions, was outlawed from racing in some states, including Indiana, and many white cyclists refused to compete with a 'Negro'. Spectators threw cold water in his face and nails under his wheels. When he crossed the finish line just ahead of another cyclist, it was the runner-up who was declared the winner. I even read that they gave him the number 13, hoping to bring him bad luck. On top of all that, he endured all kinds of intimidation, including death threats before the start of many races.

But Taylor had great mental strength. Rather than destroying him, all the humiliation and aggression that he experienced only made him stronger. Due to the hatred shown towards him by certain whites, he did not race primarily for money but rather for equality, to show the world who he was and to assert his pride. He was courageous and also extremely intelligent. He tricked his competitors by making them think he was tired or by pretending to launch attacks during races. One of his most noteworthy tactics, however, was simply to lead from the front. From the beginning of the race he would go to the front and let no one past him. For if he allowed himself to be caught by the peloton, the other riders might ambush him like a lynch mob! In order for everything to turn out smoothly, he had to stay out front, a move all black people are familiar with. In order to be accepted, Taylor, and other black individuals of the time, had to excel. They had to be better than everyone else.

In 1898 he won an impressive number of bicycle races, including the mile from a moving start, the mile from a stationary start, and the half-mile. In 1899 he garnered 22 victories, including the world speed championship, the world mile championship, and the US speed championship. In 1900 he set a new world record for speed riding behind a motorcycle. Imagine what else he might have achieved had it not been for segregation and the incessant humiliations inflicted upon him!

In 1901, tired of the harassment, Taylor decided to leave for Europe. France was an El Dorado for him. He quickly established himself as a leading racer, distinguishing himself in all the races of the Old Continent, as well as in Australia and New Zealand, where he was welcomed as a star and (almost) treated like a man. Of course, his body type was 'scientifically' examined in order to try and make sense of his victories, just as others were being studied in 'human zoos' during the same period.

Eventually, he just got tired. In 1904 he quit competition and returned home, hoping to rest on his laurels until the end of his days. But his time in Europe had, temporarily, made him forget the malicious power of segregation. Unable to bear it, he took to his bicycle again in 1907 and travelled back to Europe where he was better accepted and where the racism was less aggressive. He continued to race there until his retirement, in 1910, at the age of 32.

The Hell of the Human Zoos

Ota Benga
1881 (1884)–20 March 1916

The Head of Indigenous Affairs was obliged to
deploy false promises and strategic pressure in
order to convince a hundred Kanaks to travel to
the 1931 Colonial Exhibition in Paris, where they
thought they would be presenting their culture …
The Kanaks were not housed within the exhibition
at Vincennes, as they had expected. Instead, they
were brought to the other end of Paris, to the
Jardin zoologique de l'acclimatation in the Bois
de Boulogne. Originally built to showcase exotic
plants and animals, it had served as the location
for several exhibitions of indigenous peoples. A
few shacks were quickly built, and the show could
begin.
    Alice Bullard and Joël Dauphiné, *Human Zoos*

Among the 'polygamous and cannibalistic savages' who were installed
in the Jardin zoologique de l'acclimatation in 1931 (less than a
hundred years ago!) was Mr Wathio De Canala, the grandfather of
Christian Karembeu, my former teammate on the French national
football team.

When he told the story, Christian's grandfather was still filled
with rage.

The story of Ota Benga, a pygmy from the Belgian Congo, can help
us to better understand what we refer to as 'human zoos'. He had
lost his entire family during a massacre perpetrated by the troops
of King Leopold II of Belgium. He was one of the few survivors.
In 1904 he was sold by people traffickers to a missionary named

Samuel Phillips Verner. He brought Benga to the United States in order to exhibit him at the World Fair in St Louis, Missouri, held to accompany the third Olympic Games. The missionary's eyes lit up at the thought of the money he would make from this 'savage' whose teeth were filed into vicious fangs! At these Olympics, as required by the laws of segregation, there were separate games organized for so-called 'people of colour': these were billed as 'anthropological days' with lance-throwers, boomerangs, and other 'exotic' sports.

Ota Benga was driven from fair to fair until, in 1906, he arrived at the Bronx Zoo in New York City. He was immediately placed in a cage, alongside an orangutan and a parrot, in order to provide a 'convincing' representation of his jungle habitat. The final touch that perfected the image of him as a cannibal? His cage was littered with bones. He slept in a hammock, and, as instructed, spent his day shooting arrows at a target when visitors walked by.

A panel next to his cage offered information on the 'specimen' it contained:

Ota Benga
Height: 4 feet, 11 inches; Weight: 103 lbs
Age: 23
Visiting hours: Every afternoon during the month of September

It's true that Ota Benga was sometimes permitted to leave his cage and walk in the gardens. But the fearful and aggressive reactions of the visitors forced him to stay behind bars.

To understand human zoos, you have to imagine a world in which very few people travelled. These zoos thus offered a profound sense of excitement and the thrill of new, disorienting experiences. They allowed visitors to travel vicariously but they were also informed by a distinct educational impulse. Children discovered in the zoos the same exoticism that stimulated their imaginations through books like Jules Verne's *Captain at Fifteen* or Livingstone's travel writing. In the days before television, this was the classic Sunday outing, a family picnic at the zoo. It was a venue for staging all kinds of fantasies, where the 'savage' could be seen live and nearly naked, at a time when whites were decorously dressed at all times, even when they went swimming.

By the time visitors left the zoo, they had come to believe profoundly and completely in the existence of the savage, and felt that they understood his natural environment and his customs. Why doubt the 'reality' displayed in these human zoos? The 'savages' were all the more realistic to them because they were paid to growl, to eat raw meat, to climb trees, and to hang from the branches by one arm! There is no point in blaming the organizers of these deceitful shows. As the savage never actually existed, it was clearly necessary to bring in an actor to play the role!

The director of the Bronx Zoo believed wholeheartedly in the pedagogical mission of his Prehistoric Park. For him, this pygmy embodied the proof of a missing link between monkeys and men – and by 'men' he was referring exclusively to white men of course.

Science supported this. In the mid-nineteenth century, the main difficulty for anthropology was locating specimens. Very few anthropologists actually went to the colonies to take their measurements. They didn't have Pygmies, Antilleans, or Aborigines on hand, and lamented their lack of access to resources to carry out their research. But the circuses and zoos, and, later on, the universal exhibitions, helped spur the development of their discipline. At the great exhibitions in Paris more than 140 anthropologists would gather to record their observations. The mornings were reserved for scientists. A stream of racist treatises were published between 1860 and 1910, all based on these specimens who were paid to 'play the savage'.

This success, however, ultimately undermined the small business model of the missionary Samuel Phillips Verner. Some men of good conscience took offence at his exhibition. More importantly, influential religious figures demanded it be outlawed due to its support for Darwin's theory of evolution and the idea of a 'missing link', which contradicted Christian doctrine.

Ota Benga was thus placed in the Howard Orphanage and Industrial School in Brooklyn, New York, which was directed by Reverend Gordon. Then he was brought to Virginia, where his filed teeth were covered and he was dressed in European-style clothes. Touched by his suffering, the poet Anne Spencer encouraged him to educate himself at the Baptist school in Lynchburg. But he thought only of returning home. And in order to do that, he had to earn some money. So he worked in a tobacco factory, saving up his wages over ten years. After a decade, though, the First World World War put an end to his hopes of ever seeing his home again.

Benga fell into a deep depression and, on 20 March 1916, after having lit a fire as tradition dictated, he shot himself through the heart.

People wondered why he did it. Samuel Phillips Verner claimed that Ota Benga committed suicide because he had 'failed to integrate'!

To better understand the mechanisms that allowed something as monstrous as the human zoo to exist, I turned to Pascal Blanchard, historian, author of books on contemporary Africa, and co-editor of the excellent collection of essays *Human Zoos: Science and Spectacle in the Age of Colonial Empires* (2008).

In the late nineteenth and early twentieth centuries, he explained to me, there were more than ten million black people in the United States. Many whites feared the prospect of interracial marriage. 'The mixing of different races lowers the physical and mental level', declared one eugenicist treaty. The white race had to be protected. To convince people of the danger, blacks from Africa were brought over to the US. They were put on display, and the American people were placed on alert: 'See what the Negro is really like! Imagine, just for a moment, what would happen if mixed marriages were allowed! See what your children would look like!'

The Eugenics Record Office shot movies in these human zoos, distributing them across the United States. Partly as a result, from 1910 onwards, 43 states voted to outlaw interracial marriage, a situation that lasted through to the 1950s.

The West has always exoticized and exhibited the Other. The Romans displayed the Gauls in their arenas. Only a few decades ago, you could go to rural fairs in the United States to see bearded ladies, obese ladies, panther ladies, men without arms or legs, Siamese twins, and what were known as 'Ethnic Shows' or 'Freak Shows'. And black people were often found right alongside the bearded ladies and men without arms or legs!

At the beginning of the nineteenth century, however, very few people were exhibited in theatres or in the enormous Barnum marquees. The major shift took place when Carl Hagenbeck, the owner of a zoo in Hamburg, noticed that the audience applauded the camel-riders much more than the camels! 'Damn!' he thought to himself. 'That's the real business opportunity!' This revelation pushed him to scale up his enterprise to industrial levels. He started importing groups of children and adults from Africa, Asia, and Greenland, exhibiting them in travelling circuses throughout Europe, America, and Japan.

For the 'universal exhibitions', those massive events of that era, entire villages of so-called savages were uprooted. The production line of exoticization was in full swing. The list of cities where these exhibitions took place is too long to recite in full. No European city of more than 50,000 people was forgotten. Governments kept asking for them, since these exhibitions supported colonial business interests and dazzled the population: 'Look at how well we are civilizing them!' 850 million Westerners visited these human zoos, events that transformed scientific racism into mass racism.

It strikes me that black people are still often seen as different beings. I often hear sentences begin with: 'Blacks are...'

Which reminds me of a story... One day, a coach came to me for advice: 'I don't know how to communicate with the young black men on my team.'

I replied: 'How about if you spoke to them normally?'

For many people, it is obvious that blacks exist as a separate category. They talk about a 'black people' or 'black thought' or a 'black soul'... Blacks are not seen as individuals, but as an indistinct mass. Though human zoos no longer exist, some people still look at blacks with incomprehension, as a kind of mystery. They still wonder, 'What makes them tick?'

Back to Africa

Marcus Mosiah Garvey
17 August 1887–10 June 1940

> If you haven't got confidence in self, you are twice
> defeated in the race of life. With confidence, you
> have won even before you have started.
> Marcus Garvey

Two years before Marcus Garvey was born in Jamaica, a treaty cut Africa into pieces and divided the pieces up between the European powers. From 15 November 1884 until 26 February 1885, 14 imperialist powers* gathered together for the famous 'Berlin Conference', at the behest of Otto von Bismarck, Chancellor of the German Empire. At its conclusion, they proclaimed: 'In the Name of God Almighty [...], wishing in a spirit of good and mutual accord, to regulate the conditions most favourable to the development of trade and civilization in certain regions of Africa [...]; and concerned at the same time as to the means of furthering the moral and material well-being of the native populations.' Despite these pious declarations, they paid no attention to the native peoples' own claims to the territories, and acted on the assumption that colonized lands were a good that could be exchanged, abandoned, sold, or transformed at will. So it was that absurd, artificial borders were drawn up solely on the basis of the needs of Western powers, placing together ethnic groups that were profoundly different in terms of language, beliefs, etc. This, in turn, created great disparities in agricultural and mining resources. The contemporary borders of Africa, inherited from the colonial period, are often the source of conflict between neighbouring nations.

---

* [Author's note] Germany, Austria-Hungary, Belgium, Denmark, Spain, France, United Kingdom, Italy, Holland, Portugal, Russia, Sweden-Norway, Turkey, and the US.

Members of the African diaspora had seen their families scattered, and the land of their birth denigrated. They had no home they could call their own anywhere on the Earth. This feeling of alienation explains the rise of a movement that encouraged a return to one's roots, the pan-Africanism inspired by Marcus Garvey and W. E. B. DuBois.

Marcus Garvey was the youngest of 11 children in a Jamaican family, and he left school when he was 14 to work in a printing shop. He would later say that, like most black people, his education had come from (the experience of) poverty. Soon he began working as a militant in a political organization called the National Club. Energetic, enterprising, and an eloquent speaker, he became the first secretary of the organization. A member of the printers' union, he led a strike to obtain better pay – in Jamaica, the black population, freed from slavery in 1833, was still subject to an oppressive regime at the hands of the white planters. Garvey was fired from the position, but quickly found another job and established his first newspaper, *The Watchman*.

Throughout his life, Marcus Garvey was a tireless traveller, an inciter of rebellions, and a founder of newspapers that gave voice to the oppressed. Between 1909 and 1911 he travelled across South America: Panama, Ecuador, Nicaragua, Honduras, Colombia, Venezuela, and Costa Rica. Everywhere he went, he encouraged workers to form unions and published newspapers that criticized discrimination, racism, and poor living conditions.

He then travelled to Britain where he studied the history of Egypt and read voraciously, from the Bible to Shakespeare. For several years, the book always on his bedside table was *Up from Slavery* by Booker T. Washington. This black ideologue of the American South emphasized the need for black people to integrate into American society. He supported peaceful coexistence with whites, and argued that the black community could carve out a place in society through hard work and good hygiene. This approach effectively meant that the progress of the black community was subject to the approval of whites, and it limited blacks to the role of manual labour.

Whites were particularly eager to promote *Up from Slavery* as it allowed them to drown out another voice which was far more disturbing, that of W. E. B. DuBois, who called for equal rights, the formation of a black intellectual elite, and a struggle against all forms of injustice. Gradually, Garvey distanced himself from Booker T. Washington.

In London, Garvey studied the institutions of the British Empire and sat in on debates at the House of Commons. Where are the black governments, the black empire, the black presidents, the black army, the black navy, the large black corporations, the black religion? They don't exist, he realized. So he decided to create them. 'I saw before me then', he said, 'even as I do now, a new world of black men ... a nation of sturdy men making their impression upon civilization and causing a new light to dawn upon the human race.'

After returning home to Jamaica in July 1914, Garvey created the mass movement to which he would devote the rest of his life: the United Negro Improvement Association (UNIA). Following parallel paths, he and DuBois would henceforth serve as the fathers of 'pan-Africanism': a form of thought-in-action rooted in the call for pride in one's African heritage and for the restoration of black dignity. It was also inspired by the ideal of forging solidarity across the global African diaspora – the 'unity of African peoples' – and encouraged a return to the African homeland.

Two years later, in 1916, Garvey moved the UNIA to Harlem. Between 1900 and 1930 this neighbourhood in New York underwent a complete transformation from a white residential area to one of the blackest ghettos in the United States. Here, Garvey discovered a population comprised of black migrants who had fled the South, poverty, and the Ku Klux Klan. There were also soldiers who had returned from the horrors of the First World War and were trying to escape discrimination and the threat of lynching. The KKK wanted these 'Negroes' to understand that serving their country would not lead to any new rights.

What would later be called the 'Harlem Renaissance' was born in this period, but concerned only a small elite. The vast majority were not concerned with poetry, jazz, or modern art, but they drank up the words of hope offered by Marcus Garvey. Ordinary black people began to share his dream: 'If only I had a flag and a country of my own!' Garvey spoke to these women and men about their roots, about the lands from which they came. They were, of course, former slaves, but Garvey pushed them to take pride in themselves. He didn't want them to feel inferior. They came from great civilizations, many older than those of the Europeans. 'You did not come from the cotton fields and the ghettos', he told them. 'You came from Africa. Whether you are a black person from Brazil, the Caribbean, or North America, you all have African ancestors.'

Garvey refused the idea of black victimization and the notion that black history began with slavery.

You are 'African Americans', he repeatedly told them. His insistence on this term was not insignificant, for at the time many blacks rejected their African heritage. They wanted to be 'Black Americans', thereby cutting themselves off from their origins and trapping themselves in a terrible contradiction. Without roots, how can one build an identity? On the one hand, they felt American because they had been born and had grown up there. But on the other hand, they were 'Negroes' because they didn't have the same rights as white citizens. They were prisoners of this paradox, and could only express their personality through fear or revolt.

Marcus Garvey was convinced that it was necessary to decolonize people's minds and spirits in order to forge a powerful identity. 'Like the great Church of Rome, Negroes the world over MUST PRACTICE ONE FAITH, that of Confidence in themselves, with One God!' They should be proud of their colour, proud of their civilization, and proud of their ancestors. Garvey celebrated *blackness* and demanded the right of 'repatriation' to Africa for blacks throughout the world, for he was certain that African Americans would never find respect and liberty outside Africa. His message clearly caught on as his movement gained over a million followers!

In 1920 Garvey organized his first convention. Thousands of delegates came from 25 countries spanning Central America, the Caribbean, Africa, and the United States. During a meeting held at Madison Square Garden, he announced to 25,000 enthusiastic spectators: 'We will mobilize 400 million blacks on the planet and plant the banner of liberty in Africa ... If Europe is for the Whites, then Africa must be for all the Blacks of the world.' The conference ended with a vast procession through the streets of Harlem.

This small, stocky, indefatigable, and slightly disorganized man was galvanized by this success, and he would never take a moment's rest. He purchased a 6,000-seat auditorium in Harlem, which he named Liberty Hall and which served as the headquarters of UNIA. He also founded a series of newspapers, starting with *The Negro World*, which was published in three languages and, at its height, regularly sold 250,000 copies. The newspaper updated readers on UNIA activities from across the world, published the texts of Garvey's speeches, and reported on events and information censored by other newspapers.

Garvey also founded a 'Black Orthodox Church'. In effect, for him, the very devout and Christian black community could only rid itself of its sense of inferiority if it changed its perception of the white God that had long been imposed through the racialized representations created by Westerners. If God created man in his image, for a black person, God is black!

Marcus Garvey launched companies managed by blacks and catering for blacks 'in the large industrial centers of the United States, Central America, the Caribbean, and Africa, to produce all types of commercial products'. He created the Negro Factories Corporation and established hotels, restaurants, laundromats, clothing and food shops, a factory that produced 'black dolls for negro children', a publishing house, printing shops, etc.

The crowning achievement of his 'utopia of return' came on 26 June 1919 with the creation of the Black Star Line. This autonomous shipping company, which belonged to the UNIA, was entirely funded by 'subscriptions and the emission of stocks purchased by ordinary black people, attracted by the idea of emigration towards an independent black nation'. The Black Star was to serve as a link between blacks around the world 'in their commercial and industrial relations'. It was also intended to link the different headquarters of the UNIA scattered around the world, raising money for the association, and making the 'return to Africa' a reality (on boats free of racial segregation).

The first of these ships, called the *Frederick Douglass*, launched on 31 October 1919. It is said that everywhere the *Frederick Douglass* docked, joyful crowds rushed to greet it, covering the ship with flowers and fruit. People even left work to catch a glimpse. But the *Frederick Douglass* was in poor condition and soon proved unseaworthy. The second ship enjoyed even less luck than the first: it sank while anchored in the Hudson River. The third ship foundered off the coast of Cuba. Slated to deliver migrants to Liberia, the fourth was purchased but never delivered to the Black Star Line.

No matter. Garvey created a new company and bought a fifth ship, the *Booker T. Washington*, which was to carry the first wave of emigrants to the land of their ancestors.

This return to Africa was his most cherished dream, and it was only natural that his thoughts should turn to the state of Liberia as the ideal location for the realization of this dream. Liberia was founded in 1847 and was administered by an independent black government. Garvey sent an emissary to meet the leaders of the Liberian government, who encouraged Garvey and his followers to settle in their country. The emissary then sent two missives to Garvey: the official one was enthusiastic, but the other one, for

Garvey's eyes only, spoke privately of the corruption that reigned in the country and of the colonialist manner in which the blacks who hailed from the United States treated the native blacks. This behaviour, he concluded, was something that would have to be 'remedied once we are on the ground'.

In 1921 Garvey dispatched a team to Liberia to negotiate the terms under which the 'Garveyites' would settle in the country. The 'Back-to-Africa' operation was making progress: they acquired 200 hectares of land at Cape Palmas and received equipment and supplies sent to support the project. But then things became complicated. Garvey denounced the enormous privileges and concessions offered by the government of Liberia to Firestone, the leading US tyre manufacturer. The US immediately warned the president of Liberia, C. B. D. King, that it 'would not tolerate the presence in Liberia of an organization working for the overthrow of European supremacy in Africa'. Meanwhile, Great Britain and France refused to accept an incursion into territory that was their exclusive preserve. Swayed by the arguments of his allies, the president of Liberia declared his opposition to the 'incendiary politics' of the UNIA under Garvey's leadership.

This change of fortune, along with poor management, led to the bankruptcy of the Black Star Line and the sale of all its property to the UNIA. The *Booker T. Washington* was seized, and Garvey was arrested, accused of having organized the sale of stock in the Black Star Line despite knowing the financial difficulties of the company. He refused to hire a lawyer and, in court, made a declaration that left his audience in tears:

> I do not regret what I have done for the Universal Negro Improvement Association; for the Negro race, because I did it from the fullness of my soul. I did it with the fear of my God, believing that I was doing the right thing. I am still firm in my belief that I served my race, people, conscience and God. I further make no apology for what I have done. I ask for no mercy. If you say I am guilty, I go to my God as I feel, a clear conscience and a clean soul, knowing I have not wronged even a child of my race or any member of my family. I love all mankind. I love Jew, Gentile, I love White and Black. I have respect for every race. I believe the Irish should be free; they should have a country. I believe the Jew should be free and the Egyptian should be free, and the Indian and the Poles. I believe also that the Black man should be

free. I would fight for the freedom of the Jew, the Irish, the Poles; I would fight and die for the liberation of 400,000,000 Negroes. I expect from the world for Negroes what the world expects from them.

As history shows us, those who attack the interests of the powerful are often destroyed (Toussaint Louverture, for example, or Patrice Lumumba, to mention just two examples). At the close of his trial in 1925, Garvey was sentenced to five years in prison without parole in the federal penitentiary in Atlanta. There is no question that he had mismanaged his financial affairs, but his trial was still highly political. The white press admitted as much: 'One day, Black Africa will be free, she will no longer be shared between France and Great Britain. Garvey's problems started when he began stepping on the feet of these two nations...' (*Evening Bulletin*, New York); 'It is a question of great importance to know whether justice was truly served in the affair of Garvey, "president of the Republic of Africa"' (*Evening Times*, Buffalo). These criticisms were repeated across the press, eventually leading to Garvey's sentence being commuted by President Coolidge. In 1928 Garvey was exiled to Jamaica.

He returned to his country of origin a hero. Having refused to renounce any of his ideals, he continued his involvement in the UNIA but also in local politics. He founded yet another newspaper (his seventh), *The Black Man*, and fought tirelessly against discrimination on the island. He also organized a new convention (his sixth) in which 12,000 delegates participated.

Garvey was beginning to pose a real threat to the British Empire and to the United States. The two governments considered assassination as a solution, but decided instead to smother him with court cases, fines, libels, and rumours. He nevertheless succeeded in being elected to the Municipal Council of Kingston, where he lived. At the seventh convention of the UNIA in 1934, it was resolved that the group's headquarters would be transferred to Britain, where the black nationalist leaders hoped to benefit from a semblance of democratic rights.

In 1935 Garvey moved to Britain, but he frequently travelled back across the Atlantic to attend various conferences held in Toronto, Canada, where he eventually established the School of African Philosophy in 1938.

Marcus Garvey died in 1940, almost forgotten.

His most important idea – that the black condition should not only be considered in a particular national context – continued to be highly relevant. And his successors were influenced by his thinking. In fact, traces of his thought can be found in the ideas of Martin Luther King, Jr, and of the Black Power movement. His presence is felt in the words of Malcolm X, Cheikh Anta Diop (the 'restorer of black consciousness') and even those of Bob Marley, Nelson Mandela, and Barack Obama.

The seeds of the twenty-first century were sown by Marcus Garvey.

He taught us that in order to succeed, we must first learn to take pride in ourselves. That is why I named my youngest son Marcus.

'No Time Rest, All the Time Make War, All the Time Kill Blacks'

Thierno Diop, Ouijaran Ollian, Siriki Kone, Dyne Sylla, Tiemcoumba

(... –1914) (... –1915) (... –1916) (... –1917) (... –1918)

1914. **Thierno Diop**. A *tirailleur* [colonial infantryman] with the rank of private in the 1st BTS (Battalion of Senegalese Tirailleurs): 'Under enemy fire, a short distance from his trench. Had the strength and character to make it back to our lines. Refused to abandon wounded comrade who was unable to move.' Military medal.

1915. **Ouijaran Ollian**. *Tirailleur* in the 13th BTS. 'Attacked by group of enemy soldiers. Showed incredible willpower in continuing to fight. Though shot three times and stabbed twice, lay on his weapon to prevent enemy from seizing it, until help arrived. Died of his wounds.' Mentioned in dispatches.

1916. **Siriki Kone**. Corporal in the 1st Somali Battalion. 'Extremely brave officer. Served as bugler. During the attack on 24 October 1916, followed the commander of his company to the end. Fell into shell-hole occupied by several Germans. Was able to disarm one of his adversaries, kill two, and wound two more. Stabbed with a bayonet nine times.' Military medal – mentioned in dispatches.

1917. **Dyne Sylla**. 24th BTS. Warrant Officer. 'Badly wounded by shell explosion. Didn't want to be evacuated. Claimed that "one of his hands was enough to kill several Krauts". Bandaged himself and returned to his post. Wounded again, very seriously. Had himself carried to the commander of his company to hand over his weapons and said he had had enough.' Military medal – mentioned in dispatches.

1918. **Tiemcoumba**. Corporal in the 15th BTS. 'A liaison officer, very brave and energetic. Killed while leading his group in a bayonet charge against an enemy stronghold.' Mentioned in dispatches.

The simple act of listing those who 'died for France', for liberty and justice, would fill a whole pile of books. But what were they doing in that hell, these 200,000 natives of Equatorial and Western Africa who didn't even enjoy the benefits of French citizenship? How did they come to bury themselves in the vile, muddy trenches of France's coldest regions?

According to the newspapers of the period, they rushed to the defence of their imperial masters, with flowers in their rifles, to play at being heroes, because it was in their nature, because they had the 'warrior's vocation, a sense of obedience, courage, hardiness, endurance, tenacity, the instinct for combat, a lack of fear...'

Throughout the war, posters and postcards showed them, smiling and jaunty, even though they never once returned to their homeland in five years. Popular songs recounted their sexual exploits, and above all, their exploits on the battlefield. A brave *tirailleur* was happy to die:

For them the most beautiful tomb
Is the one that is dug on the field of honour.

A year before these words were written, the *tirailleurs* had already been a great success. During the Bastille Day parade in July 1913, at the Longchamp racecourse, the Legion of Honour was awarded to the 1st regiment of Senegalese *tirailleurs*. Elegant women dressed in black and white shouted, 'Long live the *Negroes!*'

Beginning in 1857, battalions of Senegalese *tirailleurs* were recruited from among the ranks of recently freed former slaves. They were immediately enlisted by General Faidherbe, the governor of Senegal – which France had begun to colonize in 1854 – for a term of twelve to fifteen years! It is important to remember that the Senegalese *tirailleurs* played a major role in the French colonial empire. They helped invade other countries for France's benefit, allowing France to be an important player on the international political stage, and contributing to the country's wealth. Recall that, at its height at the beginning of the 1930s, the French colonial empire stretched over 12,347,000 square kilometres – 22 times the size of France itself. In total, France colonized 60 countries or territories. Today, those who fail to understand how someone from black Africa, Asia, or the Maghreb can be French don't know their own history.

The best known of all the *tirailleurs* is 'Banania', the smiling *tirailleur* on the packaging of a powdered cocoa drink, which appeared in grocery shops in 1914. He was the 'black force of chocolate'! They may have saved France, but the 'black forces' were also used as cannon fodder. How many men were sent to die on the front lines of a country they didn't know?

General Charles Mangin, known as the 'butcher of the blacks', explained in his 1910 bestseller, *The Black Force*, that the French race had been weakened by democratic ideals, resulting in a lower birth rate than Germany. While waiting for a renewal that would come from a higher birth rate – he himself fathered eight children – the relative lack of French troops had to be compensated for by calling on African soldiers. The idea was to create a 'colonial reservoir'. This was greeted with scepticism by the merchant houses of the Colonial Union, which worried the result would be a lack of manpower in the colonies. The finance minister also worried about the potential costs. But, little by little, Mangin's strategy won people over.

Some of the generals, meanwhile, were delighted. 'The impetuous savagery of bayonet charges will bring success more easily than long slaughters', an ecstatic General Bonnal claimed. 'Black troops have no equal when it comes to delivering the final blow. A division of ten thousand men will be able to open a breach three or four kilometres wide in the enemy lines.' What was the role of a Senegalese *tirailleur*? An elite soldier who left the safety of his own lines, lay in ambush, fired on the enemy, and then returned to his comrades. Indeed, the battalions of Senegalese *tirailleurs* were regularly deployed throughout the war. They were used, in particular, in assaults aimed at breaching enemy lines, which exposed soldiers to the greatest dangers. The army commanders recognized in them a particular aptitude for holding their ground. They were incomparable 'shock troops', Mangin concluded, who would ensure French victory within three weeks!

They still had to recruit them. It wasn't easy, because the African soldier was a volunteer, not a conscript. After an investigation, General Mangin announced to the government that he could recruit 40,000 soldiers in French West Africa!

The realities on the ground undermined these claims. A lot of promises were made: bonuses, decent pay, educational courses during their time in France, the possibility of becoming naturalized

Frenchmen, the 'prestige of the uniform', free travel, the chance to discover the Old World, 'enlistment parties', subsidies for 'families in need'. Village chiefs, and especially their wives, were used to help spread the message. But not everyone dreamed of seeing France, then dying...

Contrary to received opinion and the image projected on to Africans, they had neither desire nor reason to fight. For them, this was a 'white man's war'. News of the arrival of recruitment boards sent young men fleeing into the bush; entire villages took refuge in impenetrable areas. Meanwhile, to stymie the army, as many sick and handicapped residents as possible offered themselves up for duty at recruiting stations.

After six months of war, draft evasion increased. The only *tirailleurs* Africans saw come home were horribly mutilated; as for the others, no one even knew where they were buried. They had no way to honour the dead. So the French government began to use a raft of repressive measures against the population. 'The trade in human flesh has been re-established through the recruitment sergeant', wrote a confidant of General Mangin who, despite the raids and other forms of repression, was only able to recruit a total of 16,000 soldiers.

In France, despite efforts to 'acclimatize' them, the *tirailleurs* often succumbed to illness. Up until that point, the only success of the 'Black Force' had been in increasing the number of occupied hospital beds! And these recruits from overseas were not cheap: transport costs, daily expenses, subsidies to families... and they had yet to prove their patriotism. 'These young soldiers are not fighting for themselves and, according to the commanders, are "incapable" of understanding the patriotic sentiment that animates their white brothers!' wrote the historian Marc Michel in *Africans and the Great War*.

There were also problems of cultural 'acclimatization'. Beyond ordinary racism, there was also the language barrier, which the generals were not prepared for. Most of the *tirailleurs* came from the colonies of West Africa (present-day Mali, Burkina Faso, Guinea, Ivory Coast, Senegal, Benin, Niger, and Mauritania) and couldn't understand one another. They understood French soldiers even less. How was one to command them in such a situation? But, of course, the French military had an answer for everything. They wrote a *Manual for the French Tirailleur* with translations of common French words and phrases into 'petit nègre', a form of simplified, pidgin French. Following the principle that blacks would never be able to fully understand a language as refined as French, the military offered them a sandbox full of gibberish, simple and utilitarian: with verbs in the infinitive, no articles; the conjugation of the verb 'avoir' – 'to have' – was replaced by the all-purpose set phrases 'y a' or 'y en a' etc. The pronunciation was based on elementary-school French: *missié* for *monsieur, zambes* for *jambs* (legs), *zenoux* for *genoux* (knees). The pidgin French of Africans became commonplace in French-language culture. As Hervé wrote in *The Red Sea Sharks*: 'You no get mad, mista ... You no scream ... We not know you good white.'

This reminds me of a journey I once took to South Africa on an Air France flight. The hostess announced that we would be watching an African film in its 'original language'. I pointed out to her that Africa was a continent composed of many countries and hundreds of languages. 'Would you announce that we were going to watch a European film in its *original language*?'

But the war went on and on, beyond the three weeks predicted by the infallible General Mangin, and the French had to continue recruiting, until, on 17 November 1915, a revolt exploded in the region of West Volta, in present-day Burkina Faso. The military hierarchy's well-laid plans were encountering the realities of the African continent. It all began when the youth of the village of Bouna refused to show up at the recruitment office. The village refused to back down, even when soldiers were sent in. Fifteen other villages were similarly prepared to refuse enlistment.

This bloody and desperate revolt lasted nine months, and led to thousands of deaths. As had happened during the slave trade, Africans defended themselves against this new form of human traffic. More than a hundred villages were destroyed. A report by Vidal on 1 November 1926 offered a terrifying account: 'Large numbers of men, the elderly, women, children, in groups or on their own, chose to let themselves be killed, or to be smoked or grilled to death inside burning houses, rather than surrender, despite our promises that their lives would be spared. They didn't even take advantage of the opportunities of escape at night or the momentary retreats of our *tirailleurs* to escape the certain death that awaited them. I saw women and children burying themselves alive in their family graves, an old man who draped himself over the body of his son so he wouldn't fall into our hands.'

This happened in the twentieth century! Reading this passage, I can't help imagining the ways in which, over several centuries, my African ancestors resisted the slave trade. I also think of Louis

Delgrès and his 300 followers (see pp. 67–74) who, in Guadeloupe in May 1802, in order to prevent the re-establishment of slavery by Napoleon, committed suicide by blowing up their refuge at Matouba, shouting, 'Live free or die!'

We should not take it for granted that the recruited soldiers simply fought obediently in their trenches. One hundred years later, it is still impossible to know what they were thinking. Since most of them couldn't write, their letters were written by their commanders. But in 1917, for example, the 61st BTS refused the order to charge, chanting, 'In the Malafosse Battalion things aren't good, no time rest, all the time make war, all the time kill blacks.' They were sick of the everyday racism of their lower-level officers, of the contempt, and of the beatings. They were sick of the cold, the food, the blood spilled, of being ripped to pieces by the enemy guns as they charged with their bayonets raised.

But the war dragged on. General Mangin wanted to start recruiting in Africa once again. This time, Georges Clemenceau, the French prime minister, sensed that the politics of the situation demanded that he should confide the mission to Blaise Diagne, the black parliamentary deputy for Senegal. Of course, colonial circles fulminated against a nomination that threatened to 'weaken the prestige of the dominant race'. As for Mangin, he worried that this African man of the moment would turn out to be a kind of Toussaint Louverture who would create all sorts of problems in the colonies. How could you trust a black man, even if he was a deputy of the French Republic? We can see here the inherent, racist suspicion of black people as the 'internal enemy'.

Blaise Diagne arrived in Dakar on 18 February 1918. In his pocket he had an array of decrees allowing the natives to catch a glimpse of a better life: privileges for those who cooperated, bonuses for those who enlisted, tax relief for their families, and the payment of monthly benefits. He pursued a 'politics of incentives', offering favours to chiefs based on the 'number of men recruited': honours, medals, promises of future promotions within the colonial administration. His success was undeniable: 63,000 recruits in French West Africa, 14,000 in French Equatorial Africa. Some of these 'volunteers' were obliged to sign up, but many more were genuinely inspired by this African statesman.

The Great War ended when there was no space left to dig new graves, for either blacks or whites. The colour of mourning erased all other colours. The armistice was signed on 11 November 1918 in Rethondes, in France, at 5 a.m. France had won: it had lost *just*

1,383,000 soldiers, compared to 1,900,000 for the Germans! As for the Senegalese *tirailleurs*, their losses are estimated at 21.6 per cent of their total number. For white troops, it was 18.6 per cent.

If we take into account the fact that African troops were not permitted to fight during the winter, because of a myth regarding black people's inability to cope with the cold, we can conclude that their losses were in fact twice as heavy. General Mangin, in fact, had at one point sent a message accompanying African troops being sent to the battle lines: 'To be consumed before winter, as they can't handle the cold!'

In 1937 the poet Léon-Gontron Damas, seeing the Second World War on the horizon, offered this warning:

To the Senegalese veterans
To the future Senegalese soldiers
To all that Senegal can give birth to
Of future Senegalese fighter veterans
Of what-am-I-getting-myself-into future veterans [...]
I ask one thing
To start by invading Senegal

In 1919, after the Versailles peace treaty, French troops occupied the Rhineland. Among them were Senegalese *tirailleurs*. Their presence quickly became known as the 'Black Shame', and they were the target of a hateful campaign in the German and international press. They were accused of rape, theft, murder, and violence. There was talk of women left to bleed to death, and the spread of disease.

Four years later, in *Mein Kampf*, Hitler wrote of the 'negro blood' that had been sent to infect and subjugate the German race. In 1937 this ideology led to the sterilization of mixed-race children and the deportation of blacks to the concentration camps.

Champion of the World

Battling Siki
22 September 1897–16 December 1925

On 4 July 1910, when Jack Johnson, then the greatest boxing champion of all time, beat Jim Jeffries, there were riots in the streets. Blacks were killed, others lynched: white people saw the victory as an unacceptable insult to the white race. A few years later, wanted by the police on a trumped-up charge of immoral behaviour, Johnson fled the United States for France. In Paris, he declared to a newspaper, 'I plan to settle permanently in this city and never return to the United States.'

The stage was set for a remarkable period in the history of boxing. At the time, France was one of the few countries that allowed fights between whites and blacks. In Paris, fighters were recruited from all quarters: a major boxing card required at least one black boxer. Intellectuals and socialites were fascinated. Writers like Apollinaire, Cendrars, and Colette all attended boxing matches as readily as they would a show at the Moulin Rouge. And their expectations of an exciting night out were not disappointed by Louis Mbarick Fall, who fought under the name of *Battling Siki*.

Louis Mbarick Fall was born in 1897 in Saint-Louis, Senegal. At the age of 8, he was kidnapped by a Dutch dancer on her way home from a tour in India. Some say she made him her own sexual plaything, others that he became her house servant. Whatever the case, he arrived in Marseille with his abductor, only to be abandoned there a few weeks later, like an unloved toy. He had to find menial work, whether with a mop, a sponge, a paintbrush, or a trowel. During one of his many street-fights, he met some fairground workers who ran a boxing club. When they asked him his name, he responded 'Siki', which means 'clever' in Wolof, the primary indigenous language of Senegal. This was how he came to boxing.

After the First World War broke out in 1914, Battling Siki found himself fighting in the trenches, having volunteered on a whim for the French Army. He reappeared in Paris in 1919, as a decorated war veteran, recipient of both the *Croix de Guerre* and the *Croix de Mérite*. He started boxing again, and, between 1921 and 1922, he won at least 86 matches, demolishing each of his opponents. One of his victories saw him beat the champion of Holland in Rotterdam and, while he was at it, he won the heart of a pretty blonde girl with blue eyes, Lintje van Appelteere, whom he brought back to Paris. Madly in love, they were soon married with a child. If people wanted to talk, so be it!

How many insults his wife must have suffered for having dared to marry a black man! Of course, Siki also suffered, so much so that he felt obliged to write, in a September 1922 issue of the magazine *L'Auto*: 'My wife is Dutch, with white skin, blonde hair, and blue eyes. I love her very much, she loves me very much, we truly love each other.'

All of France awaited the return to the ring of Georges Carpentier, the greatest of all the middleweight champions, who was scheduled to fight in September at Buffalo Stadium in Montrouge, in the Parisian suburbs. Battling Siki, who had won every single one of his matches, was the obvious opponent. But apparently, the world champion thought that defending his title against a black man was beneath him. He believed Battling Siki to be unworthy, a sub-par challenger, who was not 'qualified for such a sudden and excessively flattering elevation in status'.

Initially, the press was unanimous in its support for Carpentier but eventually it became obsessed by the idea of a fight between the two men. There wouldn't be the same 'biological stakes' in a fight between two white men. The fight was scheduled. Shortly before it took place, a journalist for the newspaper *Paris-Midi* wrote: 'The question is to know whether one white is worth two blacks – as is the case in musical notation.' Another journalist, referring to Battling Siki, remarked: 'He is agile, like all those of his race, and dodges punches ... by backing up rapidly on quick legs ... This tactic, or rather this primitive method, can it be considered equal to the more classical style of the world champion? Obviously not...'

In fact, some concluded that this was to be a fight between a man and an animal, who shouldn't be viewed in the same category. Battling Siki was thus nicknamed the 'Championzee'.

Georges Carpentier arrived at Buffalo Stadium in a limousine. He had a taste for seedy nightlife, and a reputation as a dandy, leading him to be nicknamed 'the orchid man'. He had already reserved a table at a fancy restaurant where he would eat after the fight with showbusiness stars and politicians. He entered the ring, looked at the forbidding sky, and with his legendary smile, shouted to the crowd, who were already under the spell of his film star good looks: 'Let's get started! It's going to rain!'

The bell rang...

In order to understand this boxing match, one needs to know what was being planned behind the scenes. 'When you fight Carpentier, you'll earn a lot of money', Siki's coach told him, 'but only if you allow yourself to be beaten.'

In his book *Battling Siki*, Jean-Marie Bretagne describes this momentous fight. The first round was a pale imitation of a boxing match. Siki entered the ring fully intending to lose, just as he had been asked to. Carpentier knew he couldn't lose so he let down his guard and started to provoke Siki so as to give the spectators some entertainment. But when the crowd started booing, he took a gentle swipe at Siki, who doubled over, writhing in pain. The referee was offended by such behaviour. 'Mister Siki', he exclaimed, 'do us the pleasure of standing up!'

Siki began to brood over his predicament, but he took up the fight again. Carpentier, once again, waltzed lithely around him. He could easily have used a right hook to finish off Siki and walk away with his title and his earnings, but he wanted to string out the fight as long as possible for the cameras. Reporters wanted something worth filming. The idea was to prolong the show.

The first round ended. In his corner, Carpentier stared at his opponent with hate-filled eyes. Okay, the match was fixed, but so what? Was it really necessary for Siki to exaggerate his role as the fall guy so much?

In the second round, Carpentier delicately jabbed at Siki's chin, hoping he wouldn't decide to fall down! Then Carpentier got angry and hit a little harder. Siki responded gingerly, with tentative jabs, which merely stung the world champion's pride.

At the start of the third round, Carpentier decided that the masquerade had gone on long enough. Tired of dealing with this negro, he let his fists fly. Siki hit the floor once again, but then, to everyone's surprise, he quickly got back on his feet and began to skip lightly around the ring. It looked like a Charlie Chaplin film. Once again Carpentier punched him furiously. Siki collapsed on to the canvas but then sprang to his feet immediately!

The fourth round... By this stage, Carpentier had had enough and he unleashed a flurry of punches. Siki asked him to stop, as this wasn't part of the deal. But Carpentier was enjoying himself and was no longer holding back. To escape this punishment, Siki sank to his knees. The referee counted, 'One, two...' But then Siki got up yet again and simply absorbed his opponent's blows. He had resolved that he wasn't going down again, that nothing Carpentier could throw at him would knock him down. Then, out of nowhere, he landed one massive punch on Carpentier ... who promptly hit the canvas. He tried to get up, but his feet slipped out from beneath him as though he were on an ice rink...

'In the fourth round', Siki would later recall, 'when I saw myself on my knees in front of 50,000 people, I said to myself, "Look here, Siki, you've never been defeated by any other boxer ... You've never been on your knees the way you are at this moment." And my heart skipped a beat. I got up and I punched [...] I did it even though [my manager] Hellers was hissing in my ear, "Why are you acting like an idiot? Have you forgotten the agreement?" It had been agreed that, in the fourth round, I would be laid out flat on my back, arms spread wide. If I had done as planned, Hellers would have won 200,000 francs. But I didn't want to.'

The referee counted: 'Three, four, five, six...' The cameras were rolling.

Finally, Carpentier got back to his feet.

In the fifth round, the world champion was little more than a spectator.

Then, in the sixth round, an exhausted Carpentier clung to Siki before collapsing. Once he hit the canvas, he suddenly remembered his acting lessons. Grabbing his ankle, he cried out in pain and accused his opponent of having tripped him. The referee knew it was a trick, of course, but what could he do? He consulted with the judges who recommended that he award the fight to Carpentier in order to appease the crowd.

'Georges Carpentier is the winner!' the referee announced. But the judges had made the wrong call. The 50,000 spectators cried out: 'Siki is the winner! Siki is the winner!' An hour of discussion ensued. Finally, the referee approached Siki and held up his arm, signalling that he had won.

But it was unacceptable for a black man to be champion of France, Europe and the world. Few journalists dared defend Siki after the fight. The exception was a young law student, Nguyen Ai Quoc, who wrote in a communist newspaper: 'As long as colonialism has existed whites have been paid good money to beat up blacks. This time, a black was paid to do the same thing to a white.' Thirty years later, under the name Hô Chi Minh, this one-time law student would liberate Vietnam from the grip of French colonialism!

In the 1920s prejudice began to be challenged. Blacks began to make their voices heard. In 1921 René Maran, a Martinican from Fort-de-France, won the major literary prize, the Prix Goncourt, for his novel *Batouala*! In a newspaper article from September 1922, one journalist declared: 'Blacks, until now, have worked in the shadows like *niggers*. From time to time, they have shown up on stage in a jazz band [...] All of a sudden, the black cloud burst and Mr René Maran published *Batouala* [...] In the wake of this literary prize, the gladiator's prize is now held by the black man Battling Siki.'

The newspapers continued harping on the themes of national decline, the difficulty of integration, etc.

I'm very aware of the range of different theories offered throughout history to explain the success of black people. First, people insist that 'black athletes are incapable of doing this or that'. Then, when they are successful, the initial response has always been to write it off as 'luck'. Thus, the day after his epic battle, it was decided that Battling Siki had taken a wild swing at Carpentier and hit him 'by chance'!

Finally, when blacks continue to prove their 'ability' and it is no longer possible to attribute their success to luck, it is claimed that it is just 'natural for them' – that it is physical, genetic, related to body type, psychological. In short, their success is the result of everything except their intelligence and hard work. 'The Carpentier–Siki fight highlights the fragility of the white body compared to the granite-like frame of the black man', one newspaper declared.

The supposedly superior physical strength of the black man is tied to his past, which invariably posits slavery as the source of his exploitable strength. Slavery equals physical effort.

For example, 'natural' was also the word used when Jesse Owens, an American track and field athlete, won his medals at the Olympic Games in Berlin in 1936. Here is how one reporter described his famous long jump: 'The "black lightning bolt" from Ohio is the fastest thing in the world without wheels. His stride is fluid. He seems to flow like water along the track. It is his natural speed that ensures his superiority in the long jump. He doesn't have to worry about working hard to produce a massive effort in the forward rotation phase like others do. All he has to do is lift up his legs and hold his breath for a moment, and as soon as he lands he has already broken the record.'

No one bothered to discuss his technique. In fact, the reason Jesse Owens was so successful was that he revolutionized sprinting technique. As Etienne Moreau notes, Owens introduced 'an explosive push phase at the beginning of races, and his cruising speed mid-race was much faster thanks to a short, rapid stride pattern, while holding the torso in an upright position'. When journalists described the Guadeloupe-born Marie-José Pérec, another fantastically successful French track and field athlete, they often underlined her 'natural ability', overlooking the hours of training, effort, and pain that went into preparing her races.

As for Battling Siki, he was a victim of his time. Eventually, his title, his boxing licence, and his prize money were all stolen from him by the 'wise men' of the Boxing Federation. Battling Siki had spoken publicly about the deal that had been arranged by his coach before the fight. But rather than criticize Carpentier for his insulting and unsportsmanlike conduct, people accused Siki of having taken advantage of his adversary's relaxed attitude to knock him out!

In the communist newspaper *L'Humanité*, Paul Vaillant-Couturier drew this conclusion: 'There is something much more serious at issue here than the fixing of a sporting competition. This is a characteristic symptom of the campaign organized against men of colour, a situation emblematic of colonialism itself. Carpentier was a sort of national symbol ... who could not be beaten by a Negro. It was too dangerous. If he were beaten, the Negro would have to be punished. And so he was.'

A disgusted Siki left France for the US, stopping off en route with his wife and child in Holland, where he was received with honours by the queen. But Siki didn't know New York, and he didn't yet understand the power of segregation. However, he had never backed down from a fight, and he vowed never to be subjugated. Years before Rosa Parks appeared on the scene (see pp. 199–206), Battling Siki resisted segregation by not giving up his seat on buses, by not using the bathrooms reserved for blacks, and by not taking the black elevators. 'You have a Statue of Liberty', he said, 'but it's a lie.' He continually refused to obey the rules of a segregated society. You say that the black man is a monkey, a bigamist? Fine. Siki remarried a white American woman and he walked the streets of New York with a monkey on his shoulder...

His eventual fate comes as no surprise. On a winter morning in December 1925, Battling Siki, the man who liked white women, white cars, and white ties, was gunned down: seven bullets in the back. He was not yet 30.

Decades later, his exploits were symbolically recognized when Fernandez Mell, who fought under the command of Che Guevara in Cuba, chose 'Siki' as his *nom-de-guerre*.

The Black Dragonfly

Panama Al Brown
5 July 1902–11 April 1951

> You are a blue Negro who boxes
> equators, equinoxes
>
> Sun, I can take your punches
> your heavy punches to my neck
>
> It's still you I prefer
> sun, delicious hell
>
> Jean Cocteau, *Drums*

I'd like to tell you the story of the 'black dragonfly', Panama Al Brown, who, in the 1930s, was the new star of the boxing ring, a genius, champion of the world.

Alfonso Teofilo Brown was born in Colon, Panama. His father was a former slave from Tennessee who, after his liberation, had travelled to Panama to work on the famous canal.

Brown started boxing when he was 17, racking up a long list of knockouts, and was soon noticed by an American businessman who ran the Winter Velodrome (known as the Vél d'hiv) in Paris, a popular indoor sports and entertainment venue. He had the perfect build for a boxer: he stood 5 feet 7 inches tall, and weighed 115 lbs, tall enough to deal with a straight left, arms long enough to parry punches from a distance, and long, thin legs.

In 1927 he won several fights at the Vél d'hiv in front of 20,000 spectators! He then went to the US where he continued to rack up victories. Upon his return to Paris, he knocked out his first opponent in 18 seconds! No opponent could go the distance against him. He was ready to fight for the world title, which he won, in 1929, after going the full 15 rounds against Gregoria Vidal. Eugène Huat, known as the 'Tiger Cat', challenged him for the title but

Brown beat him easily. He held on to his title for six long years. It was said that Al Brown threw such heavy punches that he would even have beaten heavyweight contenders.

Paris fell in love with him. People were fascinated by his elegance, his intelligence, his gift for languages: he spoke seven languages fluently. They couldn't get enough of tales of his eccentric night-time adventures in the clubs that he frequented until the early hours of the morning, high on drink and drugs. Some were disturbed by his fondness for champagne; he regularly took a bottle into the ring, where he drank and smoked cigarettes while waiting for the bell. And Brown continued to win because his strategy in the ring was never to be in the place where his opponent thought he would be, the element of surprise allowing him to land the killer blow.

Al Brown's winning streak lasted until 1 June 1935, in Valencia, when he lost his crown to Baltazar Sangchilli. But the fight was fixed. Brown's own agent, bribed by the challenger's team, had spiked the champion's water bottle. Not understanding what was happening to his body, Brown fought until he passed out. The referee knew what was happening but did nothing. He was in on the fix. In the ring, the referee is the boss, a king who lays down the law as he sees fit. Disgusted by the bribes and cheating, by corrupt managers, and by crowds that turned a blind eye, Brown laid down his gloves for good.

He started over with a band that played at the Caprice Viennois, a restaurant in the Pigalle district of Paris. Alcohol and opium gradually destroyed him and the former champion became a truly pathetic sight. The poet Jean Cocteau called him 'a black diamond in a trashcan'.

By then, Brown had become the laughing stock of Paris. His situation moved Cocteau, who wanted to find a way to bring him back to his rightful place in the ring. But Brown refused. His right hand was a constant source of pain. He told Cocteau: 'I don't want anyone to touch me any more. I've got glass wrists.' But in the end, Cocteau convinced him.

Of course, the fact that a young poet wanted to play at being a boxing manager only gave Parisians more of a reason to jeer. Everyone knew Cocteau was attracted to men, but that was not solely what drove him to help Brown. He, too, had struggled to break a drug habit. He, too, had needed to achieve success before he could openly admit to his sexual 'colour'. He had genuine empathy for Brown. 'I like boxing', he wrote, 'and that is why, one day, I persuaded Al Brown to dive back into this active form of poetry, the mysterious syntax that was the glory of his youth. I became attached to the fate of this boxer, because for me, he represented a kind of poet, a mime, a sorcerer, who had created between the ropes the perfect success of a human enigma: the prestige of presence. Al was a poem in black ink, a eulogy for spiritual strength that was more powerful than pure strength.'

Of the two men's romantic relationship, little is known. Many people simply could not accept the idea of a homosexual being an athlete, especially a boxer – and even more so a black boxer. Growing up in the West Indies, I used to think that there was no such thing as a black homosexual. We live in a society full of prejudices against homosexuality, which I believe are identical to those surrounding skin colour or religion. A few years ago, a member of parliament in the north of France described 'homosexual behaviour' as a 'threat to the survival of humanity'.

The Black Panther Party had it right. On 5 August 1970 Huey P. Newton, the group's minister of defence, declared: 'We must relate to the homosexual movement because it is a real thing [...] They might be the most oppressed people in society [...] And maybe here I'm injecting some of my own prejudice when I say that "even a homosexual can be revolutionary". Quite the contrary, maybe a homosexual can be the most revolutionary.'

Like racism, homophobia is a problem of the collective imagination. Our societies are driven by received ideas, and the most homophobic among us are those who have never spent time in the company of homosexuals. Did you know that 25 per cent of adolescents and young adults who commit suicide are homosexual? Violence, insults, and contemptuous remarks are commonplace in schoolyards and throughout society. We all need to learn how to respect others. We need to help these young people to accept their sexuality and to stay alive.

Today, so-called homosexual practices are still punishable by death in six countries: Afghanistan, Iran, Mauritania, Pakistan, Sudan, and Yemen. In 84 countries, they are illegal and can result in imprisonment! In France too, the inequalities persist; same-sex marriage was only recently legalized, while adoption is still often closed off to couples of the same sex. Is a society where some have more rights than others truly a just society?

In the end, it was love that saved Al Brown. Guided by Cocteau, he went through a drug rehabilitation programme at Saint Anne's Hospital in Paris. It was likely the hardest-won of all his fights. He re-entered the world of athletics a new man. 'Imagine, today', wrote

Cocteau, 'something (it is impossible to say someone) that moves like thunder, fortune, rage [...] like an epidemic.'

Finally, on 4 March 1938, Panama Al Brown entered the great hall of the Palais des Sports, a famous indoor arena in Paris's 15th *arrondissement*. His opponent was, once again, Baltazar Sangchilli. As the fight started, Brown was in a bad way, sick with the flu, and with his kidneys reacting badly to the champagne he had drunk to give himself courage. The boxing match was like a fight between frightened kids.

Brown managed to dominate his opponent for nine rounds, but he then visibly began to age. His knees grew weak, and he threw punches blindly, grimacing and bleeding. With every wild blow from Brown, his opponent almost seemed to have one foot in the grave. With both men on the verge of collapsing, the referee pulled them apart. Brown was declared the winner.

Panama Al Brown had teetered dangerously on the brink of catastrophe. Cocteau wrote to him: 'Give up boxing. You hate it. You wanted an act of justice, and you got it. The celebrated elite, for whom four rounds of fatigue erase 11 rounds of miracles, don't deserve that you should exhaust yourself for them. The crowd has proven that they love you. Try something new.'

Al Brown would have liked to follow this advice, but he didn't know how to live without boxing. In the end, it was alcohol that delivered the final knockout blow.

A Pen of Rage

Richard Nathaniel Wright
4 September 1908–28 November 1960

In 2008 a pre-Obama United States celebrated the 100th anniversary of the birth of the African-American author Richard Wright. For once, the proverb 'No one is a prophet in their own land' was turned on its head. And, moreover, it was turned on its head by a black man. Yet this man had voluntarily left his country in 1947, openly declaring that he was going to France in order to denounce segregation in the land of his birth. Until his final breath, Richard Wright strove to change a culture that offered people like him just three options: to chase futile ambitions, to drown in bitterness, or to rise up in revolt. Wright's protagonists are a mix of rage and fear, and they still haunt America today.

Richard Wright was born in Natchez, Mississippi. In the nineteenth century, the town had been home to one of the largest slave markets of the American South. In the racist and segregationist state of Mississippi, conditions for blacks hadn't changed much since abolition: 'sawmills, cotton factories [...] a swamp, a prison; roads, fits of the Blues, travels, accidents, and, of course, various forms of violence'. The grandchild of slaves, Wright endured a childhood of poverty, caught between a violent family life, a suffocating religiosity, and 'white terror'.

He was six years old when his father left the family for another woman. His mother worked as a cook for a white family; she left early in the morning and, when she could, brought leftovers home for dinner. Wright was left on his own all day long. He would follow the black workers and the unemployed around town, as they drowned out their sense of oppression at the local bar. The men had a game: filling the youngster with alcohol and getting him to repeat a string of obscenities. That was his education. 'My father was statistically destined for delinquency', remarked his daughter, Julia Wright, whom I met with in order to write this chapter.

Richard Wright's attitude and life can be summarized in two words that sound similar: *hunger* and *anger*. The quest for food, both physical and intellectual, was his primary motivation, dominating his entire life and framing his vision of the world. It was the desire to satisfy his hunger that initially led to his awareness of racial division. 'Watching white people eat would make my empty stomach churn', he wrote, 'and I grew vaguely angry.' The combination of anger and hunger transformed a physical obsession into an existential, and soon an intellectual, quest. For culture, too, is nourishment. Politicians provide sports facilities for teenagers, when what they really need are cultural centres where they can find books written by women and men like them! Education isn't only about finding work. It is also a way of learning to feel comfortable in one's own skin.

But books were inaccessible, practically outlawed, for the poor black kids of the South. Wright was both passionate and ingenious in his quest for reading material, willing to resort to whatever means necessary to get his hands on a book. To steal words was like stealing fire. They were to be treated with veneration and fear.

'I had never in my life been abused by Whites, but I had already become as conditioned to their existence as though I had been the victim of a thousand lynchings', he wrote in *Black Boy*. His uncle was murdered in Arkansas. As a child he heard adults speak in low voices about lynchings. In these conditions, some black people turned to religion, hoping for a better world in the afterlife. Others translated their suffering into the Blues or jazz, or drowned the fire within them in alcohol. Still others rebelled, becoming 'bad Negroes'. Wright knew all kinds of 'bad Negroes' during his childhood, like the one who terrorized him and his playmates: 'I suspect that his end was violent', he later wrote. Or another whose violence was directed against white people: 'He was in prison last I heard.' Or the one who challenged white people: 'He was shot in the back by a white cop.' There was also one who attacked segregation laws and talked about all kinds of taboo subjects: 'White women; the Ku Klux Klan; France and how Negro soldiers fared there; French women; Jack Johnson; the northern states; the Civil War; Abraham Lincoln [...] slavery; social equality; Communism; Socialism...' This last one apparently ended up in a mental institution.

Reading and writing kept Richard Wright from becoming a delinquent. They gave him the words, the distance, and the experience that allowed him to establish a bridge between himself and the world. Blacks were not allowed in the local library, so it took the goodwill of a white man, who loaned him his reader's card, for Wright to be able to check-out books under the man's name. He brought these treasures home wrapped in newspaper, as though they were a form of contraband.

Then he went to Chicago, attracted by the great myth of equal opportunity. In fact, blacks were treated just as poorly there as in the South. Living in poverty in the midst of great material wealth, Wright worked as a deliveryman, a busboy, a postman, and used literature to distract himself from his impatience, his rage, and his feeling of rejection. He found refuge in the John Reed clubs, linked to the Communist Party, which reached out to writers and artists. They published a magazine called *Left Front*, where Wright first discovered the revolutionary writers Maxim Gorki and André Gide, and where he first learned about sociology, psychology, and Marxism. It was also there that he produced his first published texts.

He was always grateful to the Communist Party for having pulled him out of the ghetto. But it didn't take him long to understand that there was a price to pay: strict party discipline and intellectual orthodoxy. Nothing truly comes for free: in the end, there's always a price to pay. It's just that sometimes the price tag isn't visible... When Wright left the Communist Party, it wasn't because he was rejecting Marxism or socialism, but because he wanted to think for himself. Aimé Césaire would express this same notion in 1956 in his *Letter to Maurice Thorez*:

> One fact that is paramount in my eyes is this: we, men of color, at this precise moment in our historical evolution, have come to grasp, in our consciousness, the full breadth of our singularity, and are ready to assume on all levels and in all areas the responsibilities that flow from this coming to consciousness.
>
> The singularity of our 'situation in the world,' which cannot be confused with any other. The singularity of our problems, which cannot be reduced to any other problem. The singularity of our history, constructed out of terrible misfortunes that belong to no one else. The singularity of our culture, which we wish to live in a way that is more and more real.
>
> What else can be the result of this but that our paths toward the future – all our paths, political as well as cultural – are not yet charted? That they are yet to be discovered, and

that the responsibility for this discovery belongs to no one but us?

Wright's passion was always evident, not solely in his role as a militant within the Communist Party, but in everything he ever did. He became a pillar of the John Reed clubs, and his name was soon widely recognized. In 1938 he published a short story collection titled *Uncle Tom's Children*, its title citing the famous *Uncle Tom's Cabin* by the 'white' abolitionist Harriet Beecher Stowe. Wright's book was deemed to be a 'terrifying expression of racial hatred'.

Wright's *Native Son* was published two years later in 1940. A hard-hitting and challenging novel, it denounced racist America, the wilful blindness of the communists, the self-satisfaction of the Left, religious people trying to show themselves off in a good light, a city that strangles all sense of humanity, and a society that denies fundamental rights to poor people and blacks.

The story illustrates the poverty and the fate of black people during those years. Bigger Thomas is a young black man living in the Chicago ghetto, who commits a double murder in a state of panic because words quite literally fail him. He is illiterate and tongue-tied. Each of his acts can be explained by an injustice. He finds work as a chauffeur for some rich whites. But on his first day, their daughter, a communist sympathizer, orders him to drive her in secret to a communist meeting and then to a black neighbourhood on the South Side. When they get back to the house she is dead drunk, and it is very late. If her parents find them together, he will lose his job. On the other hand, it is absolutely forbidden for him to carry her to her room. To do so would be to transgress the rules of racial segregation and would leave him open to accusations of rape. He knows he should probably call her parents to help him, but he doesn't want to betray her. So Bigger decides to act on his own and carry her to her room. But, as he steps into the bedroom, her mother hears a noise and calls for her daughter. In terror, he places the corner of a pillow over her mouth to stop her from speaking and ends up accidentally suffocating her. 'He was a murderer, a Negro murderer, a black murderer!' He thinks of running away. But his fingerprints would surely give him away. He places the girl in a trunk and later burns her body in a furnace. Eventually, he flees, after killing his girlfriend out of fear that she will betray him. After a manhunt, Bigger Thomas is captured and sent to the electric chair.

When it was published, *Native Son* was a huge success. Wright was called a 'black Dickens', a 'sepia Steinbeck'. He was praised for his literary talent and his insight into society. The poor black community was proud that one of their own had achieved such fame. But middle-class blacks and those in the professional classes accused him of exaggeration and pessimism. Why did he choose to make such an anti-social black man his hero? In so doing, didn't he risk discrediting all blacks? Zola had been similarly criticized for showcasing an alcoholic hero in his novel *L'Assommoir*. The emerging black middle classes were climbing the social ladder and they feared controversy; they wanted to believe that solutions to the problem of race had already been found. 'Having narrowly escaped the Bigger Thomas reaction pattern themselves', Richard Wright wrote in the postscript to his novel, 'they would not relish being publicly reminded of the lowly, shameful depths of life above which they enjoyed their bourgeois lives. Never did they want people, especially *white* people, to think that their lives were so much touched by anything so dark and brutal as Bigger.'

'Here is the tragic son I leave to you', he told the American people. 'We'll see what you do with him.' The novelist refused to create a clear distinction between blacks and whites. Bigger is not always black. He is also white. In fact, millions of Biggers, products of the United States of America, products of a society ravaged by a savage form of capitalism, carry within them the potential for crime.

As for the Communist Party, it was displeased by this book in which the protagonists were not 'painted as immaculate knights heroically charging the enemy'. But – as Michel Fabre explains in a book devoted to the writer – for Richard Wright, describing blacks in a way that conformed to the political theories of the Party would have meant betraying Bigger and betraying himself. As a result he distanced himself from communism, but not from his socialist convictions.

In 1947 he left the United States for France. Over the years, his anger had turned to rage. Two years earlier, something happened that was just too much. His daughter, Julia Wright, recalled: 'I was three years old. We lived in New York. Since my father was writing, he asked Connie, a white friend, to take me out for a few hours. Connie brought me to Bergdorf Goodman, a very chic store on Fifth Avenue. She looked at dresses while I followed, holding onto her skirt. Finally, I told her I needed to go pee. She walked up to a counter and asked a saleswoman where the bathrooms were. She kindly showed her where to go. But when we walked away from the counter, I suddenly became visible! The woman cried: "Miss, you can go, but not her!" When we got home, she told my father what had happened. I can still remember – I was in the dining room. Connie and my father were in the study next door. And I heard my father shout. His shout was like the cry of a wounded animal!'

He had suffered countless other personal humiliations, like having to trek over to Harlem just to get his hair cut, or not being able to buy a house in certain districts reserved for white people. He was never allowed to forget the different ways in which blacks were scorned.

The reasons behind his emigration were emotional – he didn't want to raise his daughter in that kind of climate – but they were also intellectual and literary. To go to Europe was to follow in the footsteps of Ernest Hemingway and to meet French writers he admired, like Albert Camus and André Gide.

When he arrived at the Saint Lazare railway station, he was greeted by the writer Gertrude Stein. Just along the street, he noticed a car with tinted windows from the American Embassy. The FBI surveillance had begun! And it would never stop.

In no time at all, Wright was meeting French leftists of various shades – for example, the Trotskyist Maurice Nadeau, or the communist Paul Éluard, as well as writers with no particular political affiliation, like André Breton, Jacques Prévert, André Gide, or Jean-Paul Sartre. His wife, Ellen Wright – white, American, Jewish, and communist – became Simone de Beauvoir's literary agent. Since Wright did not belong to any political party, people spoke freely in his presence, and, as time passed, the Left's contradictions became more apparent to him. As did the schisms between groups. Wright found it difficult to hold himself back, for when he saw injustice, he wanted to do something about it. Smooth talk and bluffing held no attractions for him. What mattered was direct action. Wright had no interest in leading a bourgeois life in Paris, surrounded by the intellectual stars of the Left Bank, nor did he wish to enjoy the comfortable life of a bestselling novelist, although he could well have done so. His autobiography *Black Boy*, which recounts his childhood in Mississippi, sold a million copies. And *Native Son* sold 600,000 copies!

Paris served, rather, as a springboard for Wright's travels and for his tireless activism on behalf of the oppressed. In 1952 he met the great Ghanaian statesman Kwame Nkrumah, who at the time was passionately demanding the independence of colonized black Africa. In April 1955 Wright was to be found in the city of Bandung, in Indonesia, attending the first conference of the 29 non-aligned nations (that is, countries which, during the Cold War, did not rely upon either Russia or the United States). He met the first Indian prime minister, Jawaharlal Nehru, the first premier of the People's Republic of China, Zhou Enlai, the first president of Indonesia, Sukarno, and the second Egyptian president, Gamal Abdel Nasser. Wright also published an account of the proceedings called *The Color Curtain: A Report on the Bandung Conference*.

While back in Paris between trips, he would devote most of his time to the struggle against racism. He created a group whose goal was to denounce all the injustices happening to black people in the United States – the lynchings, the propaganda being broadcast throughout the world – and to defend blacks facing racism and discrimination at the hands of American companies in France.

Wright played the role of father figure for all the expatriate writers and artists of the period. And there were lots of them, for there was a fascination with Paris and the freedom it seemed to offer. He brought together great black authors like James Baldwin, who went into exile in France in 1948 and who, like Wright, combined literary expression and political engagement, and Chester Himes, author of *A Rage in Harlem*, who went into exile in France in 1953, and whose prose Wright said was 'so intensely blinding that it burns your eyes'. There were other exiled Americans, such as William Gardner Smith, a journalist, editor, and novelist, and the cartoonist Ollie Harrington, one of the greatest artists of the twentieth century, whose most famous character, Bootsie, took a stand against racial segregation through the use of humour and mockery.

The growing alliance of all these black intellectuals undermined US propaganda, which sought to make people believe the black problem had been solved, that discrimination was no longer relevant. 'Wright's venom', wrote one journalist in 1956, 'continuously dispensed by expatriates at sidewalk cafes, along with years of headlines about the Dixie lynchings, has succeeded in poisoning European thinking about racial problems in America.' The FBI tightened its surveillance of Wright. He was listed on the National Security Index as a menace to US national security. It was the middle of the Cold War between East and West, and the witch hunt was reaching its climax.

Those conservatives who advocated white racial supremacy in the United States could not tolerate the fact that a black elite had formed a community in France. So they fell back on the classic tactic of divide and conquer. 'It's a murderous struggle in which brother is set against brother, in which threats of physical violence are brandished by one Black against another, in which people vow to hurt and kill one another', Richard Wright wrote. The supposed conflict between Wright and Baldwin was entirely fabricated by the FBI. Manipulation by the US Cultural Services played a key role in the harsh criticism of Wright by Baldwin, the famed author of *The Fire Next Time*. It was an effort to prove that two black stars didn't have the right to coexist.

The intimidation didn't stop there, for Wright was incorruptible, and therefore a potential danger who had to be carefully watched at all times. 'Of course, I don't want anything to happen to me', he wrote in a letter to Margrit de Sablonière, another author, on 30 March 1960, 'but if something does happen, my friends will know exactly where it came from. If I tell you these things, it is so you know what is happening. From the point of view of the Americans, I am worse than a Communist, for my work has cast a shadow over their policies in Asia and in Africa. That is the problem: the Americans have asked me many, many times to work for them, but I'd rather die.'

Wright meant what he said. Eight months later he was dead.

His last actions, writes Michel Fabre, 'were all aimed at revealing the sinister maneuvers of the American secret service in Paris. It is symbolic that as he was born into rebellion, this final chapter of his life should end in it.' On 8 November 1960 Wright gave a lecture in which he argued that the US government was silencing black intellectuals and artists. He described the racial tensions on US naval bases in Europe, denounced the surveillance of the black expatriate community in Paris, and unveiled the infiltration methods of the FBI and the CIA in the 'black zones'.

The walls began to close in on him; he received criticism from all sides. He responded by writing 817 short poems, in the form of haikus: tiny sparks of light at this dark moment in his life, truths in a world full of pretence:

Squeezing his eyes shut,   haiku 385
The cat yawns as if about
To eat the spring world.

Even the sparrows   haiku 192
Are attempting to thaw out
The frozen scarecrow.

On 28 November 1960 it was announced that he had died of a heart attack. Some people talked of poisoning. But it is more likely that, like many other African-American writers, Richard Wright died a victim of hate. His heart gave out, worn down by the relentless need to take up a pen of rage to denounce injustice.

The Silent Resistance Fighter

Addi Bâ

25 December 1913–18 December 1943

You, Senegalese *tirailleurs*, my black brothers
    with warm hands under ice and death
Who will be able to sing of you if not your
    brother in arms, your brother in blood?
I will not leave the words to the ministers
    not to the generals
I will not leave – no! – the praise of disdain
    bury you furtively
You are not poor men with empty pockets
    without honor
But I will tear down all the *banania* laughs
    on all the walls of France
          Léopold Senghor, 'Liminary Poem'
                Black Hosts, 1948

Colonel Rives welcomed me to his apartment near Fontainebleau, a suburb of Paris, not far from where I spent my childhood. He told me stories of the Second World War: of its procession of victims, dead and wounded; of the 'native' soldiers from Africa and elsewhere.

When the war – which was never supposed to happen – was declared, Maurice Rives was 16. In 1944, at the age of 20, he escaped to join the Resistance movement, and then became a career military man. He served in Vietnam, Algeria, Laos, Cameroon, the Central African Republic, Martinique, Djibouti … anywhere the Republic needed him. After his retirement, he was astonished to discover that his former comrades-in-arms from the colonies were suffering discrimination regarding their pensions. The issue was brought home to him when, one day in the northern Parisian suburb of Sarcelles, he ran into an old army comrade, a commander in the

Legion of Honour, France's highest honour: he had lost all his teeth, as he was unable to pay for dental care.

One might have thought that the Republic would honour all its soldiers – many of them wounded in action and handicapped for life – equally, regardless of whether they were from the former French colonies or elsewhere. However, soldiers from Africa, including those conscripted to fight under the French flag, were given a miserable military pension based on the median incomes of their home countries and calculated in their often devalued currencies.

Colonel Rives was determined to denounce an injustice that dishonoured his country, and he decided to take up arms once again, this time employing the primary weapon of peacetime: the media. He wrote over a hundred articles and made appearances on radio and TV shows a dozen times. But it was all in vain. Discrimination is still alive and well today, despite more recent efforts, like Rachid Bouchareb's 2006 film *Days of Glory*, which shows soldiers of all colours and religions united in the struggle to free France during the Second World War.

Convinced it was his duty, that his honour compelled it, Rives shared with me one particular story of a man very dear to his heart: Addi Bâ, a truly 'unknown soldier'. Of course, Rives could have chosen to tell me about a more famous figure, such as Félix Éboué (1884–1944). Appointed governor of Guadeloupe in 1936, Éboué was the only black person ever to reach the top of the hierarchy in the French colonial administration. On 18 June 1940, not long after the start of the Second World War, and while governor of Chad, he formally joined the Resistance, rallying support for General Charles de Gaulle's Free French movement. He raised an army of 40,000 soldiers. The 'only hope' for a free France lay in Africa, since the imperial homeland was Nazi-occupied. 'For this hope to materialize', wrote General de Gaulle in his *Mémoires de Guerre* (translated into English as *The Complete War Memoirs of Charles de Gaulle*), 'real support from Africa is required. The first and very effective support came from a colonial administrator originally from Guiana, Félix Éboué.'

But Éboué's role in the Resistance has been recognized. On 20 May 1949 his ashes were transferred to the Pantheon, the grand building in the Latin Quarter of Paris that houses the remains of France's national heroes, to lie alongside those of great Resistance figures such as Jean Moulin, the abolitionists Abbé Henri Grégoire and Victor Schoelcher, and those guardians of France's social conscience, Émile Zola and Jean Jaurès. As for Addi Bâ, he remains a black star lost in the French sky. To honour him, Colonel Rives – with the support of the local residents – had a street named after him on 11 May 1991 in the town of Langeais, part of the department of Indre-et-Loire, in west-central France.

Addi Bâ was born in 1913 near Conakry, in the French West African colony of Guinea. He eventually moved to mainland France, where he found a job with a local dignitary in Langeais. In 1939, with the war imminent, the military command suddenly recalled the 'indigenous' forces who had fought so courageously in the First World War. Addi Bâ signed up to fight. An African familiar with Nazi propaganda, he knew that a Germany victory would represent a return to a kind of slavery. Aimé Césaire expressed this same sentiment in 1948 in the introduction to a new edition of *Slavery and Colonization* by Victor Schoelcher:

> It would be hard to imagine what that terrible period, stretching from the beginning of the seventeenth century to the middle of the nineteenth century, was like for the residents of the Antilles, had history not taken on the task of furnishing a few bases for comparison.
> Imagine Auschwitz or Dachau, Ravensbrück and Mauthausen, but all on an immense scale, over centuries, over continents, America as a world of concentration camps, the striped uniforms imposed on an entire race; imagine all of that, along with all the dregs of history, along with all the humiliations and all the sadism; let us add them up and multiply them, and we'll understand that what Nazi Germany did was to implement on a smaller scale in Europe what Western Europe had implemented for centuries against races that had the audacity or the clumsiness to find themselves in her path.

In April 1940 Addi Bâ was assigned to the 12th regiment of Senegalese *tirailleurs*. On 10 May 1940 these troops were sent to put their bodies on the line to hold back the German army's advance. African troops would go on to suffer the worst losses of the whole army; 520,000 *tirailleurs* had been mobilized to occupy the front lines. A quick comparison reveals the scale of the losses: the mortality rate of the 'French from France' in 1939–40 was 3 per cent; that of soldiers from West and Central Africa was 40 per cent!

In May and early June 1940, Addi Bâ – badly equipped, squelching through the mud – fought in the Ardennes Forest and along the banks of the Meuse in terrible, bloody battles, sometimes engaging in hand-to-hand combat. His regiment was decimated on 18 June 1940, in Harréville-les-Chanteurs, a commune of the Haute-Marne department in north-eastern France. Some soldiers were killed during the actual battle, while others were massacred after their surrender: 500–600 *tirailleurs* were ruthlessly executed by the Germans. A bullet in the back of the neck.

Violating all traditional rules of war, the Nazis organized manhunts throughout the Sarthe and Côte-d'Or departments and elsewhere. The 'Senegalese' soldiers were imprisoned in France, rather than in Germany, because the Germans feared tropical illnesses and, even more, the possibility of sexual relations between black men and white women.

It was the unspeakable behaviour of the Nazis towards black soldiers that radicalized Jean Moulin, the future president of the National Council of the Resistance. He was the prefect of the department of Eure-et-Loire, when he was arrested by the Germans on 18 June 1940, and pressurized to testify publicly that the Senegalese *tirailleurs* had carried out atrocities and generally behaved like savages. But Moulin refused to sign the paper placed in front of him, appalled by 'such an indignity', a refusal for which he was beaten and insulted. He tells the story himself in his book, *Premier Combat*.

One of the Nazis managed to calm him down, and attempted once again to persuade him that all the evidence showed that the black soldiers really were committing unspeakable crimes. Moulin asked to see this evidence and was handed a report describing how the black army units 'retreated along the railroad tracks, beside which were later found, about 12 kilometres from Chartres, the mutilated bodies of women and children'.

'How can you be sure that the Senegalese *tirailleurs* actually passed through the precise location where the corpses were discovered?' Moulin asked.

'We found their abandoned gear', replied the Nazi. He added that the victims had been examined by specialists and that the 'violence to which they were subjected showed all the characteristics of crimes committed by Negroes'.

'The characteristics of crimes committed by Negroes!' Moulin almost laughed in the face of such stereotypes.

As violence and persuasion had both failed to elicit his signature, the Nazis brought the prefect to the supposed site of the carnage, where they showed him nine horribly disfigured corpses, including those of several children. Moulin immediately recognized that these were victims of a bombing. The Nazis were furious and threw him into a tiny cell, next to the mangled corpse of a woman whose limbs had been torn off.

Night was now falling, and Moulin still had not complied, despite the fact that he was so weak by that point that the Germans decided to lock him in a room at the Notre Dame de Chartres Hospital, promising to continue the interrogation the next day. A Senegalese *tirailleur* lay on the mattress next to him. 'Now that we know how much you love Negroes, we thought it would make you happy to be able to sleep with one of them', his Nazi jailers sneered.

Why such insistence that Jean Moulin should sign that document, which eventually led him to take a shard of glass to his own throat (though, luckily, he did not succeed in killing himself)? Because the Germans needed the official cover provided by a French prefect to hide their own war crimes against the Senegalese *tirailleurs*. I have read that 'by the end of 1940, there were 165 Senegalese buried in the zones of the battle of 16 June [...] including 120 "unknowns" from whom the Germans had removed their military dog tags to ensure their anonymity. They were among the many other soldiers gunned down like animals on 17 June following their capture...'

But what happened to Addi Bâ? While the fighting continued, and the black battalions fell one after another in the early summer of 1940, he was captured and brought to Neufchâteau, in the eastern French department of Vosges. But soon after that, he was able to take advantage of a night of drinking by the prison guards, and managed to escape along with 40 of his fellow prisoners. They disappeared into the night, but not before they had armed themselves with abandoned weapons.

They took refuge in the woods of the commune of Saint-Ouen-lès-Parey, where they struggled to survive. Some among them were wounded. Addi Bâ took the risk of making contact with the local population. The mayor of Tollaincourt and the village schoolteacher took care of the wounded and provided food for the men. A few were hidden in homes in the village. It took a lot of courage, or recklessness, to hide an African in this new, Aryan France. There were obvious logistical difficulties, but, more significantly, the reprisals were terrible. There are some truly incredible stories, like that of the Senegalese *tirailleur* disguised by some local farmers as a woman and asked to watch over their cows. This was in the middle of the war!

The presence of Addi Bâ and his companions in an enemy-occupied zone was very risky. And he knew it. He sought to flee the region. In the commune of Épinal, some gendarmes put his group in touch with smugglers. After burying their weapons, they were secretly transported to Switzerland, arriving in early 1941.

But Addi Bâ stayed behind in France, in Tollaincourt, disguised as a farm labourer, and continued to fight. In October he made contact with two future members of the network 'Ceux de la Résistance' ('Those of the Resistance').

Many people are unaware of the immense contribution made by blacks who fought to liberate France in the Second World War. As early as 1940, black people were to be found in the first Resistance networks. In 1944 they swelled the ranks of active Resistance fighters. In the Vercors region, for example, in July 1944, the French Forces of the Interior (FFI) included 52 Senegalese *tirailleurs* (escaped prisoners of war), whom their chief considered 'the best units in the area'.

Addi Bâ occupied an important role and demonstrated great skill as he carried out his duties. On several occasions he went to the demarcation line between Nazi-occupied and Vichy France in order to receive instructions from a high-level commander. And he himself began to pass on intelligence.

He also discovered a British pilot whose bomber had been shot down by the Germans. After nursing him back to health, he helped him escape to Switzerland. Along with a companion, he formed the first group of Resistance fighters in the Vosges in March 1943, at a place that became known as the Chêne-des-Partisans. In July his clandestine organization, known as the 'Camp of Deliverance', included 80 escapees from the Forced Labour Service, 18 Russians, and two Germans who said they were deserters from the Wehrmacht (Germany's armed forces). But on 11 July these two pseudo-deserters left the camp and betrayed its location to the Kommandant of their unit. Two days later, over a thousand German soldiers surrounded the small hill where the group was hidden. Luckily, the local farmers, who supported the Resistance fighters, had warned them in advance, and they were all able to escape.

But for Addi Bâ things were more difficult than for the others: his skin betrayed him. On 15 July he was captured at La Fenessière. No sooner had he been thrown into prison than he jumped out of the window of his cell. A soldier fired at him with a submachine gun and hit him in the thigh. Addi Bâ was then taken to the prison in

Épinal, where he was brutally tortured. The Germans wanted him to disclose the names of other Resistance fighters but he refused to say anything. He was soon joined in the prison by one of his comrades, Arburger, captured two days earlier by the Gestapo as he was trying to lead his comrades in arms from the 'Camp of Deliverance' to other hideouts.

On 18 December 1943, after relentless torture, Addi Bâ and his friend Arburger were executed on the Plateau de la Vierge in Épinal. Neither of them had revealed a single name.

Though he had played a major role in the Resistance from the very beginning, Addi Bâ only received the Médaille de la Résistance posthumously in 2003, sixty years after his death. Is it really all that surprising, though? Even before the liberation had been completed, France was attempting to whitewash the Resistance movement. As Colonel Rives told me: 'No trace remained but a footprint in the sand quickly erased by the winds of the desert.' This whitewashing extended to the entire army. Despite the fact that half of the men who took part in the landings in Provence in August 1944 were African, they were not seen marching on the Champs-Élysées on 14 July 1945. After the war, not a single one of their names was listed in the annals of France's liberation. As for the various monuments erected to honour the fallen, rarely do they mention an African soldier.

Let us return to the matter of Colonel Rives' sense of injustice when he learned that the surviving veterans from the overseas territories still weren't receiving the same pensions as French veterans, and were still not recognized as the freedom fighters they were. The crowning achievement of national 'recognition' for their service was a decree signed in 1959 by Valéry Giscard d'Estaing, then the Secretary of State in the Ministry of Finance, freezing the retirement benefits and pensions of the veterans of the former French empire in Africa. As France's empire began to disintegrate, these pensions, retirement benefits, and subsidies were transformed into annual indemnities, calculated on the basis of prices at the moment of each country's independence.

What a betrayal on the part of the French state! That 1959 decree was ratified by General Charles de Gaulle, then the president of the French Republic, the same man who, on 18 June 1940, exclaimed on BBC radio in his famous statement, 'France is not alone! She is not alone! She has a vast empire behind her!'

Colonel Rives spoke movingly about these African veterans: 'For me it is something terrible because we fought together, some died in my arms, some took care of me when I was wounded. We are soul brothers. What is to be done? We hear grand speeches about their sacrifice, about their bravery, but there is no talk of their pensions, of the basic minimum they would need to live decently!'

The politicians are not that worried, though: these veterans are so old! They'll be dead soon enough...

The Genius of Black Scientific Pioneers

Scientists, Inventors, Researchers

The list of black scientists, inventors, and researchers that I offer here is by no means exhaustive. It begins in the second half of the nineteenth century for the simple reason that, before the abolition of slavery, there was no formal authorization process for the registration of patents.

In fact, this list could begin hundreds of thousands of years earlier, at the dawn of time. Since Africa was the cradle of humanity, I could have cited stone carvings, the mastery of fire, pottery, astronomy, medicine, writing, agriculture, mathematics... Whatever their environment, early humans in Africa had to resolve all kinds of problems: crossing rivers, building shelters, gathering food, treating ailments, etc.

Humankind has always been forced to invent and has grown more intelligent in the process. This may seem obvious, and the list of inventions that we owe to black people would be superfluous if it weren't for the fact that there are still people today who doubt their intellectual capacity.

The following names of scientists are drawn from the works of Otha Richard Sullivan and Yves Antoine.

Household Inventions

Dr Martin Luther King, Jr said, 'Before leaving for work each day, know that half of all the things and appliances we use at home were invented by black people!'

- The system for opening and closing elevators: Alexander Miles, in 1867.
- Clothes wringer: Ellen F. Eglin, *circa* 1880.
- Electric light (first incandescent bulb with carbon filament): Lewis Howard Latimer (1848–1928) and Joseph V. Nichols, in 1881.

- Shoe-making machine that allowed soles to be durably attached in one minute: Jan Ernst Matzeliger, March 1883.
- Egg-beater: Willis Johnson, in 1884.
- Satellite dish: Granville T. Woods (1856–1910).
- Refrigerator: John Stenard, in 1891.
- Bottle caps: William Painer, in 1892.
- Ironing board: Sarah Boone, in 1892.
- Clothes-dryer: George T. Sampson, in 1892.
- Mop: Thomas W. Stewart, in 1893.
- Panel to protect beds: Lewis A. Russell, in 1895.
- Security mechanism for elevators: James Cooper, in 1895.
- Curtain rod: William S. Grant, in 1896.
- Juicer: John T. White, in 1896.
- Pull-out couch and bed: John H. Evans, in 1897.
- Steam-cooker: George W. Kelley, in 1897.
- Folding bed: Leonard C. Bailey, in 1899.
- 'Hot Comb' (for straightening hair): Walter H. Sammons, in 1920.

Garden, Leisure, Writing, School
- Swinging chair: Payton Johnson, in 1881.
- Lantern or storm lantern: Michael C. Hamey, in 1884.
- Folding bed and roll-top desk: Sara E. Goode, in 1885.
- Lawn sprinkler: Joseph H. Smith, in 1897.
- Merry-go-round: Granville T. Woods, in 1899.
- Improvements to the player piano and reed organs: Joseph H. Dickinson, in 1912.
- Photographic printing and negative wash machine: Clatonia Joaquin Dorticus, in 1895.
- Golf tee: George F. Grant, in 1899.
- Fountain pen: William Purvis, in 1890; also invented the hand stamp.
- Pencil sharpener: John L. Loove, in 1897.
- Ink made from sweet potatoes: George Washington Carver (1864–1943).

- Postmarking and mail-cancelling machine: William Barry, in 1897.

Industries
- Procedure for fabricating paint and dyes: George Washington Carver (1864–1943)
- Shoe-lasting machine: Jan Ernst Matzeliger, in 1884.
- Automatic stop-plug for natural gas and petroleum pipes: William F. Cosgrove, in 1885.

Food
- Practical technique for pollinating vanilla orchids: Edmond Albius (1829–80).
- Synthetic production of flour, ink, tapioca, starch, rubber … from potatoes! George Washington Carver (1864–1943).
- Corn and cotton planting machine: Henry Blair (1804–60).
- Fabrication of sugar cubes: Norbert Rillieux, in 1846.
- Improvements in refrigeration: Thomas Elkins, in 1879.
- Harvester (gear rolling machine): H. L. Jones, in 1890.
- Churn: Albert C. Richardson, in 1891.
- Kneading machine: Joseph Lee, in 1894.
- Corn-shucking machine: Robert P. Scott, in 1894.
- Potato-digger: F. J. Wood, in 1895.
- Refrigerated trucks, train-cars, and boats allowing for the preservation of food during transport: Frederick McKinley Jones (1892–1961).
- Process for food preservation through rapid drying: Lloyd A. Hall (1894–1971).
- Refrigeration system for trucks and railroad cars: Frederick McKinley Jones, in 1949.

Transportation
- Propeller allowing steamboats to navigate in deep water: Benjamin Montgomery (1819–77).
- Chimney for locomotives: improved by Landron Bell, in 1871.

- Electrification of railroads; tunnel construction for electric railroads: Granville T. Woods, in 1888.
- Metal frame (for cars): Carter William, in 1892.
- Trolley for electric trains: Elbert R. Robinson, in 1893.
- Train alarm: R. A. Butler, in 1897.
- Bicycle frame: Isaac R. Johnson, in 1899.
- Points and switches for railroads: William F. Burr, in 1899.
- Combustion engine: Andrew J. Beard (1850–1910); also invented the linkage apparatus for train cars, in 1899.
- Apparatus for freight transport; luggage rack for trains: John W. Butts, in 1899.
- Traffic light: Garrett A. Morgan, in 1923.
- Automatic transmission for cars: Richard Spikes, in 1932.
- Soy-based manufacturing/production of plastic automobile parts; cotton-based insulating boards, paper, ropes, and cement blocks for the construction of highways: George Washington Carver (1864–1943).
- Road signage system: Lewis W. Chubb, in 1937.

Security
- Fire escape hatch and improvements in rescue ladder: Joseph R. Winters, in 1878.
- Safety glasses: Powell Johnson, in 1880.
- Security doors (for drawbridges): Humphrey Reynolds, in 1890.
- Motorized street sweeper: Charles Brookes, in 1890.
- Gas mask: Garret A. Morgan (1877–1963).
- Method and equipment for regulating thermostats and air conditioning systems: David N. Crosthwait, Jr, in 1928.
- Techniques to remove smoke from buildings and to clear fog from airport runways: Meredith Charles Gourdine (1929–98).

Health, Biology, Pharmacology
- First open-heart surgery: Daniel Hale Williams (1856–1931).
- Shampoo, soap, bath powder, and shaving cream, all made from peanuts: George Washington Carver (1864–1943).

- Product to treat baldness, other cosmetics: C. J. Walker (1867–1919).
- Research on cells and fertilization: Ernest Everett Just (1883–1941).
- Syphilis screening test: William A. Hinton (1883–1959).
- Necklace for cervical fractures: Louis Tompkins Wright (1891–1952).
- Intradermal vaccination method against smallpox: Louis Tompkins Wright (1891–1952).
- Curling iron: Marjorie Stewart Joyner (1896–1994).
- Chemical synthesis of medicines from plants; pioneer in the industrial synthesis of human hormones: Percy Lavon Julian (1899–1975).
- Blood transfusion: Charlies Richard Drew (1904–50).
- Devices to assist amputees with feeding and independence: Bessie Blount Griffin (1913–2009).
- The use of chemotherapy and combination therapy in fighting cancer: Jane Cooke Wright (1919–2013).
- Pacemaker; air filter: Otis Boykin (1920–82).
- Second kidney transplant: Samuel L. Kountz (1930–81).
- Device for improved measurement of blood pressure: Michael Croslin (b. 1933).
- Development of X-ray imaging: George Edward Alcorn (b. 1940).
- Use of lasers for cataract surgery: Patricia E. Bath (1942–2019).
- First bone transplant in a child: Yvette Bonny (b. 1938), in 1980.
- Separation of craniopagus conjoined twins: Benjamin S. Carson (b. 1951).

Mechanical
- Improvement of the lubrication of steam cylinders: Elija McCoy, in 1876.
- Functioning rheostat: Granville T. Woods, in 1896; also invented the electrical relay, in 1887.
- Foot-activated propulsion hammer: Minnis Headen, in 1896.

- Rotary motor: Andrew J. Beard, in 1892.
- Lubricator: Elijah McCoy, in 1898.
- Lifting and loading mechanism: Mary Jane Reynolds, in 1899.
- Booster system for internal combustion engine: Joseph A. Gamell, in 1876.

Communications

- Printing press: W. A. Lavalette, in 1878.
- Railroad telegraph: Granville T. Woods, in 1888; also invented device for electrical transmission of messages, in 1885.
- Instrument for the transfer of mailbags: J. C. Jones, in 1917.
- Instrument for loading and unloading airmail: Gus Burton, in 1945.
- Power source for antennae to coordinate two tracking radars: James E. Lewis, in 1968.
- Cellular telephone: Henry T. Sampson, in 1971.
- Floppy disk (drive): John P. Moon (b. 1938).

Mathematics, Electronics, Atomic Research, Astronomy

- Measurement of the movement of stars and prediction of the 1789 solar eclipse; creation of a famous Almanac of Astronomy that allowed farmers to better understand the phases of the moon for planting crops: Benjamin Banneker (1731–1806).
- Electronic apparatus for guided missiles and for certain IBM computers: Otis Boykin (1920–82).
- A system allowing a TV set to receive several different channels; the introduction of electricity in nuclear control devices: Raoul-Georges Nicolo (1923–93).
- Co-inventor of new laser technology: Earl Shaw (b. 1937).
- The camera that travelled to the moon on Apollo 16, in April 1972: George R. Carruthers (1939–2020).
- Magellan probe sent to Venus in 1989, Galileo probe sent to Jupiter in 1989, Ulysses probe sent towards the sun in 1990, Observer and Pathfinder probes sent to Mars in 1996: Cheick Modibo Diarra (b. 1952).

- CM-2 Connection Machine supercomputer (the fastest computer in the world): Philip Emeagwali, in 1989.
- Magnetic recording roll for computers: Larry T. Preston, in 1971.
- Director of NASA: Charles Bolden (appointed in 2009).

Every year since 1976, black Americans have celebrated Black History Month in February, the birth month of Abraham Lincoln and Frederick Douglass. During this period, people recall the fundamental role that black people have played in their country's history, as scientists, inventors, artists, writers, artisans, athletes, etc. White people also participate in the commemorations in schools, churches, and town enterprises throughout the country. Over the years, mentalities have changed, a fact not unrelated to the election of President Barack Obama in 2008.

Canada too, lamenting the fact that the 'contribution of Blacks to the history of Canada is one of the best kept secrets of our collective past', established its own Black History Month in 1995. Great Britain and Germany have also followed suit.

'Southern Trees Bear a Strange Fruit'

Billie Holiday
7 April 1915–17 July 1959

Café Society was a unique nightclub in 1930s New York. Its clientele was made up of women and men of all colours, its walls painted by 'leftists'. A Hitler figurine with a monkey's head was hung from the ceiling. Charlie Chaplin, Errol Flynn, Judy Garland, Nelson Rockefeller, and other celebrities were regulars. Despite the economic crisis, with unemployment rates rising frighteningly high, the richest had seen their incomes increase. As for those of more modest means, they went deeper into debt. Against this backdrop of global crisis, Café Society was a haven in which people could forget all about segregation. So much so that, on one occasion, a young black singer took to the stage and, showing her disdain for the rowdy and largely white audience, turned her back, pulled up her dress, and showed them all her 'ass'!

That woman was named Billie Holiday.

It was 1939, and she was 24. The song she was about to sing was the most moving, the most terrifying of her repertoire: 'Strange Fruit'. The fruit to which she was referring were the black people killed by lynching: hanging, scalding tar poured on skin, pyres – so many forms of torture, which were still a fact of life in the southern United States. Between 1889 and 1940, these crimes were responsible for the deaths of more than 3,800 black people, along with some whites who had shown solidarity with blacks. Lynchings would continue until 1960.

'Strange Fruit' was written by Abel Meeropol. A Jewish teacher of Russian origin and a militant communist, Meeropol wrote poetry, composed music, and worked as a high school literature teacher in the Bronx. One day in 1930 he saw a photograph of two black men hanging from a tree. The image haunted him.

But what truly terrified him was learning, in 1939, that six out of ten white people still approved of lynching! In the South, these lynchings had replaced weekly outings to the 'fairground or the theatre'. Lynchings were seen as joyful occasions. Men, women, and children participated, dressed in their Sunday best. At the end of the lynching, the penis of the victim was cut off and marinated in a jar as a trophy. It was a way of definitively annihilating the alleged 'sexual power' of the black man, which so frightened people.

Billie Holiday got ready to sing. The audience and the staff in the bar stopped talking. People put out their cigarettes. The room was plunged into darkness, and then a projector lit up Billie's face, her ruby lips, the gardenia she wore over her ear, her hands cupping the microphone. She closed her eyes, tilted her head back, and began to sing in a subtly haunting voice:

> Southern trees bear a strange fruit,
> Blood on the leaves and blood at the root,
> Black bodies swinging in the southern breeze,
> Strange fruit hanging from the poplar trees.

I am mesmerized by this song. Every word weighs on my chest. I feel like I am at 'the foot of the tree'.

> Pastoral scene of the gallant South,
> The bulging eyes and the twisted mouth,
> Scent of magnolias, sweet and fresh,
> Then the sudden smell of burning flesh...

I can smell flesh burning; I feel as if the scene is taking place in front of me.

> Here is fruit for the crows to pluck,
> For the rain to gather, for the wind to suck,
> For the sun to rot, for the trees to drop.

Then, for the last line, her voice rises like a cry:

> Here is a strange and bitter crop.

The note remained in the air, suspended, and then there was silence. The lights went out. No one applauded. Finally, in the funereal silence, someone clapped nervously. Then the audience, overwhelmed with emotion, erupted into applause.

When the lights came up, the stage was empty. Billie never came back out to acknowledge the audience after 'Strange Fruit'. No matter how much people applauded.

By 1939 Billie Holiday had lived through enough nightmares to know what it meant to sing this song. The taste of this fruit, of this pain, had been in her mouth since she was a child. No one could sing the word 'hunger' the way she could. 'I got my lumps and scars', she wrote in her memoirs. 'All the Cadillacs and minks in the world – and I've had a few – can't make it up or make me forget it.' No one could sing the word 'love' like she could. Clarinettist Tony Scott said that 'When "Lady" sang "my man left me", then you see the bags are packed, the cat's going down the street, and *you know he ain't never coming back.*' With her, the emotions never slipped into sentimentalism; they were part of a pain that came from the gut, and they burst on impact into the listener's heart.

Billie was born in Baltimore in 1915. Her parents were very young, as many parents in the ghetto still are today. Her father, Clarence Holloway, was 13, and her mother, Sadie Fagan, was 14. In fact, her parents only knew each other long enough to conceive her, at a dance. They met and split up in a single night. Clarence was a jazz guitarist, who spent his nights in clubs. Sadie did odd jobs and worked as a prostitute. She had neither the time nor the inclination to look after her daughter, and left her in the care of a particularly brutal aunt. The only person who gave her any affection was a great-grandmother who died one night in her sleep, her arm wrapped around the little girl's neck.

Billie Holiday's childhood was a living nightmare. At the age of 10, she was raped by a neighbour. He was sentenced to five years in prison. As for the girl, she was locked up as a juvenile delinquent in a religious institution where the mistreatment and the humiliations never ceased.

When Billie was 13, her mother suddenly remembered her daughter. Conscious of her 'potential', she set her up in a brothel where she became a 'twenty-dollar call girl'. At that time, segregation ended at the door of the brothel. In public, on the other hand, it was unacceptable for a black woman to be seen in public with a white man. 'The only time I was free from this kind of pressure was when I was a call girl as a kid and I had white men as my customers.

Nobody gave us any trouble. People can forgive any damn thing if they did it for money [...] How many times have I been in court in my life? It started when I was 10, then again when I was 14, then there are couple of times in between.'

Then Billie discovered Harlem, the underground clubs, the sound of jazz all around. Almost by chance she landed her first gigs. She was 15 and started believing there was light at the end of the tunnel. In 1933 a producer at Columbia Records heard her sing with a black orchestra. A few weeks later she recorded 'Your Mother's Son-in-Law' and 'Riffin' the Scotch'. She sang with all the great figures that jazz aficionados worship today: Lester Young, who nicknamed her 'Lady Day', Duke Ellington, Louis Armstrong, Count Basie... These great musicians were wowed by her voice, her intonation, her phrasing, her truthfulness. Billie soon found herself appearing on stage with the popular white jazz band led by Artie Shaw. But a black singer in a white band couldn't be tolerated for long. The tour ended abruptly. Billie returned to New York and sang in the only place that accepted racial mixing: Café Society.

'Strange Fruit' gave new meaning to her life. She silenced the white racists, or *crackers*, named after those dry cookies that snap like a whip when you break them. She screamed the truth and stirred up a sense of resistance. The song had an effect on black liberation comparable to Rosa Parks' refusal to give up her seat to a white man on a bus on 1 December 1955. It is said of this song: 'If Billie Holiday didn't light the fuse, she unquestionably fed the flame.' For Angela Davis, the Marxist and feminist militant, 'Strange Fruit' played 'a catalytic role' in 'rejuvenating the tradition of protest and resistance in African-American and American traditions of popular music and culture'.

Billie Holiday struggled to convince her label to let her record the song, but when she finally did, it was sold and distributed like a propaganda pamphlet.

Billie paid the price. The Federal Bureau of Narcotics was aware of her drug consumption. She was accused of offences to which, until then, people had turned a blind eye. Federal agents suspected her of communist sympathies, and she became caught up in the witch hunts of that period. When a woman as famous as Billie Holiday is imprisoned, who is the target? The drug addict? The black woman? The singer of a song against lynching? The police hounded her, often preventing her from singing, until her premature death at the age of 44. Drug squads broke into her hotel rooms, searched her, humiliated her. For the musicians who worked with her, there was no doubt in their minds that the police had it in for Billie, just as they had it in for Charlie Parker and for the be-boppers in general, because these artists openly criticized the injustices of their era and fought against segregation.

'Our Time Has Come'

Aimé Césaire
26 June 1913–17 April 2008

I met Aimé Césaire on several occasions, most memorably when the French national football team played a game in Martinique in 2005. I presented him with a jersey. He hung it up in his office, and I felt proud. In return, he signed a book for me.

I have chosen to talk about this great poet and politician because, within the Negritude movement – which also includes Léon-Gontran Damas and Léopold Sédar Senghor – he is the one who, through his poems, plays, pamphlets, open letters, and speeches, most forcefully defended, in a never-ending struggle, not only the black man but the dignity of humankind.

Aimé Césaire was born in Basse-Pointe, in Martinique. His father was a teacher and later a tax inspector, and his mother was a tailor. The young Césaire attended the high school, Lycée Schoelcher, in Fort-de-France, where he befriended a young man from French Guiana named Léon-Gontron Damas. Damas would also become a great poet of Negritude. Césaire was an excellent student and he received a scholarship to pursue his studies in France, leaving for Paris in September 1931. He was 18 when he began studying at the renowned Lycée Louis-le-Grand for the *hypokhâgne*, the first of two years of preparatory school in literary studies leading up to entrance examinations for the Grandes Écoles, the most prestigious French universities. On Césaire's very first day at Louis-le-Grand, he made the acquaintance of the Senegalese Léopold Sédar Senghor. The Antilles and Africa were finally united! The moment was historic, for, at that time, Africans were still considered to be savages. The Negro inhabited Africa. And the Antillean despised the African. From the meeting between these two men was born a new consciousness that would develop into the concept of Negritude.

All the young black men in the preparatory schools, these A1 students of the French Republic, sometimes dismissively called 'Classical suit-and-tie' Negroes, were trained in the greats of French culture: Hugo, Molière, Corneille... In the Antilles, they only had access to *white* knowledge, to history as told by whites. As for the literature, art, and philosophy of the Antilles, it could only be the product of Europeans. Frantz Fanon notes this clearly in his celebrated book *Black Skin, White Masks*: 'A European familiar with the current trends of Negro poetry, for example, would be amazed to learn that as late as 1940 no Antillean found it possible to think of himself as a Negro.' The same opinion is expressed by René Menil, a surrealist writer and philosopher from Martinique, who denounced Antillean alienation: 'We have read other people's cultures [...] All our cultural manifestations so far have been nothing but copies ... useless mirror images.'

The Martinican writer René Maran was a notable exception. An administrator in the Ministry for the Colonies, he was the first black person to win the Prix Goncourt, still the most prestigious prize in French literature, which he received in 1921 for his novel *Batouala*. It was not just any novel: neither 'exotic' nor saccharine, it denounced the crimes committed in the name of colonialism at a time when Empire was a widely accepted fact of life. What courage it must have taken for this black man to attack the 'civilizing mission' of the Europeans! In fact, the following lines of his preface to *Batouala* got him fired from the Ministry: 'Civilization, civilization, pride of the Europeans and charnel-house of innocents [...] You have built your kingdom on corpses. You are not a torch, you are a conflagration. You devour whatever you touch...' Maran also asserted, 'If we knew of what vileness the great colonial life is composed, of what daily vileness, we should talk of it less, we should not talk of it at all. It degrades a man bit by bit.' This novel, frowned upon by the colonial authorities, was read in secret by Césaire, Damas, and Senghor.

Ten years after *Batouala*'s publication, the Nardal sisters, Paulette and Jane, founded the French- and English-language literary journal *The Review of the Black World*. Césaire devoured this journal when he arrived in Paris. Among other things, he discovered the works of the black writers of the Harlem Renaissance, who opened his mind to black issues and provided the foundation for his idea of Negritude. 'Yes, we do constitute a community, but a community of a very particular type', he would say years later in his speech 'Discourse on Negritude', delivered at the University of Miami in 1987. 'First, it is a community forged out of oppression suffered, imposed exclusion and discrimination. And to its honor, it is also a community of continued resistance, of stubborn struggle and of indomitable hope. At least, that's what negritude was to us then as young students [...] Negritude has been all this...'

In 1932 the fiery journal *Self-Defence* was published by the young Martinican students René Ménil, Jules Monnerot, and Etienne Léro. They embraced their own sense of difference, whether in terms of culture, history, experience, or skin colour. Committed to leftist politics, they rebelled against colonial capitalism and called for class struggle. There was only one issue of *Self-Defence*, but it set in motion the 'New Negro' movement in France.

In 1934 a new journal, *The Black Student*, created by Aimé Césaire, Léopold Senghor, and Léon-Gontran Damas, sought to take this exploration of identity even further. The founders of the journal were passionate about traditional African poetry and non-Western literature. They distinguished themselves from *Self-Defence*, which, in their opinion, was too invested in the communist idea that political revolution must precede cultural revolution. This was yet another expression of the 'assimilationist' ideology that saw no value in black culture, whereas these students were demanding emancipation. In his contribution, Césaire wrote: 'Black youth want to act and create. They want to have their poets and their novelists who will speak to it. They want to have their own misfortunes and its greatness.'

Léon-Gontran Damas' poetry collection, *Pigments*, published in 1937, included the following poem, entitled 'Whitewash':

It may be
they dare to
treat me white
though everything within me
wants only to be black
as Negro as my Africa
the Africa they ransacked

White

Abominable insult
they'll pay me dearly for
when my Africa
the Africa they ransacked

is determined to have
peace
peace
nothing else but peace

The concept of Negritude initially appeared in Césaire's first major text, *Notebook of a Return to the Native Land*. During that period between 1935 and 1939, Césaire confronted a variety of personal difficulties. His eyesight became weak, and he suffered from migraines. Above all, he was locked in a struggle to carve out his own identity. It was the concept of Negritude that would lead him to this identity.

I say hurray! The old negritude progressively cadavers itself
the horizon breaks, recoils and expands
and through the shredding of clouds the flashing of a sign
the slave ship cracks from one end to the other...

Notebook of a Return to the Native Land came to symbolize Negritude. It did away with the traditional exotic image of 'enchanted Caribbean islands'. Rather, it speaks of 'the hungry Antilles, the Antilles pitted with smallpox, the Antilles dynamited by alcohol...' It describes Antillean populations, alienated by 400 years of slavery, who no longer bother to revolt: 'And in this inert town, this squalling throng so astonishingly detoured from its cry [...] this throng detoured from its cry of hunger, of poverty, of revolt, of hatred, this throng so strangely chattering and mute.'

This magnificent text ends with a vow: to always confront one's destiny. Césaire wanted to be 'the mouth of those calamities that have no mouth' and urges his brothers to escape their submissive state and to fight, not with 'date hearts' but with 'men's hearts'. Césaire's revolt was never a solitary act; it was always carried out in collective solidarity. 'Negritude' is not only made up of the word 'Negro'; it doesn't stop at skin colour, Césaire tells us. The cry of Negritude is the cry of anyone who is mistreated, tortured, or unjustly imprisoned. Negritude can be found under every dictatorship. Under such conditions, how is one to live, to speak freely, to fight against fear? The answer to these questions lies in Negritude, which means existing in spite of oppression; it gives a voice to all those oppressed, a voice to all those humiliated, to the men and women whose histories have been denied. Césaire's words urge them to take the bull by the horns, and to speak up, even if doing so disturbs people; to refuse to be, in the words of Frantz Fanon, 'locked in his blackness', confined to one camp. Negritude goes beyond the colour black.

Before the Second World War, Martinique's inhabitants included 2,000 white people who were well integrated into everyday life. But soon the island sided with the Vichy regime and, in 1941, more than 2,000 racist Europeans arrived. A new literary review, *Tropiques*, founded that same year by Césaire and Suzanne Roussi, along with other Martinican intellectuals, took on a special significance within the Antilles. Césaire continued to defend the 'virtuous colour' of the Negro, proclaiming that 'it-is-beautiful-good-and-legitimate-to-be-a-nigger', and repeatedly insisting that 'paint the tree trunk white as you will, the roots below remain black'. Césaire and his friends used *Tropiques* as a platform from which to denounce those Antillean intellectuals who, in their view, were simply imitating the work of white writers. In doing so, Césaire's group explored the links that exist between the Antilles and Africa, beginning with the fact that Antilleans are the grandchildren of enslaved Africans.

With the end of the war in 1945, the time had come for actions to match words. The move from poetic action to political engagement was a natural evolution for Césaire, for whom politics was a 'manifestation of culture'. He ran for office in the municipal and legislative elections in Martinique as the head of the communist list. His success was immediate and overwhelming. He was elected mayor of Fort-de-France and, at the same time, a deputy to the French National Assembly. His two high school friends followed similar paths: Senghor was elected as Senegal's deputy to the National Constituent Assembly that same year, and Damas, the deputy for Guyana in 1948.

As soon as he was elected, Césaire began to focus on the various problems facing his island. For example, he ordered schools to be opened. In a book about education in the Antilles, Sylvère Farraudière writes that: 'Before 1947, primary education in the former French colonies was not obligatory, except in a few areas, mainly urban, that had the necessary resources. Until then, school had not been state-run, free, or obligatory for the majority of the population living in the rural areas, which was the majority of the island's total population. The result was under-education on a mass scale, over the course of several generations. Universal education only started in the Antilles during the 1980s, almost a century after the educational policies implemented by Jules Ferry.' Césaire called for budget increases, in addition to a change in the official status of the French Antilles and of Reunion Island: 'Departmentalization' would place these former colonies on a level footing with the administrative units of mainland France. Departmentalization was voted into law, as Césaire had wanted; however, it was applied only half-heartedly. In fact, it soon became clear that the law in itself was incapable of bringing about any real change. On 18 September 1946 Césaire gave a speech to the French National Assembly in which he criticized the government, arguing that it was trying to 'build a democratic republic, a social republic', even as it sought to 'perpetuate a colonialist system that carries within it racism, oppression, and servitude'.

To make matters worse, in December 1947 the French government issued a decree effectively legalizing inequality in the salaries paid to civil servants of Antillean origin and those from metropolitan France. Strikes, conflict, and several deaths ensued.

In 1948, in the middle of this political and social unrest, the *Anthology of New Negro and Malagasy Poetry in French*, edited by Léopold Sédar Senghor, was published. The anthology brought together poems by 16 rebel authors, among them Damas and Césaire. In order to understand colonialism, one must listen to the colonized, but with the expectation that many of the things one hears will be disturbing. When a person who has been attacked, humiliated, and terrorized finds their voice, they will not tell you that everything is fine. They will speak the truth.

'When you removed the gag that was keeping these black mouths shut, what were you hoping for?' Jean-Paul Sartre asks in his preface to the *Anthology*, titled 'Black Orpheus'. 'Did you think that when they raised themselves up again, you would read adoration in the eyes of these heads that our fathers had forced to bend down to the very ground?'

Hot on the heels of Senghor's collection came Césaire's celebrated *Discourse on Colonialism* in June 1950. It is a text I reread often, one of Césaire's greatest works. The text was greatly influenced by the repressive colonial violence of 1948 in Madagascar, and it gave Césaire the opportunity to express things that he had been unable to say in his speeches to the National Assembly. Césaire has sometimes been admonished for not being a 'political animal'. But that is because, as a man steeped in both poetry and politics, he decided instead to be the voice of conscience:

First we must study how colonization works to *decivilize* the colonizer, to *brutalize* him in the true sense of the word, to degrade him, to awaken him to buried instincts, to covetousness, violence, race hatred, and moral relativism; and we must show that each time a head is cut off or an eye put out in Vietnam and in France they accept the fact, each time a little girl is raped and in France they accept the fact, each time a Madagascan is tortured and in France they accept the fact, civilization acquires another dead weight, a universal regression takes place, a gangrene sets in, a center of infection begins to spread; and that at the end of all these treaties that have been violated, all these lies that have been propagated, all these punitive expeditions that have been tolerated, all these prisoners who have been tied up and 'interrogated,' all these patriots who have been tortured, at the end of all the racial pride that has been encouraged, all the boastfulness that has been displayed, a poison has been instilled into the veins of Europe and, slowly but surely, a continent proceeds towards *savagery*.

In 1994 *Discourse on Colonialism* was included as part of the baccalaureate exam in French literature, but was subsequently deemed too subversive and withdrawn by the French Ministry of Education. It seems the state was concerned that too many beautiful ideas – the refusal to accept oppression, the struggle against racism, a sense of fraternity and justice – would start to shape the minds of young people. It is not part of the educational programme today because we still have a very restricted vision of history. The day that this text is restored to the school curriculum will be a sign that French society has developed greater understanding of the past.

Césaire continued his subversive ways throughout his life. In 1956 he – a 'Negro' – dared to resign from the French Communist Party (PCF). For the first time, a well-known intellectual had the audacity to break with the Party. 'Our time has come', he wrote on 24 October 1956 in a letter to Maurice Thorez, the general secretary of the PCF, a few hours before the tanks rolled into Budapest. In the letter, he criticized the PCF's refusal to denounce the crimes of Stalinism, as well as its support for brutal colonial repression in Algeria. He also returned to the concept of Negritude.

For my part, I believe that black peoples are rich with energy and passion, that they lack neither vigor nor imagination, but that these strengths can only wilt in organizations that are not their own: made for them, made by them, and adapted to ends that they alone can determine.

Césaire proclaimed his 'desire to distinguish between alliance and subordination, solidarity and resignation'. One must recall that, for him, the word 'Negritude' designated, above all, 'the rejection of cultural assimilation; the rejection of a certain image of the Black as submissive, incapable of constructing a civilization. The cultural premium of politics.'

Césaire went on to argue in his letter to Thorez that 'There is a veritable Copernican revolution to be imposed here; so ingrained in Europe (from the extreme right to the extreme left) is the habit of doing for us, arranging for us, thinking for us – in short, the habit of challenging our possession of this right to initiative of which I have just spoken, which is, at the end of the day, the right to personality.'

Until his final breath, Aimé Césaire resisted: 'A Negro I am, a Negro I will remain.'

It is this consistency of his resistance that makes him a beacon for us today. He will never be forgotten, unlike his friend Senghor who, although incredibly talented, wrote like Claudel, like Saint-John Perse, and thus never became truly emancipated. Overly committed to French interests, Senghor had declared with a 'white' voice that 'Emotion is black, just as reason is Greek.' He was rewarded with a cocked hat and a sword by the Académie Française. Nonetheless, his French friends failed to show up at his funeral in 2001.

A few months after the ratification of a law on 23 February 2005, which decreed that schools should teach the 'positive aspects of colonization in the overseas territories', Césaire, then 92 years old, refused to meet with the French minister of the interior, Nicolas Sarkozy. 'As the author of the *Discourse on Colonialism*', he wrote, 'I remain faithful to my doctrine, a resolute anti-colonialist.'

After a part of this law was abrogated, Césaire agreed to meet with the minister, but made sure to present him with a copy of *Discourse on Colonialism*:

They talk to me about progress, about 'achievements', diseases cured, improved standards of living.

I am talking about societies drained of their essence, cultures trampled underfoot, institutions undermined, lands confiscated, religions smashed, magnificent artistic creations destroyed, extraordinary *possibilities* wiped out.

They throw facts at my head, statistics, mileages of roads, canals, and railroad tracks.

I am talking about thousands of men sacrificed to the Congo-Océan. I am talking about those who, as I write this, are digging the harbor of Abidjan by hand. I am talking about millions of men torn from their gods, their land, their habits, their life – from life, from the dance, from wisdom.

At Aimé Césaire's funeral in April 2008, I went up to his coffin, and I said: 'You can go in peace, for you have educated an entire population. We are your sons and daughters, we will continue to use our pens and our voices to denounce injustice.'

Returning Africa to Her Children

Patrice Émery Lumumba

2 July 1925–17 January 1961

By 1960 Belgium was no longer able to oppose the growing resistance to its rule in the Congo. It was forced to accept the independence of a country it had held captive since 1885, and to participate in the ceremony that consecrated that independence on 30 June 1960. It was to take place at the parliament building in Léopoldville in the presence of the Belgian king, Baudouin I, and members of his government. Also in attendance would be the president of the Congo, Joseph Kasa-Vubu, the prime minister of the coalition government, Patrice Lumumba, and all those politicians who had just been elected in the first free elections in the Congo.

Before attending the ceremony, Patrice Lumumba showed his speech to Thomas Kanza, whom he had just appointed as the Congolese ambassador to the United States. Skilled diplomat that he was, Kanza explained to Lumumba that his speech was excellent, but that the ceremony at the parliament would be neither the time nor the place to speak in such radical terms.

Upon his arrival at the parliament, Kanza spoke to the Belgian prime minister Gaston Eyksens and to the Belgian minister of foreign affairs, Pierre Wigny. He advised them to delay the presentation of the independence proclamation for just a few minutes so that there would be time to reason with Lumumba. 'Because he won't stay silent!' he warned them. But they didn't listen to him and failed to understand the urgency of the situation. Indeed, a speech by Lumumba was not even on the programme. They thought that Kanza was being the typical diplomat, worrying unnecessarily about etiquette!

Baudouin I opened the ceremony with a speech that, as expected, glorified the role of Belgium and the accomplishments of his great-uncle, the cynical and bloodthirsty Leopold II, whose statue stood in front of the National Palace within the parliament compound. He predicted a neocolonial future full of promise and essentially exhorted the Congolese to show themselves 'worthy of the confidence' he as king was according them: 'Do not worry about turning to us. We are ready to remain by your side, to advise you, and to train with you the technicians and administrators that you will need!'

Thomas Kanza could imagine Patrice Lumumba's feelings of revolt and rage as he listened to this paternalistic, colonialist, and racist speech. In a panic, he tried to catch the eye of the two Belgian ministers, who pretended not to see him and to be unaware of his anxiety.

It was at this moment that President Kasa-Vubu stepped on to the platform to reply to the king. The sovereign was relaxed, for Kasa-Vubu's speech had been submitted and approved in advance by the Belgian government. The president 'thanked the King', celebrated the virtues and the accomplishments of the colonial regime, and even called on God to 'protect our people and enlighten all our leaders...' This moderate speech was tailored to please the monarch, to laud his colonial policy and his Catholic beliefs. But it appalled Lumumba and all those who had led the resistance against the worst colonizer Africa had ever known. The Belgian occupation had represented a new form of slavery, one that Joseph Conrad, the author of *Heart of Darkness*, described as 'the vilest scramble for loot that ever disfigured the history of human conscience and geographical exploration'.

Overcome with indignation, Lumumba quickly improvised some changes to his speech and demanded that he be allowed to speak. To the great surprise of Baudouin and his prime minister, Gaston Eyskens, the president of the National Assembly, Joseph Kasongho, let him speak. Eyskens tried to catch the eye of his Congolese ally, President Kasa-Vubu. Neither of them had read Lumumba's text and – oh, my God! – the entire international press was there.

Men and women of the Congo,
Victorious independence fighters, I salute you in the name of the Congolese Government!

From the beginning, Lumumba addressed his words to his wounded people. Forget the king, the diplomatic corps, the colonists... Baudouin I turned pale.

I ask all of you, my friends, who tirelessly fought in our ranks, to mark this June 30, 1960, as an illustrious date that will be ever engraved in your hearts, a date whose meaning you will proudly explain to your children, so that they in turn might relate to their grandchildren and great-grandchildren the glorious history of our struggle for freedom.

Although this independence of the Congo is being proclaimed today by agreement with Belgium, an amicable country, with which we are on equal terms, no Congolese will ever forget that independence was won in struggle, a persevering and inspired struggle carried on from day to day, a struggle, in which we were undaunted by privation or suffering and stinted neither strength nor blood.

The crowd burst into applause. Not in the parliament, of course, which was paralysed by his words, but outside where the speeches were being broadcast through loudspeakers. The Congolese population exploded with joy. The deafening silence within the parliament only served to reinforce the people's enthusiasm. And then Lumumba began his description of the 'colonial system' and the struggle against it.

It was filled with tears, fire and blood. We are deeply proud of our struggle, because it was just and noble and indispensable in putting an end to the humiliating bondage forced upon us.

That was our lot for the 80 years of colonial rule and our wounds are too fresh and much too painful to be forgotten. We have experienced forced labour in exchange for pay that did not allow us to satisfy our hunger, to clothe ourselves, to have decent lodgings or to bring up our children as dearly loved ones.

Morning, noon and night we were subjected to jeers, insults and blows because we were 'Negroes'. Who will ever forget that the black was addressed as 'tu' [the informal form of 'you'], not because he was a friend, but because the polite 'vous' was reserved for the white man?

We have seen our lands seized in the name of ostensibly just laws, which gave recognition only to the right of might.

We have not forgotten that the law was never the same for the white and the black, that it was lenient to the ones, and cruel and inhuman to the others.

We have experienced the atrocious sufferings, being persecuted for political convictions and religious beliefs, and exiled from our native land: our lot was worse than death itself.

We have not forgotten that in the cities the mansions were for the whites and the tumbledown huts for the blacks; that a black was not admitted to the cinemas, restaurants and shops set aside for 'Europeans'; that a black travelled in the holds, under the feet of the whites in their luxury cabins.

Who will ever forget the shootings which killed so many of our brothers, or the cells into which were mercilessly thrown those who no longer wished to submit to the regime of injustice, oppression and exploitation used by the colonialists as a tool of their domination?

The wild enthusiasm of the crowd grew stronger as the official representatives in the parliament sank further and further into a stony silence.

But Lumumba was actually holding back in his description of colonial reality. If he had wanted to condemn out of hand the actions of the king and his henchmen, he could simply have quoted the words of one of the leading figures in the crusade against Belgian colonialism in the Congo, E. D. Morel, an employee of a British shipping company: 'I had stumbled upon a secret society of murderers with a King for a croniman.' The Congo had, after all, been the site of atrocities that had led to the first international scandal of the modern era. As he listened to Lumumba, King Baudouin probably feared a repetition of this scandal. And there were only a few weeks until his marriage to the Spanish noblewoman Doña Fabiola!

The horror of Belgian colonization consisted of exploiting a free labour force to the point of its destruction, just as had been done during the period of slavery. In the Congo of Baudouin's great-uncle, a village or an entire region would be burned to the ground if it failed to meet its rubber quota; children had their hands or feet amputated if they made even the smallest show of complaint about their work. The Congolese people were hanged, decapitated, burned, 'smoked', starved, their wells and limited reserves of food destroyed. The scale of the slaughter was so great that the Belgian colonizers actually suffered labour shortages.

Since 1919 the total population of the territory had been cut in half! Incredible? No. The logic of terror had replaced the logic of economics. 'Once under way, mass killing is hard to stop; it becomes a kind of sport, like hunting', notes Adam Hochschild in his book *King Leopold's Ghost* (1999). As for Aimé Césaire, in his *Discourse on Colonialism*, published in 1950, he deemed that these 'hideous butcheries' proved that 'colonization, I repeat, dehumanizes even the most civilized man; that colonial activity, colonial enterprise, colonial conquest, which is based on contempt for the native and justified by that contempt, inevitably tends to change him who undertakes it; that the colonizer, who in order to ease his conscience gets into the habit of seeing the other man as *an animal*, accustoms himself to treating him like an animal, and tends objectively to transform *himself* into an animal.'

There is nothing surprising about the fact that, at the end of the twentieth century, the director of *Apocalypse Now*, Francis Ford Coppola, found inspiration in Joseph Conrad's *Heart of Darkness* to describe the bloodthirsty madness of the Americans in Vietnam.

Patrice Lumumba continued:

> All that, my brothers, brought us untold suffering.
>
> But we, who were elected by the votes of your represent-atives, representatives of the people, to guide our native land, we, who have suffered in body and soul from the colonial oppression, we tell you that henceforth all that is finished with.
>
> The Republic of the Congo has been proclaimed and our beloved country's future is now in the hands of its own people.
>
> Brothers, let us commence together a new struggle, a sublime struggle that will lead our country to peace, prosperity and greatness.
>
> Together we shall establish social justice and ensure for every man a fair remuneration for his labor.

At the time Lumumba was giving this speech, the country lacked Congolese administrators. Baudouin claimed that Belgium wished to help the free Congolese and 'to train with you the technicians and administrators that you will need'. But Belgian colonialism had never offered blacks more than a rudimentary education. In the 1960s, after more than fifty years of Belgian colonialism, only a few dozen Africans had gained access to higher education! No doctors, engineers, or officers. Within the civil service, only three out of 5,000 positions were occupied by Africans!

We shall show the world what the black man can do when working in liberty, and we shall make the Congo the pride of Africa.

We shall see to it that the lands of our native country truly benefit its children.

We shall revise all the old laws and make them into new ones that will be just and noble.

We shall stop the persecution of free thought. We shall see to it that all citizens enjoy to the fullest extent the basic freedoms provided for by the Declaration of Human Rights.

To anyone who is aware of the horrors of colonization, aware of the extreme poverty in which the wounded country found itself after these atrocities, it is little wonder that Lumumba's words were greeted with a wave of applause … outside the parliament, that is.

Economic planning was nearly impossible. With independence imminent, government companies had quickly left the Congo, receiving massive compensation from the state. 'All the companies opted for Belgian law, thus eluding their tax obligations to our country', Lumumba explained a few months later, on 1 December 1960, to a foreman in Kasaï who sheltered him in his home for a few hours. (By then, Lumumba was on the run and had less than two months left to live.) 'The gold reserve of the Bank of the Congo was sent to Belgium, and colonists and merchants transferred most of the fortunes acquired through the spoliation of the natives...'

We shall eradicate all discrimination, whatever its origin, and we shall ensure for everyone a station in life befitting his human dignity and worthy of his labor and his loyalty to the country.

We shall institute in the country a peace resting not on guns and bayonets but on concord and goodwill.

Applause!

And in all this, my dear compatriots, we can rely not only on our own enormous forces and immense wealth, but also on the assistance of the numerous foreign states, whose co-operation we shall accept when it is not aimed at imposing upon us an alien policy, but is given in a spirit of friendship.

Applause!

Thus, both in the internal and the external spheres, the new Congo being created by my government will be rich, free and prosperous. But to attain our goal without delay, I ask all of you, legislators and citizens of the Congo, to give us all the help you can.

I ask you all to sink your tribal quarrels: they weaken us and may cause us to be despised abroad.

I ask you all not to shrink from any sacrifice for the sake of ensuring the success of our grand undertaking.

Finally, I ask you unconditionally to respect the life and property of fellow-citizens and foreigners who have settled in our country; if the conduct of these foreigners leaves much to be desired, our justice will promptly expel them from the territory of the republic; if, on the contrary, their conduct is good, they must be left in peace, for they, too, are working for our country's prosperity.

The Congo's independence is a decisive step towards the liberation of the whole African continent. Our government, a government of national and popular unity, will serve its country. Our government, strong, national, popular, will be the health of our country.

Sire, Excellencies, Mesdames, Messieurs, my dear fellow countrymen, my brothers of race, my brothers of struggle – this is what I wanted to tell you in the name of the Government on this magnificent day of our complete independence.

Applause!

I call on all Congolese citizens, men, women and children, to set themselves resolutely to the task of creating a prosperous national economy that will assure our economic independence.

Glory to the fighters for national liberation!
Long live independence and African unity!
Long live the independent and sovereign Congo!

A massive ovation accompanied the final words of the Congolese prime minister.

It is said that Lumumba's speech, one of the most famous in African history, effectively signed his death warrant. That it filled King Baudouin and his ministers with hate; they could not possibly forgive the way in which he had drawn attention to the crimes they had tried so hard to conceal. Indeed, the speech was a slap in the face, and it is claimed that Prime Minister Eyskens had great difficulty convincing the king not to return immediately to Brussels. But to reduce a major political crisis to a settling of scores between individuals would be far too simple. When the Belgian government, aided by the Americans, had Lumumba assassinated, it was not done in order to restore its self-respect (which had been lost a long time before). Rather, it was because the Congolese prime minister had essentially set himself up in opposition to the economic interests of these two Western nations, and because he was uncontrollable, impossible to manipulate. In reality, these world powers intended to give only the appearance of ceding control of the colonies, and to keep them under their control as protectorates.

Patrice Lumumba's speech was explosive precisely because it set the stakes of decolonization so high. And because it was so politically committed. In Lumumba's view, political independence alone was insufficient to liberate Africa from its colonial past; the continent also needed to break out of its role as an *economic* colony of Europe. 'His speeches set off immediate alarm signals in Western capitals', writes Adam Hochschild. 'Belgian, British, and American corporations by now had vast investments in the Congo, which was rich in copper, cobalt, diamonds, gold, tin, manganese, and zinc [...] His message, Western governments feared, was contagious. Moreover, he could not be bought.'

Was Lumumba a communist lackey? Accused of turning to the Soviet Union for support, he responded that it was the lesser evil when all the other governments were abandoning you or, worse still, seeking to subjugate and corrupt you. And he added that the Negro had always been 'communist', repeating something Aimé Césaire wrote in *Discourse on Colonialism*: 'They were communal societies, never societies of the many for the few. They were societies that were not only ante-capitalist, as has been said, but *anti-capitalist*. They were democratic societies, always. They were cooperative societies, fraternal societies. I make a systematic defense of the societies destroyed by imperialism.'

American and European multinationals held Lumumba in contempt. His days were numbered. From July 1960 he took measures to Africanize the Congolese government. The Belgians immediately countered with a campaign of internal sabotage and the spreading of 'fake news' to the general public. On 1 December 1960 Lumumba described Belgium's underhand tactics:

Not powerful enough to impose themselves by use of force, Belgium decided to use deception. The adage of 'divide and conquer' was, as ever, the order of the day, and they secretly facilitated the creation of ethnic and regional parties, that would be easy to control and that would reawaken old hatreds dating back to the dawn of time:

Under the deceitful pretext of protecting their endangered nationals, the Belgians sent in their troops [...] There had been calm in Thysville when suddenly news arrived of the absurd bombing of the Matadi camp by a Belgian boat, causing the death of 13 Congolese soldiers [...] When this news was announced, in addition to the attack on the airforce base at Delcommune in Elisabethville, a general riot broke out and the mutiny spread throughout the region...

Blacks had proven that they were incapable of self-government! UN troops arrived, and soon Lumumba found himself bound hand and foot. He would now witness first hand the ugliness of American capitalist might.

Several months earlier, in September 1960, Joseph Kasa-Vubu, the weak-willed president, had dismissed Lumumba and the other nationalist ministers. But Lumumba had held steadfastly to his position, and, at his request, parliament removed President Kasa-Vubu from office.

The Americans concocted a plan to poison this man whom they just couldn't seem to get rid of. Dr Sidney Gottlieb was entrusted with the pharmacological part of the operation, but it proved impossible to get near the target. Brussels even dispatched a hitman, but he fared no better.

As a last resort, the United States and Belgium bribed a henchman, Joseph Désiré Mobutu, who recruited a team of executioners. With the financial backing of the US, Mobutu formed a coalition that included Kasa-Vubu as well as Tshombe, the pro-Western president of the Katanga region, which he had encouraged to secede in July.

On 1 December 1960 Lumumba, under house arrest, escaped the capital and attempted to make his way to Stanleyville, hoping to wrest back control of the Congo. Under Mobutu's orders, though, he was arrested the very next day, before he could reach his destination, and transferred along with Maurice Mpolo (a rival of Mobutu's) and Joseph Okito (a candidate to replace Kasa-Vubu) to the military camp of Thysville. On 17 January 1961 the three men were brought by plane to Elisabethville, in Katanga, and handed over to the local authorities. The transfer was organized by the Belgian authorities. They were brought to a small house under military escort, savagely beaten by Belgian and Katangan officials, and then killed by soldiers under the command of a Belgian officer.

The next day, two Belgian secret agents were given an important mission: to oversee the dismemberment of the three bodies and to have them dissolved in acid. This was similar to the destiny of Dona Beatriz, 'the Joan of Arc of the Kongo', whose ashes were three times burned and scattered. Or to that of Ruben Um Nyobé, the hero of Cameroonian independence, whose body was dragged through the mud for miles, leaving his face unrecognizable. As if acid, mud, or ashes could erase the memory of free men! I remember the square in Bois-Colombes where I grew up, and these words from General Charles de Gaulle carved in stone: 'The flame of the Resistance must not go out and will not go out.'

The dictator, Mobuto, supported by Belgium, France, and the United States, would go on govern the Democratic Republic of the Congo until 1997! Then, as a result of the massacres in Rwanda, he was forced to cede power to Laurent-Désiré Kabila. This country of approximately 905,410 square miles (four times the size of France) is potentially the richest country in all of Africa, often described as a 'geographical anomaly' because of its natural resources: dense forests and massive reserves of gold, diamonds, copper, uranium, cobalt (without which we would not have mobile phones). But the country now lives in dire poverty and destitution, having been ransacked by its own leaders and by foreign powers. I wonder how it was possible for the Congolese president, addressing the Belgian Senate in 2004, to say that 'the history of the Democratic Republic of Congo is also that of the Belgians, the missionaries, the administrators, and the entrepreneurs who believed in King Leopold II's dream of building a state in the middle of Africa. We want to honour all of those pioneers...'

Today, the situation of the Democratic Republic of the Congo is catastrophic. International human rights organizations continually denounce the conflicts and the humanitarian crisis that cost the Congo the lives of 5.4 million people between 1998 and 2007. In February 2008 the writer and activist Odile Tobner wrote that 'The apocalyptic vision of the world's worst contemporary humanitarian disaster has been met with global indifference, largely because it has not endangered the interests of the great powers. While massacres took place, business continued as usual. The age-old pillage of rare and precious metals, which abound in the Congo, has not stopped;

the war has in fact intensified the pillage as a source of revenue for all the warring parties.'

So the pillage of Congolese mineral resources continues. According to the investigative report published by Congolese Senator Mutamba Dibwe in Kinshasa on 24 September 2009, 'Despite the regulatory dictates of the Mining Code [enacted on 11 July 2002], and while the mining sector is built on vast and varied mineral resources, the Code, due to poor governance, has yet to make even the slightest contribution to finding a response to the cries for help of the Congolese population condemned to live in sub-human conditions.'

Black Skin, White Masks

Frantz Fanon
20 July 1925–6 December 1961

I am talking about millions of men in whom fear has been cunningly instilled, who have been taught to have an inferiority complex, to tremble, kneel, despair, and behave like flunkeys.

Aimé Césaire, *Discourse on Colonialism*

Frantz Fanon was born in Fort-de-France, Martinique, in 1925. Over the course of his short life – he died at the age of 36 – he wrote many books and articles, among them *The Wretched of the Earth*. But for me he remains the author of *Black Skin, White Masks*, which describes the lived experience of an Antillean facing up to his identity in a white world. I have read and reread this book. I even gave it as a present to the black players in the French national football team at the European Championship tournament in Portugal in 2004.

Frantz Fanon was the fifth oldest child in a family of eight. His father was a customs inspector, his mother, a shopkeeper. This Antillean family, their heads filled with inherited personality complexes, taught Fanon what were considered 'good manners', those of the dominant white class, who were considered the model to follow.

School picked up where his family left off: he was forbidden from speaking Creole. Fifty years after Fanon, I experienced the same thing. When we spoke in Creole in school, we were punished, even though our parents spoke it at home! Still today, French remains the default language of social advancement.

Some time ago, a younger cousin interrupted me while I was speaking Creole to her mother.

'You're speaking Creole to my mother, you don't respect her', she declared. 'You have to speak to her in French!'

What was it that the Guyanese poet Léon-Gontran Damas said in his collection, *Pigments*?

be quiet
have I or have I not
told you to speak French
the French of France
the French that Frenchmen speak
French French

In Fanon's era, children's books always featured white heroes who vanquished the bad guys, who were almost always blacks or Indians. Through a perfectly natural psychological process, the young Fanon thus came to identify with these 'good' white heroes and began to unconsciously absorb the negative discourse on blacks, and thereby, on himself.

Some manage to escape such a fate, others never do. They internalize the discourse on the hierarchy of different skin colours. Either they develop a strong, even violent, resentment of white people, or they develop an inferiority complex and low self-esteem.

When my mother was young, it was considered preferable to marry someone with light skin in order to 'dilute the colour'. There is an expression in Guadeloupe for lighter-skinned children: their skin is said to be 'chapée', that is, it has 'echapée du noir' or 'escaped from the black'! Mireille Fanon-Mendès-France, the daughter of Frantz Fanon, whom I met while preparing this chapter, told me that, when her son was born, he had blond hair and blue eyes. A member of her family cried out, 'You're lucky, he came out well!'

If black people express such thoughts it is because, unconsciously, they see themselves as having 'come out badly'. 'Hence the saying in Martinique', remarks Fanon, 'that a wicked white man has the soul of a nigger ... The perpetrator is the black man; Satan is black.' Their very opposite is 'the white dove of peace'.

Antillean society has absorbed this discourse of inferiority, of classification according to the colour of one's skin, just as it has absorbed the negative discourse on Creole; although this does not prevent Antilleans from denouncing racism directed against them.

I take, as a case in point, my mother and my sisters who wear wigs and weaves! Although they tell me that these are more practical and make their hair easier to comb, the message they will transmit to their daughters and granddaughters is that they can't be beautiful with their frizzy hair. As for their sons and grandsons, they will absorb the idea that a beautiful woman has long, straight hair. When the standard of beauty is that of white society, one can easily imagine the complexes that children inherit from their parents.

Great black leaders have forced their communities to confront harsh truths. Malcolm X, for example:

> Who taught you to hate the color of your skin, to such an extent that you bleach it to get like the white man? Who taught you to hate the shape of your nose and the shape of your lips? Who taught you to hate yourself from the top of your head to the soles of your feet? (5 May 1962)

My mother and Fanon's parents belonged to those generations who were taught in school that the Gauls were their ancestors. This might seem funny at first, but it is actually tragic, as it introduced a lie into the history of black Antillean families, which effectively denied the true lineage of multiple generations. This has created the unpleasant impression of an Antillean society 'born without parents'. To understand one's identity, shouldn't one's entire history be recognized?

I have noticed that many Antilleans complain that positions of power on the islands are occupied by whites. But isn't it also true that many Antilleans have a difficult time accepting the authority of a black superior? In the era of slavery, the only thing that mattered was the opinion of the master, the property-owner, a flawless figure who had all the power, a role model who was hated, but who, at the same time, had to be imitated. The Antillean has been conditioned by the behaviour of the slave-owners, which has sown ongoing divisions among the people. The advice given to plantation owners in 1712 by Willie Lynch, a British slave-owner in the Caribbean, provides a prime example: 'You must use the dark skin slaves vs. the light skin slaves and the light skin slaves vs. the dark skin slaves.'

Just as the slave was a physical prisoner, are we not still today psychologically imprisoned? Hasn't the attitude of the 'victim' remained deeply anchored in our Antillean mentality? Don't we still seek out the approving gaze of whites?

The slightest criticism hurts us and we rapidly become aggressive. This susceptibility comes from a lack of confidence in ourselves. Some people still confuse the judgement of a particular act with the statement 'I don't like you'. Isn't it now time to speak to one another peacefully, to discuss issues like responsible human beings?

Everything was done to prevent the Antillean from rebelling. My mother used to tell me, 'Stop dragging yourself around like a *nèg marron'* – a *nèg marron* was a maroon, or escaped slave. But the maroon was precisely the one who had the courage to resist, to run away from the plantation! The maroon should be a source of pride for black people; yet, instead, we turn such an individual into a good-for-nothing, someone to be ashamed of.

Fortunately, some people in Antillean society have begun to return to these buried memories. Both the figure of the maroon and the Creole language are becoming sources of pride once again.

Our parents' generation always resisted silently, but most black women and men were afraid to make actual demands. The situation is evolving, however, and little by little we are losing the mindset that prevented us from openly denouncing anti-black racism or straightforward injustice.

Frantz Fanon described how upset he had been when, at the age of 10, he had first heard about the history of slavery during a school ceremony held in front of a monument dedicated to Victor Schoelcher, the French abolitionist. For in Antillean families, this foundational history had remained taboo. In fact, it remains so. In my family, no one ever mentioned the slave trade. Most Antilleans were so ashamed of it that they refused to imagine even the slightest link to Africa. 'The fact is', writes Fanon, 'that the Antillean does not see himself as Negro; he sees himself as Antillean. The Negro lives in Africa. Subjectively and intellectually the Antillean behaves like a white man.'

My mother didn't connect at all with her African history; she sought to maintain this clean break from her ancestors, even though the grandfather of her own grandfather had been a slave. But Antilleans cannot avoid a proper reckoning with the legacies of slavery, since it was slavery that created Antillean society. We have to talk about it, discuss it. We have to understand that wanting to show whites that we are just as capable as they are is a trap that must be avoided. As I often say, blacks have nothing to show or to prove. Their only problem is that some white people – in the past and still today – have cast doubt on their abilities, and they have come to doubt themselves as a result. At the end of the day, can't we just learn to exist, to escape the role of victims, to build something for ourselves without waiting for white society's approval? And, most importantly, hasn't the time come to take a long hard look at ourselves?

One day in Paris, I asked a high school student: 'Tell me honestly, what does it mean to you to be the descendant of slaves?'

'I'm ashamed.'

'You have to get beyond that. The only thing that you should be ashamed of is that there was a time when you were ashamed of it.'

For my part, if there is one thing that I am proud of, then it is precisely the history of my African ancestors who were enslaved in Guadeloupe and who resisted this attempt at dehumanization that lasted centuries.

Frantz Fanon received a good education at the Lycée Schoelcher in Fort-de-France, Martinique, where Aimé Césaire taught. An excellent student, he was also headstrong and dreamed only of escape from the island. For the young Fanon during the 1940s, Martinique seemed suffocating, a universe that was closed and crushed under the lead weight placed upon it by the Pétainist government.

Fanon felt like a prisoner on his own island, and the call of the French Resistance was a form of liberation for him. In 1943 he finally turned 18 and could officially take up arms. He embarked on the first boat he could find to join the Free French forces. Some friends reproached him: 'You, the son of slaves, are going to free the sons of those who put your ancestors in chains? This war is not yours. This war does not concern black people.' Nonetheless, Fanon was burning with a fiery passion and he joined the regular army once the French Antilles rallied behind General de Gaulle. He then fought in the armed forces led by General Jean de Lattre de Tassigny.

Fanon was wounded in combat in the Vosges, and was later decorated for his service. But there are two sides to every medal. He had left Martinique fuelled by the Republican ideals of liberty, equality, and fraternity, but soon encountered the racism and indifference of the French, for whom the black troops, who had arrived from different French colonies, were all uniformly thought of as Senegalese. Like so many others, his convictions were undermined and his illusions shattered. He wrote to his parents on 12 April 1945: 'If I don't come back, and if one day you should learn that I died facing the enemy, console each other, but never say: he died for the good cause [...] *I was wrong!*'

After his demobilization, Fanon returned to the Antilles briefly, but soon returned to France to study medicine. Like all young Antilleans, he was mentally prepared to leave. With no decent universities on the islands, the high achievers were obliged to continue their education elsewhere. Even today, the exodus from the Antilles of their best and brightest young people persists, preventing the islands' development.

Fanon arrived in white territory and was forced to 'rethink his life'. He recalls in *Black Skin, White Masks* that a child shouted in the street, pointing:

> 'Maman, look, a Negro; I'm scared!' Scared! Scared! Now they were beginning to be scared of me … I was responsible not only for my body but also for my race and my ancestors. I cast an objective gaze over myself, discovered my blackness, my ethnic features; deafened by cannibalism, backwardness, fetishism, racial stigmas, slave traders, and above all, yes, above all, the grinning Y a bon Banania.

He studied, analysed, and dissected his new life in France, and, in 1950, submitted his doctoral thesis titled *An Essay for the Disalienation of Black People*. The university deemed the thesis unacceptable on the grounds that it did not conform to methodological norms. What made the essay truly inadmissible, though, was that it criticized traditional colonialist psychiatry, and that it proposed to analyse the reactions of Antilleans in their desire, come hell or high water, to be accepted by whites, without any regard for their own identity.

After the rejection of his thesis, Fanon transformed it, and two years later, in 1952, the new version appeared under the title *Black Skin, White Masks*. The book gave rise to heated reactions. On the right, there was an outraged response that it was an 'incitement to racial hatred'. Centrists placed their hands on their hearts and said, 'We have always recognized the blacks as our equals.' As for the communists, they criticized his excessive 'individualism'.

A year later, in June 1953, having been unable to find a job in Martinique, Fanon found himself working as the chief doctor at the psychiatric hospital of Blida-Joinville in Algeria, whose conquest by the French began in 1830, although it had been governed since the late nineteenth century as part of France itself. In the hospital, there was unofficial segregation of the mentally ill, between the native Algerian population and those originally from metropolitan France. The School of Psychiatry in Algiers had popularized the writings of John Colin Carothers who, in a 1953 report for the World Health Organization (WHO), described the African man as 'a European with an amputated frontal lobe'. The patient from mainland France could be healed, but the native was incurable! Most psychiatrists did not share such extreme views, but they did share many of the existing racial prejudices about the mental health of Algerians. At best, they were considered representatives of a 'lazy race', liable to fake symptoms in order to get out of work.

Little by little, Fanon elaborated a psychiatric approach that respected the dignity of his patients. He introduced psychotherapy methods that took into consideration his patients' Muslim culture, and he outlined the relationship between their pathologies and the dramatic events disrupting public life. His work situated him within currents of thought that would later lead to the development of social psychiatry, a fact that, combined with his desire to decolonize psychiatry, earned him the hostility of some of his colleagues and led him naturally to political engagement.

Mireille Fanon-Mendès-France told me: 'He moved from an interrogation of the self, and others, to a form of total engagement. He wanted to free people from the psychiatric hospitals, the prisons, from alienation. But when oppression has reached a certain level, the response can no longer be individual. It has to be social.'

1 November 1954, known in France as *Le Toussaint Rouge* (Bloody All Saint's Day), marked the beginning of the Algerian struggle for independence. Pro-independence forces carried out several dozen armed attacks. Fanon joined the Algerian resistance and forged ties with the political leadership of the National Liberation Front (FLN). Fanon's hospital became a refuge for resistance fighters and he was forced to resign. In 1956 he sent a letter to the resident minister, Robert Lacoste, explaining that the 'events in Algeria were the logical consequence of an aborted attempt to lobotomize a people'.

Expelled by the colonial authorities in January 1957, he went to Paris and then Tunis, where he was able to combine both his psychiatric and his political activities. He never gave up his professional work as a doctor. Even when he went underground, even when he had been seriously wounded in several attacks, even as ambassador of the Provisional Revolutionary Government of Algeria in 1960 in Ghana, Fanon continued to practise medicine. His life was one of permanent tension between this profession he loved, the political responsibilities he considered indispensable, and his writing which provided an account of his work. He wrote articles for the French-language newspaper of the FLN, *El Moudjahid* ('the holy warrior' in Arabic), which were published in English as *A Dying Colonialism* (1959).

In December 1960 a check-up revealed that he had leukemia. During the spring of 1961, which he spent in Tunis, Fanon dictated his final work, *The Wretched of the Earth*, a manifesto for anti-colonial struggle and for the emancipation of the Third World. He died in December 1961 in Washington DC.

Frantz Fanon, Richard Wright, Cheikh Anta Diop, Aimé Césaire, and all the pan-Africanists of the 1960s were right when it came to colonialism. They forged the instruments of liberation: economic, social, cultural, civic, and political. But among Frantz Fanon's demands there is, unfortunately, not a single one that isn't still relevant today. It is as if we are still at square one. A process of recolonization has begun, as the wars in Iraq and Afghanistan show us. At the same time, migrants' rights are being eroded, as they are brutally policed, their cases filtered. Moreover, there is a veritable pillage of agricultural lands taking place, notably in Madagascar and Africa, where rich countries and large corporations control millions of acres.

'The new *wretched of the earth*', writes my friend, the historian Achille Mbembe, 'are those who are refused the right to have rights; those who it is deemed should not be allowed to move; those who are condemned to live in the midst of all kinds of confining structures in camps, transit centers, the thousand sites of detention that are scattered throughout our juridical and police structures. They are those who are turned away, deported, expelled, the stowaways and undocumented – the intruders and cast-offs of our humanity that we are eager to get rid of because we believe that between them and us there is nothing worth saving, since they fundamentally endanger our lives, our health, and our well-being…'

For, as Fanon Frantz said to a friend shortly before his death, 'We are nothing on earth if we are not in the first place the slaves of a cause, the cause of the peoples, the cause of justice and liberty.'

The Spark

Rosa Louise McCauley Parks
4 February 1913–24 October 2005

It requires real courage to say no. The story of Rosa Parks is the perfect example.

That someone became famous for having refused to stand up can seem surreal. But in the segregationist universe of the 1950s United States, this was a way of affirming one's rights...

It was 1 December 1955. Rosa Parks was sitting in the first row of the 'coloured' section of a bus in Montgomery, Alabama. The 'Jim Crow' laws, promulgated in southern states between 1876 and 1965, enforced the racial segregation of all public buildings and services. A white man got on at one of the bus stops. Since there were no more unoccupied seats in the section reserved for whites, the driver asked Parks to give up her place. The segregationist laws stipulated that, when the number of white passengers exceeded the first four rows assigned to them, they could fill the seats for the blacks (who typically made up 75 per cent of passengers). Therefore, there was no alternative for black people but to pack themselves into the back of the bus or to stand on the open-air platform at the rear.

Rosa Parks' calm and dignified refusal was not a result of her being more tired than usual. It was that her patience had run out. She was certainly not the first to refuse to comply with this iniquitous law. There were other celebrities, like the great baseball player Jackie Robinson, who refused to give up his seat to an army officer, or many boxers, including Sugar Ray Robinson, Battling Siki, Joe Louis... The most significant before that day, though, had been Claudette Colvin, a 15-year-old high school student, also in Montgomery, who was slapped, thrown off a bus, arrested, and heavily fined for 'disorderly conduct'.

Edgar Daniel (E. D.) Nixon, the leader of Montgomery's local chapter of the National Association for the Advancement of Colored People (NAACP), had wanted to use the case of this young woman to denounce and reject the segregation of buses. A number of black leaders had collected money for Claudette's defence. But, soon after her arrest, it was discovered that she was pregnant with the child of a married man, who, it was rumoured, was also white. This transgression threatened not only to scandalize religious members of the black community, but, more importantly, it would be used by the white press to delegitimize her. She was not the ideal person to represent the black community's quest for equal rights.

A certain Mary Louise Smith also refused to give up her seat on a bus. But her father was an alcoholic, so she couldn't provide the image of respectability needed to represent the black cause. The strategists of the NAACP continued to search for a new plaintiff who was both respectable and determined enough to travel the perilous road all the way to the Supreme Court. A truly brave individual was needed to drag the justice system itself through the courts. It required an individual with a powerful political sense that would allow them to play a potentially historic role.

Rosa Parks was one of the most respected members of the black community, her morality was exemplary, her conduct irreproachable, and her education untarnished. Her sense of determination was profoundly rooted in her from childhood and had been enriched by twenty years of fighting racial discrimination. Who could be a better standard-bearer for the black cause?

Rosa McCauley was born in Tuskegee, Alabama. Her father was a carpenter and her mother a teacher. Given the very mediocre schooling offered to black girls, her mother decided to home-school her until she was 11. Then she sent her to the Industrial School for Girls in Montgomery, an institution founded for black children by wealthy white families from the North.

Daily racism left its mark on little Rosa. She always remembered the water fountains reserved for whites: 'The public water fountains in Montgomery had signs that said "White" and "Colored". Like millions of black children before and after me, I wondered if "white" water tasted different from "colored" water. I wanted to know if "white" water was white and "colored" water came in different colors.' It was an impression shared by many black children who suffered the same discrimination. An Antillean friend told me once that her grandmother, who owned a small plot of land where she grew sugar cane, would nevertheless go out and 'steal' a bit of cane from the whites because it was considered better for the children.

Rosa had experienced the worst of times, particularly the horrors of the Ku Klux Klan, which twice burned down the Industrial School for Girls. She had heard stories of lynchings and had seen her grandfather watch over the farm at night, clutching his rifle, prepared to defend his family from the 'Loyal White Knights' (a particularly militant faction of the KKK), their faces masked as they burned crosses. Rosa, too, was ready to fight and to advance the cause of justice. Among the many forms of daily racism, those experienced on the buses were the most visible. Not only were 'Jim Crow' laws applied on public transportation but, in addition, black children were not allowed on school buses and so had to use the public buses. 'The bus was among the first ways I realized there was a black world and a white world', she said.

Indeed, the 'public' transportation system revealed home truths about social life. As the name indicates, it should serve the community and symbolize equality. It was public transportation that first brought home the full extent of racism to Mahatma Gandhi, a great source of inspiration to the black liberation movement in the US. Upon his arrival in South Africa in April 1893, he was kicked off a train, even though he had a valid ticket, because he refused to move from the first-class section to third-class. Another day, travelling this time by stagecoach, he was beaten by the driver because he refused to move to the running board to make room for a white passenger.

Rosa Parks had committed herself to the struggle for justice and equality long before the protest of 1955 that made her famous. In 1932 she married Raymond Parks, a civil rights activist and member of the Alabama NAACP. The first battle in which they fought together was the 'Scottsboro Boys' case. On 25 March 1931 nine black boys, the youngest of them only 12 or 13, illegally boarded a train in Chattanooga, Mississippi, bound for Alabama. A group of white men asked them to leave the train. The young men declared in no uncertain terms that they would do no such thing.

At the next stop in Paint Rock, Alabama, an armed, white mob was waiting for them on the platform. They forced the nine boys off the train, fully intending to lynch them. But the police intervened, and they were brought to the prison in Scottsboro. The next day, two white women, Ruby Bates and Victoria Price, claimed that they had been raped on the train the previous night and lodged a formal complaint against the nine young black men. However, the two women were examined by white doctors (unlikely to sympathize with the black cause), who concluded that they had not suffered any sexual violence. Nevertheless, on 9 April 1931, after a parody of a trial, all nine men, except for the 12-year-old, were found guilty and sentenced to death! It took every ounce of the NAACP's strength to obtain a stay of execution and force a retrial, during which the boys were eventually proven innocent. Nonetheless, they each served between six and nineteen years in jail.

Parks had been obliged to interrupt her secondary education relatively early in order to care for her sick mother, but she returned to school and completed her studies in 1934. She was convinced that her community needed educated people, who knew how to argue their case. In particular, they needed people who could wield the law in defence of the black cause. She showed remarkable determination, since at the time, only 7 per cent of blacks completed secondary education.

Her political commitment only grew stronger over the years. In 1940 Parks and her husband were active members of the Voters' League. In 1943 she became the secretary of the NAACP in Montgomery, which was led by Edgar Nixon. And at the end of December 1943, she officially became a member of the American Civil Rights movement.

There was certainly no shortage of moments of indignation and discouragement throughout Parks' life. Like many other African Americans, she was distressed by the dreadful lynching in Mississippi of Emmett Till on 28 August 1955. He was only 14 at the time. Originally from Chicago, Emmett had a white girlfriend and studied in an integrated school. He couldn't for a second imagine the climate of hatred towards black people that existed in the southern states. Walking down the street during a holiday spent with an uncle in Mississippi, Emmett called out to a young white woman on the sidewalk: 'Bye, baby!' Those two words sparked a racial frenzy. The woman complained to her husband, and a few days later, the boy's corpse was found in the Tallahatchie River. His killers had used 65 pounds of cotton (a symbol of slavery) as ballast, wrapped around his neck with barbed wire. He had been castrated. His face had been smashed in, an eye torn out, and there was a bullet hole in his head. The perpetrators were put on trial, judged innocent by a white jury, and immediately released! That was how justice worked in the southern states just sixty years ago!

Despite the appalling nature of the crime, no one reacted in Chicago. People closed their eyes to this facet of their country, not wanting to see. A young black boy killed in the South? It happened every day, and it was a southern issue. But the mother of the 14-year-old child who had been horribly tortured and murdered didn't see it that way. The day of the funeral, she opened up the casket and told the press to photograph him. Those pictures appeared around the world, damaging the reputation of the United States right in the middle of the Cold War.

Three months later, Rosa Parks participated in a major ceremony in honour of the young boy. And three days after that, on a bus in Montgomery, the conductor demanded that she give up her seat for a white man… But this was not a woman who was simply 'daydreaming', who had momentarily forgotten her place. She was angry!

She was immediately arrested, put on trial, and found guilty of violation of the local segregation laws. E. D. Nixon and a young 26-year-old pastor named Dr Martin Luther King, Jr, along with Ralph Abernathy (another young pastor from the largest Baptist church in Montgomery), started a protest campaign and a boycott of the bus company. It was, in King's words, a campaign of 'massive non-cooperation against a vicious system'.

More than 50 leaders from the African-American community, assembled by King, gathered at the Baptist church on Dexter Avenue in Montgomery to discuss a plan of action. The founded the Montgomery Improvement Association (MIA), electing King as president, and printed this call to non-violent resistance and solidarity, distributed in leaflets throughout the area on 5 December 1955:

> Another Negro woman has been arrested and thrown into jail because she refused to get up out of her seat on the bus for a white person to sit down … If we do not do something to stop these arrests, they will continue. The next time it may be you, or your daughter, or mother. This woman's case will come up on Monday. We are, therefore, asking every Negro to stay off the buses Monday in protest of the arrest and trial. Don't ride the buses to work, to town, to school, or anywhere on Monday.

The leaflets also invited community members to a large gathering at the Baptist church on Holt Street.

This call was also published in *The Montgomery Advertiser*, the local black newspaper. The next morning, an army of young people distributed more than 7,000 tracts laying out four immediate demands.

- That blacks and whites be able to sit where they wanted on the bus.

While black passengers were more numerous on the buses, they were regularly forced to stand alongside the four rows of empty seats reserved for whites.

- That bus drivers be more courteous to all people.

Drivers consistently insulted and mistreated black passengers, calling them 'black monkeys', while the women were 'black cows'.

- That the bus drivers stop their harassment.

Not content with simply being rude, the drivers generally sought to humiliate black passengers. For example, black people paid their fare at the front door, but were obliged to go to the back door to enter the bus. Often, the driver pulled away just after taking their fares, before the black passengers were able to make their way to the back.

- That black drivers be hired.

The next day, a miracle occurred. Against all expectations – Martin Luther King had hoped the boycott would involve a solid 60 per cent of the black population – the buses were boycotted by the entire black community! There were no black passengers that day.

> The once dormant and quiescent Negro community was now fully awake [...] During the rush hours the sidewalks were crowded with laborers and domestic workers trudging patiently to their workplace and home again, sometimes as much as 12 miles. They knew why they walked, and the knowledge was evident in the way they carried themselves. And as I watched them I knew that there is nothing more majestic than the determined courage of individuals willing to suffer and sacrifice for their freedom and dignity [...] We came to see that, in the long run, it is more honorable to walk in dignity than ride in humiliation. So in a quiet dignified

manner, we decided to substitute tired feet for tired souls, and walk the streets of Montgomery until the sagging walls of injustice had been crushed by the battering rams of surging justice.

That same day, King went to the courthouse where Parks was to be judged. She was sentenced to pay a fine, as well as the court's costs, for having 'violated the laws of segregation'. She immediately appealed. The members of the NAACP rejoiced, for until then, trials of black people were, more often than not, abandoned, or else the 'offender' was tried for 'disorderly conduct'. This time, however, the affair directly involved segregation. It was the opportunity they had been dreaming of to contest the validity of segregation itself. Parks became the representative of 20 million black people whose rights had been violated since the seventeenth century.

The boycott lasted for 381 days. The bus company made huge losses! Dozens of public buses remained in the depot. Most of the protestors began walking to school or work. But soon there were demonstrations of solidarity, as taxis driven by black people appeared, offering group rides for the same price as the bus fare (10 cents). Little by little, thanks in part to the international coverage of the movement, funds began to trickle in, allowing for the creation of a parallel bus service, as well as for the purchase of shoes for members of the black community who couldn't afford them.

Of course, the threats were numerous and were often followed by violence: bombs exploded at King's house on 30 January 1956. But nothing could stop this revolt. The boycotters continued their protest until victory was won.

Finally, on 13 November 1956, the Supreme Court declared segregation laws on buses to be unconstitutional. The order was given to the authorities of Montgomery on 20 December 1956. The next day, Martin Luther King, Jr, was first in line to get on the bus…

Rosa Parks, through her role as initiator of the boycott, and through the tenacity, courage, and intelligence she displayed during the ensuing court case, helped to raise awareness among all Americans of the struggle for equal civil rights. From then on, she was considered the 'mother' of the Civil Rights movement. The Montgomery Bus Boycott marked a psychological turning point in the struggle against segregation. Thanks to Parks, the black community discovered and experienced the efficacy of a new weapon: non-violent resistance.

Often, history recalls just a few names. If the modest Rosa Parks is remembered, it is because, alongside her, an entire generation took their destiny into their own hands and decided to struggle against segregation. Of course, racism will not disappear overnight. But each of us can improve things for future generations. I always think of a quote by Albert Einstein: 'The world is a dangerous place to live; not because of the people who are evil, but because of the people who don't do anything about it.'

Liberty or Death

Malcolm X

19 May 1925–21 February 1965

> Education is our passport to the future, for tomorrow belongs only to the people who prepare for it today.
>
> Malcolm X

For many people, the name Malcolm X is a synonym for violence and defiance. On one side, we have the good pastor Dr Martin Luther King, Jr, and, on the other, we have nasty Malcolm X. When I decided to call my son Malcolm, it was no surprise that this decision met with a rather equivocal response from friends and family. That is why I would like to take these next few pages to make people understand how Malcolm X, initially committed to violence, ultimately escaped that mindset so completely that he chose to work with men of all colours and religions in pursuit of a more just society. He educated himself and developed a greater understanding of the world.

Malcolm Little was born in Omaha, Nebraska, in 1925. His father, Earl Little, was a Baptist preacher and a fervent follower of the great pan-Africanist Marcus Garvey, which earned him violent threats from the Ku Klux Klan. A few days before Malcolm's birth, Earl was preaching in Milwaukee when the white knights, brandishing torches, surrounded his house, smashed in the windows, and ordered his wife, Louisa, and her three terrorized children to get out of Nebraska.

Louisa's light-coloured skin already spoke of ineradicable pain: her conception as a result of rape. Malcolm never knew anything about his grandfather except that he was a source of shame for both his grandmother and his mother. And that shame would also be his, since he inherited from this ancestor his light skin and his hair colour, earning Malcolm the nickname 'Red'.

In 1926 his family gave into the demands of the Ku Klux Klan and moved to Michigan, where soon enough the trauma began all over again. Wherever they went, his family encountered terror and violence. Malcolm was four when their house was burned down. Afterwards, no fewer than six of his uncles were killed by whites, one of them lynched. Five years later, in 1931, Malcolm's own father was run over by a tram – almost certainly a murder disguised as an accident. His mother lost her mind with grief and was committed to a mental institution.

Without a parent to care for him, Malcolm's education came to a halt at the end of elementary school. He could barely read or write. He and his brothers and sister were separated and placed in group homes. At the age of 15, Malcolm found himself in Boston, where he earned a living from a string of jobs: shining shoes, doing odd jobs for a hotel, working in a bar and a restaurant car. As time went by, he was drawn into Boston's underworld scene and discovered cocaine. On 16 January 1946, only 21 years old, Malcolm was arrested for aggravated theft and a series of break-ins. The court sentenced him to ten years in prison in Charleston, Massachusetts.

While locked away, Malcolm the nihilist discovered, thanks to another inmate, the preachings of Elijah Muhammed, leader of the Black Muslims (also known as the Nation of Islam). Imprisonment and isolation create propitious conditions for all kinds of proselytism. Adrift and cut off from the world, young men were searching for some meaning in their lives. Seeking truth and certainty, Malcolm became a passionate follower of Islam, which brought him both peace of mind as well as a fervent desire to learn how to read and write. Unsure of exactly how to accomplish this task, Malcolm began spending all his free time in the prison library copying and recopying an entire dictionary. In 1950 he wrote to a friend, 'I'm just completing my fourth year of an eight to ten year term in prison … but these four years of seclusion have proven to be the most enlightening years of my 24 years upon this earth and I feel this "gift of Time" was Allah's reward to me as His way of saving me from the certain destruction for which I was heading.'

Until the end of his prison sentence, Malcolm corresponded with 'the honorable Elijah Muhammad', who presented himself as a messenger from God, having 'directly received the truth from his lips'. As with all religions, his teachings were based on rituals, rules, and doctrine. His doctrine was extremist, advocating a black and

African nationalism and a virulent anti-white racism. In effect, he could be thought of as the mirror image of white people's violence against blacks. His doctrine essentially displayed all the failings of segregation, only inverted: blacks were the superior race, the whites were inferior and impure. Black Muslims absolutely forbade the 'mixing of blood through racial integration'. As a result, the organization didn't pursue a campaign for civil rights or for any form of integration. These dangerous sentiments, as Martin Luther King, Jr, put it, 'substituted the tyranny of black supremacy for the tyranny of white supremacy'. But for a time, this particularly outspoken group had the merit of giving its disciples – the poorest of the blacks, the ex-convicts and the abandoned – the pride and dignity that white racism had refused them.

'You have made yourself [the white man's] slave', Elijah Muhammad always repeated to his followers, and called on them to join him so that they would finally 'have a sense of dignity'. In order to do that, it was necessary to choose Islam. For according to Elijah Muhammad's doctrine, the Christian religion bore the permanent stain of its links to the slave trade, to segregation, and to colonization. 'The white man', Malcolm X declared, 'kidnapped us from our high culture and civilization in Africa, stole us and then stole our religion.' The Black Muslims built an impenetrable wall between themselves and whites.

They also refused the approach of non-violence promoted by Martin Luther King, in a society they saw as irredeemably racist. 'We no longer endorse patience and turning-the-other-cheek. We assert the right of self-defense by whatever means necessary.' And moreover, Malcolm X declared, 'While King was having a dream ... the rest of us Negroes are having a nightmare.'

Needless to say, King totally disagreed with these ideas. For him, this desperate vision of black life was only 'articulating the despair of the Negro without offering any positive, creative alternative'. He considered the speeches of the Black Muslims demagogic, and believed that the tactics they preached could only bring misfortune and despair. This type of 'violent revolution', King maintained, would inevitably fail, since the blacks 'would be sorely outnumbered. And when it was all over, the Negro would face the same unchanged conditions, the same squalor and deprivation – the only difference being that his bitterness would be even more intense, his disenchantment even more abject.'

For his part, Malcolm needed the hope offered by Islam, which helped him deal with his incarceration. When he was released on

7 August 1952, he immediately went to Chicago to meet Elijah Muhammad, and offered to help him preach and convert his black brothers. From then on, he called himself Malcolm X: 'For me, my "X" replaced the white slavemaster name of "Little" which some blue-eyed devil named Little had imposed upon my paternal forbears.'

In 1954 he became the minister of Mosque Number 7, on Lenox Avenue in Harlem. Malcolm X was no longer simply a recently converted ex-convict-turned-preacher. He had become an influential and respected leader and talented orator. He opened other mosques, including one in Philadelphia. The movement found in him a leader even more effective than Elijah Muhammad's old guard. The times had changed. It was the era of 'Black Power'. People wanted control of their own destiny. They wanted to create a black movement, a black political force, to become the masters of the neighbourhoods and towns where blacks were a majority. Under his leadership, the Nation of Islam soon reached 100,000 members. In 1959 a televised documentary called *The Hate that Hate Produced* brought him to the attention of the wider public. The show generated considerable media interest in the organization as well as in Malcolm X himself.

From the early 1960s, however, major rifts were developing between Malcolm X and his former mentor, Elijah Muhammad. There were problems over a reluctance to share power, but there were also religious and moral issues. Rumours of sexual abuse committed by Elijah Muhammad were confirmed, along with the fact that he had made financial gains on the backs of the organization's members. Little by little, Malcolm realized that Elijah Muhammad was exploiting the anxieties of blacks by holding out the promise of a future paradise. His doubts led him to reconsider his own position within the organization, which he decided was not only faking its religious motivation but was also dangerously apolitical, as it wasn't participating in the Civil Rights movement. Malcolm determined that it was high time to stop waiting for some pie-in-the-sky future and he broke with Elijah Muhammad.

It was the beginning of a new life. The Cameroonian writer Mongo Beti wrote that 'The image of Malcolm X is usually reduced to a few silly clichés that present him as being driven by a convulsive, frenetic racism, which attracts the devotion of questionable admirers and deprives him of an audience that the intelligence of his thinking deserves.' Once his thought had become less tied to that of Elijah Muhammad, his speeches reflected a more humanist thinking, forceful and rigorous, though he never betrayed his convictions.

He remained faithful to a course of action that privileged the black community while refusing to condemn the violence of oppressed blacks. For him the priority was not, as it was for Martin Luther King, to unite whites and blacks, but first and foremost to succeed in uniting the black community.

In his famous speech of 3 April 1964, 'The Ballot or the Bullet', he repeatedly threatened to resort to violence in the face of oppression. 'No, I'm not an American. I'm one of the 22 million black people who are the victims of Americanism. One of the 22 million black people who are the victims of democracy, nothing but disguised hypocrisy. So, I'm not standing here speaking to you as an American, or a patriot, or a flag-saluter, or a flag-waver – no, not I. I'm speaking as a victim of this American system.' In the same speech, Malcolm declared that he was, in fact, not racist and that 'if the white man doesn't want us to be anti-him, let him stop oppressing and exploiting and degrading us ... [W]e're going to be forced either to use the ballot or the bullet ... It'll be Molotov cocktails this month, hand grenades next month, and something else next month ... It'll be liberty, or it will be death.'

Soon after this, he converted to orthodox Sunni Islam and, on 13 April 1964, he went on a pilgrimage to Mecca. He came back with the Muslim name El Hadj Malik El Shabazz. His transformation went beyond his new name, and he returned with a new acceptance of human difference. He said of his journey: 'There were tens of thousands of pilgrims, from all over the world. They were of all colors, from blue-eyed blonds to black-skinned Africans, but were all participating in the same ritual, displaying a spirit of unity and brotherhood that my experiences in America had led me to believe could never exist between the white and non-white. America needs to understand Islam, because this is the one religion that erases the race problem from its society.'

If he wanted to be faithful to himself, he had to choose between racism and Islam. From then on, he perceived racism as a form of madness, and he made this known.

In the past, I have permitted myself to be used to make sweeping indictments of all white people, and these generalizations have caused injuries to some white people who did not deserve them. Because of the spiritual rebirth which I was blessed to undergo as a result of my pilgrimage to the Holy City of Mecca, I no longer subscribe to sweeping indictments of one race [...] The whites as well as the non-whites who accept true Islam become a changed people ... True Islam removes racism, because people of all colors and races who accept its religious principles and bow down to the one God, Allah, also automatically accept each other as brothers and sisters, regardless of differences in complexion.

When asked what kinds of people Malcolm hoped to include in his movement, he responded, 'All – we're flexible – a variety [...] All groups – Nationalist, Christians, Muslims, agnostics, atheists, anything. Everybody who is interested in solving the problem is given an invitation to become actively involved with either suggestions or ideas or something.'

Malcolm X founded the Organization of Afro-American Unity, a non-religious political group. No more soldiers of God. His project was to pursue a committed political struggle, internationalize the black movement, and to bring a charge of racism against the United States government at the United Nations. 'How can you condemn South Africa? There are only 11 million of our people in South Africa, there are 22 million of them here. And we are receiving an injustice which is just as criminal as that which is being done to the black people of South Africa.'

The essential revolutionary task, in his eyes, was education and training. For blacks, but also for whites! On 8 January 1965, less than two months before his death, he was asked about the causes of racial prejudice in the United States. His response could serve as an epigraph for this book:

If the entire American population were properly educated – by properly educated, I mean given a true picture of the history and contributions of the black man – I think many whites would be less racist in their feelings. They would have more respect for the black man as a human being. Knowing what the black man's contributions to science and civilization have been in the past, the white man's feelings of superiority would be at least partially negated. Also, the feeling of inferiority that the black man has would be replaced by a balanced knowledge of himself. He'd feel more like a human being...

But there was a growing tension between Malcolm X and the Nation of Islam. On 14 February 1965 his house was bombed. Six days later, on Sunday 21 February, in a Harlem auditorium in front of a black audience of several hundred, he began what would be his final speech: "*As-salaam alaikum.*" Peace be unto you. "*Wa-alaikum salaam.*" And unto you be peace. A shout, a stirring in the audience, Malcolm saying "Hold it, hold it–" A sudden roar – *blaam!'* Three men jumped on to the stage and shot Malcolm with sawn-off shotguns and pistols.

According to Maya Angelou, one man she encountered just after the event felt it appropriate to cite the Gospels: 'Shit, you live by the sword, you die by the sword.' Nothing could be further from the truth. The non-violent Martin Luther King also died by the sword. As for Malcolm X, he did not choose violence. Violence chose him.

A Dream That Changed the World

Dr Martin Luther King, Jr

15 January 1929–4 April 1968

> I say to you, this morning, that if you have never
> found something so dear and so precious to you
> that you will die for it, then you aren't fit to live.
> Dr Martin Luther King, Jr,
> 5 November 1967

Martin Luther King, Jr's father was a pastor, as was his father's brother, his grandfather before them, and later, his only brother ... all of them were men who cared about suffering and injustice. Martin Luther King's battle for liberty was the product of a deeply humanist education.

King was a very fortunate child. He came from a stable home and his parents were sufficiently wealthy to fund his higher education. In 1948 he received a Bachelor of Arts degree in sociology from Morehouse College, in Atlanta, where he had also steeped himself in philosophy. One of the most influential texts in his intellectual development was Henry David Thoreau's *Civil Disobedience*. The book advocates passive resistance, the duty to refuse all cooperation with a corrupt regime. A few years later, in 1950, King attended a lecture where he discovered the teachings of Gandhi. He immediately saw that the non-violent methods advocated by the Mahatma could prove very effective against segregation. In 1953 he became the pastor of the Baptist church on Dexter Avenue in Montgomery, Alabama. That same year he married Coretta Scott, who was also very active in the struggle against the oppression suffered by the black community.

1 December 1955, the day Rosa Parks refused a bus driver's order to give up her seat to a white man, was a revelation for

Martin Luther King. In Montgomery and throughout the black community, this episode, to which a chapter of this book is devoted (pp. 199–206), resulted in a victory against segregation on buses. King came to understand the effectiveness of such actions, which combined the non-violent principles of Gandhi and the moral necessity of passive resistance advocated by Thoreau. Parks was one of those whom King described as 'fifty thousand Negroes who took to heart the principles of nonviolence, who learned to fight for their rights with the weapon of love...' But he knew there was still a long road ahead in the struggle 'to emerge from the bleak and desolate midnight of man's inhumanity to man to the bright and glittering daybreak of freedom and justice'.

The heroes of black resistance during this period were neither romantic nor naive. They studied the political, legal, and public relations techniques that might help them win their rights. Just as Parks was not some random, unhappy woman, tired after a day's work, who refused to give up her seat on the bus, but a determined and experienced activist, King was not the sweet, pacifist pastor we often imagine, offering his left cheek and then his right.

King's strategy was one of 'provocative' non-violence, a 'conciliatory confrontation'. He wanted to be effective, not to cause harm. His true genius lay in drawing inspiration from Gandhi, who, in 1920, declared: 'I do believe that, where there is only a choice between cowardice and violence, I would advise violence ... I would rather have India resort to arms in order to defend her honour than that she should, in a cowardly manner, become or remain a helpless witness to her own dishonour. But I believe that nonviolence is infinitely superior to violence...' It was superior not because of its 'good intentions' or because it represented a refusal to fight, but because of its political power, its ability to turn the violence of the oppressor back on himself, to expose his brutal violence for all to see. King understood this lesson. From then on, he devoted himself to revealing the violence of white southerners, and in particular the Ku Klux Klan and its accomplices within local police forces and the media. King was a true political leader, not just some faceless candidate standing for election.

In 1957 King was elected president of the Southern Christian Leadership Conference (SCLC), which coordinated the participation of African-American churches in the struggle for civil rights. Doesn't it go without saying that it is only when people share the same rights and the same duties that they can live together as citizens? Otherwise, there is a constant threat of civil war.

That is what King's actions demonstrated, and they provoked an ever-growing hatred on the part of those who wanted to maintain inequality in order to preserve their own power.

On 20 September 1958 King was stabbed in Harlem while signing his book, *Strive Towards Freedom*. The letter opener used to stab him had come so close to his aorta that the doctor told him, 'If you had sneezed during all those hours of waiting ... your aorta would have been punctured and you would have drowned in your own blood.' This attack didn't stop him, however, for King's goals were more important to him than any concern for his own life.

In 1959 King travelled to India where he met with the nation's first prime minister, Jawaharlal Nehru. King was not blind to the acute poverty and social injustice in the country. He visited a school, where a head teacher presented him as follows: 'Young people, I would like to present to you a fellow untouchable from the United States of America.' When it came to segregation, was America any better than India?

By 1960, sit-ins had spread to many shops and restaurants in the southern states. Protestors would sit together in a location generally prohibited to blacks. Although the protests carried out by King and his followers were peaceful, they led to retaliation. Targeted by the FBI, he was arrested on several occasions on various pretexts – false income declarations, taking part in a protest, driving offences, etc. Nevertheless, throughout 1961 and 1962 he continued to speak out, to take action and, as a result, he spent more and more time in prison.

In 1963 the SCLC and the Alabama Christian Movement for Human Rights launched a major protest campaign in Birmingham, widely considered to be the worst city in America for a black person to live. In Birmingham, the city fathers seemed never to have even heard of Abraham Lincoln, Thomas Jefferson, the Declaration of the Rights of Man, or the verdict handed down in 1954 rendering all segregation in schools illegal. History was denied there, along with civil rights. The governor, George Wallace, had only one slogan: '[S]egregation now ... segregation tomorrow ... segregation forever!' Then on 15 September 1963, two little black girls were killed in the bombing of the 16th Street Baptist Church. There were so many unresolved racist attacks that blacks began calling the city 'Bombingham'!

King painted a frightening portrait of the city. He described it as a place where 'human rights had been trampled on for so long that fear and oppression were as thick in its atmosphere as the smog from its factories'.

The sheriff, Eugene Connor – nicknamed 'Bull' – was a policeman by day and a member of the Ku Klux Klan by night. All aspects of civic and social life were structured by 'Jim Crow' laws: hospitals, cinemas, shops, bathrooms, fountains, cemeteries, buses, public parks... When the courageous pastor Fred Shuttlesworth won the desegregation of public parks in court, 'Bull' responded by simply closing them and setting off a bomb at the pastor's house! When it came to jobs, those offered to blacks were always lowly, with no potential for promotion and with salaries far below those of whites. The curious adaptation of democratic laws under 'Jim Crow' meant that political rights were so limited that, despite the fact that one-third of the population was black, they only constituted one-eighth of the electorate. In addition to intimidation and threats outside polling stations, King wrote of the 'slow pace of the [voting] registrar and the limited number of days and hours during which the office was open'. For example, '[o]ut of 15,000 Negroes eligible to vote in Selma and the surrounding Dallas County, less than 350 were registered'. Finally, there was the 'literacy test', designed to prevent blacks from voting and, of course, it was evaluated in a clearly biased fashion.

Churches, those sacred communal spaces, were also subjected to the 'Jim Crow' regime. 'For although your white fellow citizens would insist that they were Christians', writes King, 'they practiced segregation as rigidly in the house of God as they did in the theater.' It's hard to imagine now that a black child who entered a 'white' church to pray could be thrown out and violently beaten.

The major problem was how – in a country where whites held economic, cultural, political, and repressive power – to get white public opinion, and particularly that of a white 'silent majority', to care about the segregation under which the black majority suffered.

> [T]he Negro's great stumbling block in his stride toward freedom is not the White Citizen's Counciler or the Ku Klux Klanner, but the white moderate, who is more devoted to 'order' than to justice; who prefers a negative peace which is the absence of tension to a positive peace which is the presence of justice; who constantly says: 'I agree with you in the goal you seek, but I cannot agree with your methods of direct action'; who paternalistically believes he can set the timetable for another man's freedom; who lives by a mythical concept of time and who constantly advises the Negro to wait for a 'more convenient season'.

In Birmingham, protests began in April 1963 with a boycott of shops. As the shops seemed to cope with the boycott, the movement launched 'project C', a series of sit-ins in shops, restaurants, libraries, and whites-only churches. The objective was 'to create such a crisis and foster such a tension that a community which has constantly refused to negotiate is forced to confront the issue'.

Naturally, Martin Luther King ended up being arrested, on 12 April 1963. While in his prison cell, he wrote his famous *Letter from Birmingham Jail,* of which the following is an excerpt:

We have waited for more than 340 years for our constitutional and God given rights. The nations of Asia and Africa are moving with jetlike speed toward gaining political independence, but we still creep at horse and buggy pace toward gaining a cup of coffee at a lunch counter. Perhaps it is easy for those who have never felt the stinging darts of segregation to say, 'Wait.' But when you have seen vicious mobs lynch your mothers and fathers at will and drown your sisters and brothers at whim; when you have seen hate filled policemen curse, kick, and even kill your black brothers and sisters; when you see the vast majority of your twenty million Negro brothers smothering in an airtight cage of poverty in the midst of an affluent society; when you suddenly find your tongue twisted and your speech stammering as you seek to explain to your six-year-old daughter why she can't go to the public amusement park that has just been advertised on television, and see tears welling up in her eyes when she is told that Funtown is closed to colored children, and see ominous clouds of inferiority beginning to form in her little mental sky, and see her beginning to distort her personality by developing an unconscious bitterness toward white people [...] when you are harried by day and haunted by night by the fact that you are a Negro, living constantly at tiptoe stance, never quite knowing what to expect next, and are plagued with inner fears and outer resentments; when you are forever fighting a degenerating sense of 'nobodiness' – then you will understand why we find it difficult to wait. There comes a time when the cup of endurance runs over, and men are no longer willing to be plunged into the abyss of despair.

King was released from prison after only a week, thanks to the intervention of President John F. Kennedy and his brother Robert, the US Attorney General. But King discovered that the movement was losing steam. So he decided to turn to the younger generation, that eternal source of resistance. On 2 May 1963 a massive children's march was organized. Middle-school, high-school, and elementary-school students skipped their classes and marched downtown, chanting 'Freedom'. The youngest was 7, the oldest 18. Between 2 and 7 May, the 'Children's Crusade' never weakened. On the first day alone, more than 1,000 children were arrested. The police were forced to charter school buses to drive them to prison. By the end of the following day, 2,000 children were sleeping behind bars. And they kept coming! Some children spontaneously planted themselves in front of police stations and stood there, singing, so they would be arrested.

'Bull' Connor was beside himself with anger and let loose his German shepherd dogs, trained to target their victims' stomachs, against the peacefully marching children. He ordered the use of fire-hoses capable of ripping the bark off a tree. The next day, reporters from the national press and radio stations flooded Birmingham. Readers of every daily in the US saw photographs of incredible violence: young, defenceless women thrown on the ground and beaten, a young man propelled over a car by the gush of water issuing from a fire-hose. Most horrifying, though, were the pictures of 'children marching up to the bared fangs of police dogs'. The average American, the silent majority, was profoundly shocked by these images.

In his famous interview with Kenneth B. Clark, aired in May and June 1963, King recounted how the young, non-violent protestors were trained in advance, given 'courses where we go through the experience of being roughed up'. When asked if the children were also required to go through the training, King replied: 'Yes, it includes the children [...] In fact, none of them went out for a march, none of them engaged in any of the demonstrations before going through this kind of teaching session.'

King was attacked by high-minded individuals who criticized him for having 'instrumentalized' the children. He responded that children had been on the front lines of segregation for a hundred years and that he had never before heard anyone express any concern for them! These charitable souls almost seemed to excuse the aggressors, the dog-handlers, as though it were the peaceful children who had provoked them!

But the pictures were extremely embarrassing for Washington. King had succeeded in shaking public opinion. Criticism rained down on the US from around the world. The Soviet Union took advantage of the news to denounce Uncle Sam's attacks on human rights. As for the city of Birmingham, it was on the edge of collapse: every single downtown business had been affected. The White House was forced to dispatch Bruce Marshall and Joseph F. Dolan, aides to the Attorney General, to the city to mediate a truce and oversee negotiations.

Finally, on 21 May 1963, the mayor resigned, the police chief was fired, and, in June, all the segregationist signs were taken down: all public spaces and buildings were opened to blacks. The Kennedy government, for whom civil rights legislation had not initially been a priority, quickly decided to put forward a far-reaching legislative bill regarding such rights, which would be applicable across the US.

Martin Luther King's reputation had grown considerably. It was decided that the success of the protest would be crowned by a march on Washington, DC, intended to unite the various participants involved in the movement. On 28 August 1963, 240,000 people of all colours and religions gathered in front of the Lincoln Memorial. King was due to give a speech. He had begun drafting it the night before and had almost finished a final version of it.

King began his speech but, suddenly, the words he had spoken two months earlier during a meeting in Michigan came to him: 'I have a dream…' He pushed aside the paper he was reading from and declared to his vast audience:

I say to you today, my friends, though, even though we face the difficulties of today and tomorrow, I still have a dream. It is a dream deeply rooted in the American dream. I have a dream that one day this nation will rise up, live out the true meaning of its creed: 'We hold these truths to be self-evident, that all men are created equal.'

I have a dream that one day on the red hills of Georgia sons of former slaves and the sons of former slave-owners will be able to sit down together at the table of brotherhood.

I have a dream that one day even the state of Mississippi, a state sweltering with the heat of injustice, sweltering with the heat of oppression, will be transformed into an oasis of freedom and justice.

I have a dream that my four little children will one day live in a nation where they will not be judged by the color of their skin but by the content of their character. I have a dream … I have a dream that one day in Alabama, with its vicious racists, with its governor having his lips dripping with the words of interposition and nullification, one day right there in Alabama little black boys and black girls will be able to join hands with little white boys and white girls as sisters and brothers.

I have a dream today...

On 10 December 1964 Martin Luther King received the Nobel Peace Prize. He was 35 years old. This award also paid a wonderful tribute to the thousands of anonymous participants in the Civil Rights movement.

This 'dream' and the triumphant protest movement that accompanied it only reinforced the hatred directed at King by white segregationists. King's approach would also soon frustrate a rebellious generation of young black people. Gradually, they turned away from non-violent protest, joining movements that preached self-defence like Elijah Muhammad's Black Muslims, which featured charismatic figures like Malcolm X. Then, in 1966, Stokely Carmichael launched the Black Power movement, soon followed by the Black Panthers. For King, the 'March Against Fear' of 6 June 1966 marked the final overturning of his non-violent philosophy.

As we walked down the meandering highway in the sweltering heat, there was much talk and many questions were raised. 'I'm not for that nonviolence stuff anymore,' shouted one of the younger activists. 'If one of those damn white Mississippi crackers touches me, I'm gonna knock the hell out of him,' shouted another [...] Once during the afternoon we stopped to sing, 'We Shall Overcome'. The voices rang out with all of the traditional fervor ... But when we came to the stanza which speaks of 'black and white together,' the voices of a few of the marchers were muted. I asked them later why they refused to sing that verse. The retort was, 'This is a new day, we don't sing those words anymore. In fact, the whole song should be discarded. Not "We Shall Overcome," but "We Shall Overrun".'

Hate begets hate. King could see this clearly, and in April 1968, shortly before his death, he wrote: 'Well, I don't know what will happen now; we've got some difficult days ahead. But it really doesn't matter with me now, because I've been to the mountaintop.

And I don't mind. Like anybody, I would like to live a long life – longevity has its place. But I'm not concerned about that now.'

King knew that he risked assassination at every moment. But would that stop him?

On 4 April 1968 he was standing on the balcony of his hotel room in Memphis when a shot rang out. Just one. Martin Luther King, Jr, who wanted 'to transform the jangling discords of our nation into a beautiful symphony of brotherhood', fell to the ground.

A few days later, in the streets of Atlanta, 200,000 Americans of all colours and all religions followed the two mules that pulled the simple cart bearing his coffin.

Today, we recall the exceptional righteousness and courage of a man who never compromised on his idealism. An idealism that he explained as follows:

> On some positions, cowardice asks the question, is it expedient? And then expedience comes along and asks the question, is it politic? Vanity asks the question, is it popular? Conscience asks the question, is it right?
>
> There comes a time when one must take the position that is neither safe nor politic nor popular, but he must do it because conscience tells him it is right.

A Militant for the African People

Mongo Beti

30 June 1932–7 October 2001

In order to understand the Cameroonian Mongo Beti, the great literary explorer of righteous anger, I met with his wife, Odile Tobner.

Born Alexandre Biyidi-Awala, he chose Mongo Beti as his pen name. Mongo means 'son', and Beti is the name of his ethnic group. Thus, the name signified that he was both the son of his people and of his land. Beti arrived in France in 1951, at the age of 19, in order to pursue his studies in literature. By 1954 he had already published his first novel, *Cruel City*, in which he condemned the arbitrary and unjust nature of the colonial system.

He learned the art of storytelling as a child, at the village festivals in Akometan, Cameroon, where each person in turn had to tell a story.

The colonization of Cameroon began in 1472, when the Portuguese landed in the Wouri estuary. Thus began a system of slavery which only intensified with the arrival of the Dutch, and later the Germans, who laid claim to the colony in 1884. As a result of their defeat in the First World War, Germany lost Cameroon, which was then divided between France and Great Britain.

The art of resistance: *that* is what Mongo Beti truly learned as a child.

In 1932, the year he was born, protests against the colonial administration were violently suppressed in Douala. In 1945, while he was in high school at the Lycée Leclerc in Yaoundé, there was a series of riots and strikes. Three years later, in 1948, as he was preparing for his school-leaving baccalaureate examinations, Ruben Um Nyobé, the 'Che Guevara' of Cameroon, a charismatic leader and pioneer in the struggles for independence in Francophone Africa, founded the Union of the Peoples of Cameroon (UPC). Beti was fascinated by this orator and his arguments, and he climbed over the wall of his school to go and hear him speak: 'The colonists do not want to accept the equality of Black and White. Their vision is manifested in social relations, in the hierarchy of salaries, in medical treatment, in housing, in law and, unfortunately, in the church. Is there any liberty-loving soul who would remain unmoved before this revolting spectacle of a foreigner treating the children of this land like second-class citizens?'

In 1951 the nationalists of the UPC began their war of independence against French occupation. The bloody events that shook Cameroon between 1954 and 1960 were largely overlooked by the international community. 'The attention of the world, and particularly that of the French, was completely absorbed by the massive din of the successive wars in Indochina and in the Maghreb', Beti wrote in 'Repentance', a speech he delivered on 9 June 2001 at a conference organized by the International Research Association on Crimes Against Humanity and Genocide

Increasingly outraged at the situation in Cameroon, he published a second novel, *The Poor Christ of Bomba*, which caused a scandal. In this text, Beti sought to place himself in the shoes of two 'kind' colonizers! The main characters, a missionary and a colonial administrator, are both portrayed as sincere men of good will who are mere pawns in a wholly reprehensible system to which they are largely oblivious. This structure allows the author to offer a critical outlook without slipping into caricature. The collision between these 'kind men' and the African population is as frightening in the novel as it was in real life. The next year, Beti published *Mission to Kala* (for which he won the Sainte-Beuve prize in 1958), in which he attacked the vices of traditional Cameroonian society. His novel *King Lazarus* followed soon after. With his witty eloquence and inexhaustible imagination, Beti seemed capable of producing novel after novel, like those nineteenth-century writers who published in serial form in the newspapers. However, after the publication of *King Lazarus*, he entered a period of literary silence that lasted ten years. Why? The answer can be found in the dramatic events that accompanied the African awakening of the independence era, the tremors of which are still felt to this day.

The year 1959 saw the 'pseudo-independence' of Cameroon. 'Che' Ruben Um Nyobé, for whom Mongo Beti had boundless admiration, was killed on 13 September 1958 after having been pursued for several long months by French colonial troops. Beti would write that: 'Ruben Um Nyobé's struggle was pure madness because, truly, nothing at the time allowed him to imagine he would be successful.' It's true that resistance fighters have often been considered to be either madmen or terrorists. Take Nelson Mandela, for instance, who appeared on the political stage during a period of unimaginable repression, or Martin Luther King, or all the men in 1940 who, like General Charles de Gaulle, imagined they would overcome Nazism. Ruben Um Nyobé, Lumumba, King, Malcolm X, Mandela, and Mongo Beti will always serve as heroic examples because they never compromised.

After the murder of Nyobé, colonization endured in Cameroon thanks to a dictatorial regime. De Gaulle's France made it seem as if the decolonization of Black Africa was complete and that, if problems persisted, it was a question of 'inter-tribal' conflict. This kind of misinformation is still prevalent today. The ongoing wars over commercial interests and natural resources in Africa – and there are many, for Africa is rich – are presented as ethnic disputes.

In all his undertakings in Cameroon, General de Gaulle ignored the Declaration of the Rights of Man of 10 December 1948, whose preamble insists that 'recognition of the inherent dignity and of the equal and inalienable rights of all members of the human family is the foundation of freedom, justice and peace in the world'. At one point de Gaulle sent an expeditionary force to fight the UPC, then headed by Ernest Ouandié. Their mantra was: 'Kill them all!'

In 'Repentance', one of his final texts, Beti angrily exclaimed that 'Entire villages and city neighbourhoods were set on fire after they were surrounded by the troops so that no one could escape – children, the elderly, pregnant women.' Napalm was dropped from aeroplanes on to poor, unarmed farmers, who were trying to flee the conflict. 'In Douala in 1960, a popular district called Kongo that was known to be home to radical nationalist militants was surrounded by African soldiers under the command of white officers and burned; all the inhabitants died, with no distinction of age or sex.' Thousands were killed in this violent repression.

Ernest Ouandié was captured in an ambush in 1970. He was publicly executed on 15 January 1971 in Bafoussam. Beti was outraged by media reporting of Ouandié's trial, as well as that of a bishop, Monsignor Ndongmo. He immediately wrote *Stranglehold on Cameroon, Autopsy of a Decolonization*. Despite French government attempts at censorship, the text included various testimonies he had gathered. The book was published by Maspero, the radical publishing house, in June 1972, but was immediately banned in a decree issued by President Georges Pompidou's interior minister, Raymond Marcellin.

Beti was not discouraged. Quite the opposite, in fact. He pursued a legal case against the French state, which lasted four years. And he won. But the French press didn't pay much attention and barely mentioned the trial. The state subjected Beti to increasing bureaucratic persecution and intimidation. He was summoned to the police headquarters in the port of Rouen, and his papers were confiscated. Beti, a professor of French literature who had passed the prestigious *agrégation* examination, now found himself with no nationality. He pursued another case against the state. And he won. Once again, no one paid any attention.

This unofficial censorship by the media was a direct result of the 'scandal' around *Stranglehold on Cameroon*. There were no reviews of his numerous novels. Published in 1974, *Perpetua and the Habit of Unhappiness* paints a picture of corruption, dictatorship, and the African woman. *Remember Ruben* (1974) recounts the upheavals in Africa at the time when the likes of Ruben Um Nyobé were at the heart of the independence movement. Other novels followed: *The Almost Funny Ruin of a Buffoon* (1979), *The Two Mothers of Guillaume Ismaël Dzewatama, Future Truck-Driver* (1983), *The Revenge of Guillaume Ismaël Dzewatama* (1984), *Too Much Sun Kills Love* (1999), *Commotion in Black and White* (2000).

In the wake of the censorship of *Stranglehold on Cameroon*, and the ensuing court case, Beti decided that he needed to find his own way to publish the things no one seemed to want to read. With his wife, Odile Tobner, he founded the journal *Black Peoples–African Peoples* in 1978. It sought relentlessly to reveal the wrongs done to Africa by neocolonial regimes, and moreover, it gave young African intellectuals a platform to express themselves. The journal survived from hand to mouth; editing an independent African publication in France required a great deal of money. In addition, it had many enemies, and was pilloried as 'a vitriolic gossip column' by former colonial administrators, who had converted themselves into Africanists. Presumably they would have preferred a 'widely distributed and sentimental' journal that praised their 'contributions' to Africa.

These low-level colonial administrators who had been parachuted into positions as linguists or professors of African literature dissuaded their students from reading Mongo Beti's work. They claimed that a writer had to chose between being a true novelist and being a 'militant who writes'. Beti replied that if he were to write love stories for people who were suffering, then they would not recognize themselves in his work. He didn't want his writing to be defined as 'black skin, rose-tinted literature', or as a complacent dreamlike vision of Africa. For Beti, the work of the writer was not to give his blessing to the world as it is, but to make society 'ill at ease', to raise awareness of problems, a process without which progress was impossible. He wanted to provoke outrage, which he saw as the root of life and liberty.

After thirty-two years of exile in France, Mongo Beti returned to Cameroon in 1991. But had this son of the land ever really left? The plots of his books had always been situated in Africa, and his imagination was African.

Beti had always wanted to open a bookshop in the city of Yaoundé. For, despite common misconceptions, Africans like to read, particularly books about politics. If they do not commonly read such books, it is only because they cannot buy them in the first place. When he resettled in Cameroon, books were the rarest commodity in the country. Beti's 'Bookstore of the Black Peoples' sought to change this.

He also returned to his home village, Akometan, in order to help the locals better organize their farming practices. He hoped to create conditions in which they could develop without the need for outside help. In less than ten years, he became a major producer of tomatoes, bananas, and corn, and had begun breeding pigs and practising forestry. But he quickly became aware of the viciousness and corruption that scarred the local mindset and people's social relations. He literally killed himself trying to make his business work. As Ambroise Kom writes in his book, *Mongo Beti Speaks*: 'He struggled with a population that followed the example set by the bigwigs of the neocolonial regime, and aspired only to live a life subsidized by returned exiles.'

In *France against Africa, Return to Cameroon*, published in 1993, Beti subtly described the pervading culture and dilapidated state of the country he had rediscovered upon his return. His account constituted a denunciation of the failures of neocolonialism.

Throughout Central Africa, the neocolonial system encouraged unrestrained predatory behaviour. The large banana plantations of southern Cameroon are owned by French companies. The villages of the plantation workers remain in abject poverty. Their water is polluted, and they work 60 hours per week for a salary that keeps them below the poverty line. They are slaves on their own land, which has been stolen from them for the benefit of French capitalists.

As for timber, it is not processed on site in order to avoid the creation of any added value. For an internal timber industry would bankrupt European furniture dealers. All the profits go to foreign multinational companies, which don't pay taxes. And don't forget about the oil industry! As Loïk Le Floch-Prigent, the former CEO of Elf, the French oil company, candidly stated, the reason there are dictatorships in Africa is because 'any uncertainty' when it comes to the supply of oil cannot be tolerated!

Our global, political, and financial institutions oversee this abject situation. Joseph E. Stiglitz, winner of the Nobel Prize for Economics, explains in his 2002 book *Globalization and its Discontents* that the policies of the World Bank, and especially of the International Monetary Fund (IMF), support a kind of oppression that favours the interests of a small number of dominant countries. 'By custom or tacit agreement the head of the IMF is always a European, the head of the World Bank an American. They are chosen behind closed doors and it has never been viewed as a prerequisite that the head should have any experience in the developing world.' Some of the biggest obstacles developing countries must confront are the policies of the IMF.

It will always be possible to offer 'development aid', or at least pretend to. All of this aid combined – assistance from states, NGOs, and immigrants – represents just one-sixth of the capital stolen from Africa by multinational corporations.

As a result of all these factors, and despite its human, agricultural, and mineral wealth, Africa keeps getting poorer and poorer. It is not simply misfortune that has left Africans impoverished, or a lack of 'maturity' that has prevented Africa from opening itself up to democracy, but rather a system of frenzied exploitation established and maintained by the IMF.

Do we understand that a truly equitable market would mean a decrease in the standard of living in the West, and a decline for a certain number of developed countries? Could we accept a transfer of wealth and greater equality in standards of living? As Western nations have become corrupted by excessive consumption, is it in their fundamental interest to keep Africa in poverty?

I am always surprised that countries, including France, endlessly talk about democracy when it is not practised by any of the international institutions that govern our planet. Member countries of the IMF and the World Bank don't all share the same voting rights. The United Nations Security Council is composed of five permanent member countries which were appointed at the end of the Second

World War: China, the United States, Russia, France, and Great Britain, plus ten rotating members. But only these five nations have the right of veto. UN 'unanimity' on any matter is thus decided by these major powers.

Each of Mongo Beti's works gives voice to this pain, this injustice, and this deliberately imposed poverty. Although he had hopes that the press might play a positive role, here too, the struggle proved great. Pius Njawé, the founder and director of the newspaper *The Messenger* in Douala, the man who created the first non-government-run newspaper in Cameroon, was imprisoned ten times, and this repression was at its worst in the late 1990s.

Beti's final ten years in Africa were full of pain and suffering. He had idealized the population's desire for emancipation and journalists' desire for independence. But in the end, he came to realize that his compatriots' only desire was to deal with the system as it was and simply get by in life. He resented them enormously for this.

A few months before his death, Beti pronounced these words: 'To permanently make the relationship between Africa and France healthier, and to prevent massacres and other genocides, the most important thing will be to free those in the French media from their inhibitions, whether psychological, political or cultural, that have paralyzed them until now. As elsewhere, in developed and truly democratic countries, the day will finally have to come where a French journalist speaks objectively about Africa, even if the facts contradict their ideology.'

Mongo Beti died on 7 October 2001.

The Cameroonian government expressed its desire to 'honour' him publicly.

Loyal to his memory, his family publicly refused.

'I am Super Fast!
I Fight with my Mind'

Muhammad Ali

17 January 1942–3 June 2016

In a hundred years ... they'll turn me white ...
They did it to Jesus.

Muhammad Ali

Cassius Clay, born in Louisville in 1942, bore the name of a white general, Cassius Marcellus Clay. An exceptional athlete, he was only 18 when he won the gold medal for light-heavyweight boxing at the 1960 Olympic Games in Rome.

In 1962 Clay joined the Nation of Islam and changed his name to Cassius X. The letter X symbolized his lost African identity. It was also an homage to Malcolm X, who supported him in his fight against Sonny Liston, another black boxer. He then received the name Muhammad Ali from Elijah Muhammad, the leader of the Black Muslims. 'Changing my name was one of the most important things that happened to me in my life. It freed me from the identity given to my family by the slave-masters.' Of course, for the average American, to whom this new identity appeared as a threat, this explanation offered little comfort. 'If I had changed my name from Cassius Clay to something like Smith or Jones because I wanted a name that white people thought was more American', he declared, 'nobody would have complained.'

After Ali turned professional in 1963, he was named 'Boxer of the Year', and it was inevitable that early in 1964 he would be matched up with Sonny Liston, the world champion, who was reputed to be invincible. He surprised everyone by dominating

Liston in a contest that lasted just six rounds. After the fight, he shouted to the world:

> I'm black, I'm the strongest man in the world, I don't believe in forced integration. And why don't blacks have the right to say they are the biggest and strongest and the most beautiful! Whites say it every day. In America, everything is white. The President is white, the manager is white, the sheriff is white, even shoe polish is white, God is white, Tarzan is white, Superman too, the voice in the sky is white and women get married in white. But in America 10 percent of the men are black. They bring glory to the United States in sport, music, in song and dance. What's the point of that when no black person has any role leading the country? We don't have to apologize for being black, we don't have to act conciliatory and ask pity from the whites. On the contrary, we must be proud of our condition as black men.

From 25 February 1964 to 20 June 1967, Muhammad Ali dominated the heavyweight category. Then his legal problems began. He refused to be drafted into the US army, which had committed hundreds of thousands of troops to fighting the Vietnam War. He became a conscientious objector, famously declaring 'I ain't got no quarrel with them Viet Cong', and 'No Viet Cong ever called me nigger.' On 8 May 1967 he went before the courts, and on 20 June he was fined 10,000 dollars and sentenced to five days in prison.

Ali's boxing licence was withdrawn, and he was forced to give up his title, which Joe Frazier soon won, defeating Jimmy Ellis. Finally, in 1971, the Supreme Court recognized Ali's right to refuse military service, and he could begin his career again. Determined to win back his title, he fought Frazier and suffered his first defeat. Then, one after the other, he fought against all the best American boxers until he had regained his former sharpness. There was just one more opponent to defeat: Joe Frazier. Unfortunately for Ali, Frazier was destroyed by George Foreman on 22 January 1973.

Ali now had two opponents to beat, instead of one, to regain his title. Then, on 31 March of the same year, the boxer Ken Norton broke Ali's jaw. Now there were three! He chose to confront these three boxers in order of their greatness: Norton, then Frazier, and finally, the unbeatable Foreman.

Having left school at the age of 14, Ali did not have much of a formal education, and yet he had a real intelligence and possessed an innate sense of how to perform for his audience. Boxing provided him with a platform from which he could express his sense of rebellion. He recited poems predicting what round he would knock out his opponent in. He announced his upcoming fights to the press in a very personal style:

> I'm experienced now, professional. Jaw's been broke, been knocked down a couple of times, I'm bad! Been chopping trees. I done something new for this fight. I done wrestled with an alligator. That's right. I have wrestled with an alligator. I done tussled with a whale. I done handcuffed lightning, thrown thunder in jail. That's bad! Only last week I murdered a rock, injured a stone, hospitalized a brick! [...] Last night I cut the light off in my bedroom, hit the switch and was in the bed before the room was dark [...] You and George Foreman, all you chumps are gonna bow when I whup him, all of you, I know you got him, I know you've got him picked, but the man's in trouble, Ima show you how great I am.

Ali beat Norton on points, then Frazier. The only one left was Foreman. He had a remarkable physique. The press was unanimous: Ali couldn't beat him. People spoke of Ali before the fight as if he were about to die. 'Maybe he can pull off a miracle', said Howard Cosell, the famous sports journalist. 'But against George Foreman, so young, so strong, so fearless? Against George Foreman who does away with his opponents one after the other in less than three rounds? It's hard for me to conjure with that.'

Legend had it that all boxers, no matter how strong or how big, seemed to shrink when they stood before Foreman. It was claimed that every one of his punches sent the trainer holding the punchbag flying into the air.

But still Ali repeated to anyone who would listen: 'I'm a speed demon! I'm a brain fighter! I'm scientific! I'm artistic! I plan my strategy! He's the bull, I'm the matador!' The author Norman Mailer, a great boxing fan, who attended the fight, stated that: '[E]very interview in that period [Ali]'d say "How is Foreman going to get near to me? I'm going to dance! I'm going to dance and dance! He'll look foolish trying to find me."'

In 1974 the boxing promoter Don King organized the fight with George Foreman to take place in Kinshasa, in Zaire (which became the Democratic Republic of the Congo in 1997). As soon as he arrived, Ali set the tone: 'I'm in Africa. In Africa I'm at home. To hell with America and its values. I live there, but blacks are coming to Africa. After 400 years of slavery, I'm coming home to fight one of my brothers.' He told reporters: 'It's a great feeling being in a country operated by black people. I wish all black people in America could see this. In America, we've been led to believe that we can't live without the white man, and all we know about Africa is jungles … I used to think Africans were savages. But now that I'm here, I've learned that many Africans are wiser than we are … [W]e in America are the savages.' He ran along the Congo River, followed by joyous kids, and shouted out: 'Foreman, you're too ugly! You don't represent us colored folks. These Africans make all of us ugly. Sucker, look at you!' Then he cried out: 'Ali, boma ye! That mean kill him!'

Foreman arrived in Kinshasa with a German shepherd, the type of dog that the Belgian colonists had used against the black population! For everyone in Kinshasa, Foreman represented America, the black man in a white mask. Ali was Zaire, Africa. Ali was the 'maroon'. He knew how to talk to black people. He gave them back their dignity.

He made one public declaration after another: 'I have a lot of things to do in the black neighborhoods, we have a lot of problems we have to solve among ourselves. Prostitution, dope, gang fights. Knowledge of self. Black people have no knowledge of themselves. We have been made just like white people mentally. White people have made us so much like them it's hard to teach them about themselves, it's hard to teach them to unite and marry and be with their own. Black people are now like white people, we have to re-brainwash them now, teach them about themselves and their history and language, to do something for themselves and quit begging white people for things they should do themselves.'

He hammered home the message: 'I'm gonna fight for the prestige, not for me but to uplift my little brothers who are sleeping on concrete floors today in America. Black people living on welfare, who can't eat, Black people who don't know no knowledge of themselves or no future. I wanna win my title and walk down the alleys with the wine-heads, walk with the dope addicts, the prostitutes. I could […] help uplift my people in Louisville, Kentucky; Indianapolis, Indiana; Cincinnati, Ohio…'

When Ali also mentioned that he wanted to build a hospital, Foreman, who had a dry sense of humour, quietly remarked: 'He already thinks he needs a hospital?'

The atmosphere in the run-up to the fight was like the movie

Gladiator. Photos of Mobuto Sese Seko, the bloodthirsty dictator of Zaire – the one who had one of my Black Stars, Patrice Lumumba, killed – were posted all around the city, his watchful eyes a constant reminder of state surveillance. Beneath the stadium, which had a capacity of 100,000 people, there was a prison in which 2,000 opposition figures, delinquents, and criminals were locked up. It was said that Mobutu had ordered one hundred of them, randomly chosen, to be executed.

On 30 October the fight began at 4 a.m. Zaire time, so that it could be aired at a reasonable hour on American television screens.

Norman Mailer described the unusual scene in Ali's dressing room, just before the fight. Everyone was downcast. His friends were sure that, given his pride, he would never throw in the towel and would take a hell of a beating. It was almost like Jesus's Last Supper. Suddenly Ali asked them, 'Why are you all so sad?' When no one answered, he shouted: 'I'm going to dance tonight! What am I going to do?'

'You're going to dance.'

'Yes, I'm going to dance and that man will be bewildered. I'm going to dance, dance!'

And they all started to cry.

As soon as he was in the ring, Ali shouted to the crowd: *'Ali, bomba ye!'* The bell rang. The fight began.

Ali moved around the ring, bouncing left and right. Foreman watched him. Ali threw a glancing right hook at Foreman's forehead. A watchful Foreman readied his left hook. He cornered Ali, and then struck him with a left uppercut. Ali tried to grab Foreman's head, then managed a straight right that stunned Foreman. But he didn't fall. In fact, he let fly with a flurry of punches. Ali received two blows to the head, then a hard right just below his heart. Foreman was punishing him.

The bell rang. The nightmare Ali had feared was taking shape. Foreman was stronger, and he wasn't afraid. Then Ali gathered himself and shouted to the crowd: *'Ali bomba ye!'* One hundred thousand people echoed: *'Ali bomba ye!'*

The second round... Everyone expected to see Ali dance, but instead he backed up against the ropes! 'They were waiting for the butterfly and they saw a snail taking refuge in the ropes, sitting on them, his two elbows protecting his stomach and liver, his gloves protecting his head', writes Alexis Philonenko.

A journalist compared him to a man 'leaning out of his window to see if there was something on the roof'. He didn't look as if he were even defending himself and seemed ready to give up. Being stuck on the ropes is almost like being laid out on the canvas for a boxer. At that point, many people thought that the fight had been rigged.

For the next two rounds, Ali never left the ropes. Every once in a while, he took advantage of the fact that they were so close together to tell Foreman – who was raining blows down on him and spinning him around as if he were at the top of a mast: 'Hit harder! Show me something, George. That don't hurt. I thought you were supposed to be bad.'

Foreman was furious. He threw punch after punch, almost dislocating his own shoulder.

By the middle of the fifth round, Foreman was exhausted. Ali chose this moment to hit Foreman with a combination, and then he landed a hook that rocked his opponent back on his heels.

In the sixth round, Foreman threw a powerful jab that missed its target. He tripped and fell into the ropes, which winded him.

The seventh round went by, and the eighth began. There were 30 seconds left. Ali struck with a right hook. Another flew over Foreman's shoulder and suddenly … the perfect combination! Foreman fell to the canvas. 'Two … three … four … five', the referee counted. On 'eight', Foreman tried to get up. 'Nine … ten!' Too late!

It was over. Muhammad Ali had won by a knockout!

Ali would fight 22 more bouts. In 1976, in Manila, he beat Joe Frazier once again. Then he lost his title but won it back. Finally, in the 1980s, his body betrayed him. He was diagnosed with Parkinson's disease. The champion didn't hide his condition: he showed it openly. He didn't pity himself. Instead he fought to outlive his body, just as he had fought to convince blacks to overcome their inferiority complex. In 1996, though sick, he was chosen to carry the flame into the Olympic Stadium in Atlanta. His country was finally paying tribute to him. He forced American society to question its anti-black racism. He transformed his media celebrity into a political force. If fame serves any purpose, then that is it.

The Man who Ran the Gauntlet

Tommie Smith

Born 6 June 1944

On 16 October 1968 Tommie Smith and John Carlos approached the podium in Mexico where they were due to receive their Olympic medals for the 200-metre race. They held their running shoes behind their backs and walked on the grass in black socks, a symbol of the poverty of black people.

Tommie Smith paused, then climbed to the top of the podium, and raised his arm in the air while the crowd applauded. In his left hand he was still holding his white shoe. A black glove covered his right hand, curled into a fist. He leaned forward to receive his medal, shook the official's hand, and then stood straight again. Peter Norman leaned in turn to receive his silver medal, then John Carlos the bronze. There was an announcement: 'First place and Olympic champion, Tommie Smith, United States, 19.8 seconds.' The crowd roared even louder.

The words of *The Star-Spangled Banner*, the US national anthem, rang out:

'Oh say can you see, by the dawn's early light...'

At that moment, Smith and Carlos held their gloved fists in the air and lowered their heads. Smith wore a scarf around his neck, Carlos a necklace – references to the lynching of black people.

'Oh, say does that star-spangled banner yet wave...'

As a sign of his support, Norman, the white Australian athlete, wore a badge from the Olympic Project for Human Rights (OPHR). Carlos and Smith were sharing the same pair of gloves.

'O'er the land of the free and the home of the brave!'

In the crowd, some booing began to be heard. It began to feel like a lynch mob. A voice laced with hatred cried out: 'Dirty nigger, you are going to die tomorrow at 2 p.m.!'

What was Tommie Smith thinking at that instant? He was probably thinking about his childhood. He saw himself working in the Texas fields with his father, at sunrise. He got to school at eight in the morning, got out at four, then worked in the fields until nightfall. He received a miserable wage, and the contempt of his white employers.

He thought about when he was a little boy. 'You should be proud to be American', he was told, 'because America is the greatest country on earth.' He sat in a corner and watched the whites live a life of ease. And he felt lost. He and his father were considered subhuman, but since he knew nothing else he thought this contempt was normal.

Was he proud to be on the podium? Of course. He had worked so hard to get there! The memories came flooding back: he left the fields for the University of San José after his last year of high school and, for three years, did nothing but read and study. Finally, he had come to understand many things that a good Negro should never have learned about. Culture, education, knowledge had liberated him and allowed him to judge the world in which he lived.

Since he was tall and strong – 6 feet 2 inches – he was recruited to the track and field team and trained relentlessly. In 1966 he smashed the world record for the 220-yard race, then the 4 x 400-metre relay with the US national team. In all, while he was at university, he broke 13 world records! Not only was he acknowledged as the best athlete in basketball and track for three years in a row, but he crowned all this with a Master's degree in sociology: a healthy mind in a healthy body.

In 1967, while still at San José, he was one of the founders of the Olympic Project for Human Rights, which sought to tackle discrimination in the United States, South Africa, and throughout the world. He travelled across the United States drawing attention to the problem of civil and human rights. For the first time in history, young black athletes were mobilizing around a great common cause.

Many white Americans responded with outrage. At the Olympic Games in 1968, as Tommie Smith and John Carlos stepped down from the podium, they were greeted with cries of rage. That a black man should bow his head during the national anthem and dare raise his fist was considered to be insane! The American people do not readily accept any perceived black slight on their national symbols: one day, forty years later, during his presidential campaign, Barack Obama forgot to put his hand on his heart, and there was a general outcry. That puts Smith and Carlos's actions into context...

Before he stepped on to the podium, Smith had a contract lined up for a major American football team. As he left the stadium, he knew he had lost everything. Everything but his self-respect, and the pride of having opened the eyes of black people and denounced racism.

They took his medals from him. He had sacrificed everything, even perhaps his life. He knew there was a risk he would not make it back alive to the US.

'But what if I, along with others, had not fought? What kind of life would I have lived?' he asked. 'My father didn't have the right to look a white man in the eyes. I couldn't tolerate that. I wanted to leave something behind, a visual symbol for white and black people. I felt that need very deeply.'

The historian Pascal Blanchard reminded me: 'Just imagine that, on that day, there could have been three black athletes on the podium! Roger Bambuck, the great French sprinter, had also agreed to raise his fist if he had finished amongst the medals. Unfortunately, he ended up in fifth place. The sheer magnitude of that symbolic gesture in Mexico would have been enormous! Blacks from Europe and America, their fists raised! A diaspora speaking with one voice...'

Tommie Smith was described as a 'rebel'. The same was said of Rosa Parks, Martin Luther King, Marcus Garvey, Malcolm X, and Gandhi. But they were simply individuals who, at a specific moment in time, forced people to question themselves. The sporting world often punishes such acts rather than lending its support. The president of the International Olympic Committee, Avery Brundage, ordered Smith and Carlos to be suspended from the US team and expelled from the Olympic village. In so doing, Brundage claimed to be respecting a 'certain Olympic spirit'. The famous phrase, 'The important thing is to participate', usually attributed to Baron Pierre de Coubertin, applies to everyone except 'Negroes'. In fact, the Baron de Coubertin was angered by the 'theory [...] of equal rights for all human races, [which] leads to a policy contrary to any colonial progress. Without including in even the most lenient form of serfdom, not to speak of slavery, the superior race is justified in refusing to extend several privileges of civilized life to the lower one.'

It is not a desire for justice that leads to an evolution in people's attitudes. Blacks were allowed to participate in the Olympic Games for the first time in Paris in 1924 because the Japanese wanted to be there. If the latter were accepted, then blacks would have to be accepted also. Admittedly, sports newspapers like *Miroir des sports* in France were angered: 'We should have separate competitions … It is an injustice for the "whites" who compete within the Olympic spirit.' But French politicians understood that they had a good chance of achieving a major haul of medals thanks to their 'blacks'.

Berlin, 1936. The Nazis were in power, the 'Aryan race' was celebrated. The purest examples of the white race were sure to dominate everyone else. But who walked away from the Olympic stadium with the gold medals in 100 metres, 200 metres, the 4 x 100-metre relay, and the long jump? Jesse Owens. A black man. It led to a furore at a time when, let us not forget, black people were considered to be inferior athletes.

Today, the most common form of racial prejudice leads to the assumption that blacks have greater athletic ability than whites.

One day, a politician asked me what I planned to do after I finished playing football. I told him I was planning to work on education against racism. I want to visit schools, I told him, and offer students a way of thinking about the phenomenon of racism, to ask them questions, lead discussion and listen to what they say.

'What kind of questions would you ask them?' he asked me.

'I'd ask what are blacks good at?'

'Sport, of course!' he responded spontaneously.

'You mean at swimming, ice skating, and skiing?'

'No, at running. Sprinting, for example. Only black runners make the finals.'

'Oh yeah? Is it because they are black that they run so fast?'

'Yes, thanks to their body type … Look at the Jamaicans. They walked off with all the gold medals at the Beijing Olympic games – the women too, in fact.'

'In the top universities, the overwhelming majority of students are white. Should we therefore conclude that whites are more intelligent than blacks? That would seem the logical conclusion of your argument…'

He stammered, tied himself up in knots, and couldn't find an answer. He had never thought to understand why it was Jamaicans who won at the Olympic Games and not Cameroonians or Senegalese. All the 'dark' people had become Jamaicans. Well, if he had gone a bit deeper into the subject, he would have discovered that, for a long time now, the Jamaican government has been strongly encouraging the practice of track and field in schools from a young age.

In 2004, at Saint-Ouen in France, a gymnasium named after Tommie Smith was opened. In 2005, at the university in San José, a statue representing him on the podium with John Carlos was unveiled. In the spot where Peter Norman, the silver medallist, was standing is a plaque inviting passersby to stand in his place to support their cause.

In August 2008 at the Beijing Olympic Games, Tommie Smith offered a birthday present to the Jamaican sprinter Usain Bolt, who won three medals: one of the shoes he had worn at the Olympic Games in 1968.

From Ten Thousand Days in Prison to ... the Presidency

Rolihlahla Nelson Mandela

18 July 1918–5 December 2013

I met Nelson Mandela in 1999, in Johannesburg, when I travelled there for a friendly match organized after our World Cup victory. I remember that at the hotel we were staying in some people couldn't believe we were the French team, simply because a large majority of us were black. We have to remember that the South African people had experienced colonization since 1838, the year the Zulu emperor Dingane was defeated at Blood River by the Boers; then, from the beginning of the twentieth century until 1993, they experienced segregation and apartheid, a policy of separate development for populations based on racial and ethnic criteria.

Rolihlahla Mandela was born late in the First World War, on 18 July 1918, in the village of Mvezo in the Transkei (Western Cape). He was part of the royal family of Thembus. His father was a counsellor to the king. His first name – this was certainly a premonition! – meant 'he who creates problems'. The English school in Healdtown imposed a more traditional name: Nelson.

His father died when he was 9. His mother placed him in the care of the regent of the Thembu people, who sent him to study in the only schools open to blacks, where he proved to be a brilliant student.

In January 1934 Mandela was 15, and went through his people's initiation ceremony. According to custom, circumcision made young men free and proud. In principle, anyway ... for the reality was quite different. The crude closing speech delivered by a chief shocked Mandela and made his blood run cold:

There sit our sons, young, healthy, and handsome, the flower of the Xhosa tribe, the pride of our nation. We have just circumcised them in a ritual that promised them manhood, but I am here to tell you that it is an empty, illusory promise, a promise that can never be fulfilled. For we Xhosas, and all black South Africans, are conquered people. We are slaves in our own country. We are tenants on our own soil. We have no strength, no power, no control over our own destiny in the land of our birth. They will go to cities where they will live in shacks and drink cheap alcohol all because we have no land to give them where they can prosper and multiply. They will cough their lungs out deep in the bowels of the white man's mines, destroying their health, never seeing the sun, so that the white man can live a life of unequalled prosperity. Among these young men are chiefs who will never rule because we have no power to govern ourselves; soldiers who will never fight for we have no weapons to fight with; scholars who will never teach because we have no place for them to study.

These words sowed a seed in the spirit of the young Mandela that never stopped growing. From then on he thought only of liberty, not only for himself but also for others, since liberation could only be collective.

Three years later, Mandela registered at the high school in Fort Beaufort, and then the university in Fort Hare, the only institution of higher learning open to blacks in South Africa. It was there that he met Oliver Tambo, who would later lead the African National Congress (ANC) in exile. Following the creation of the ANC in 1912 by tribal chiefs and intellectuals, it sought to protect the interests of the oppressed African population. Mandela's meeting with Tambo and other members of the movement proved decisive. From then on, Mandela was engaged in the struggle. Elected a member of the student representative council, he organized resistance against the white administration, which quickly got him expelled from the university.

He returned home: the regent wanted to force him into an arranged marriage. Mandela ran away to Johannesburg. A real estate agent named Walter Sisulu, who would also later become a leading player in the struggle against apartheid, hired him in one of the few law offices exempt from discrimination. There Mandela met members of the South African Communist Party, who were also fighting apartheid, and who sought to convert him to their cause.

But to reduce the problems of South Africa to a class struggle was to gravely neglect their racial dimensions. Almost all the oppressive laws passed since 1913 were concerned with colour.

In 1913 the Land Act deprived blacks of 87 per cent of their territory; the Urban Areas Act created shantytowns in order to furnish cheap labour for whites.

In 1926 the Colour Bar Act disqualified blacks from skilled jobs in the mines.

In 1936 the Representation of Natives Act removed the blacks in the Cape province from the main electoral list and placed them on a separate list. Their votes would be used to send three deputies, all white, to parliament.

In 1944, along with Walter Sisulu, Oliver Tambo, and Anton Lembede, Nelson Mandela founded the ANC Youth League, whose watchwords would be: African nationalism; the creation of a nation composed of different ethnic groups; the overthrow of white supremacy; and democracy.

Four years later, the 1948 elections augured a new stage in the history of South Africa. Against all expectations, the National Afrikaner Party won the elections, despite the fact that it had openly supported the Nazis during the Second World War. Its rallying cry, its credo, was *apartheid*, which meant 'separation'; its project, nothing less than the codification through law and regulations of the practices that had oppressed people of colour since the beginning of the century. It was a system that was 'diabolical in its details, inescapable in its objective and crushing in its power'. The fact the practices of exclusion were transformed into law made them even more rigid and extreme.

That day in 1999 when I shook Mandela's hand, I would have liked to ask him to explain to me how it was that apartheid was possible, one hundred years after the abolition of slavery in France and three years after the end of the Second World War. I still can't quite understand how Western countries, having defeated Nazism, could support a racist South Africa and didn't respond more forcefully to these 1948 laws! How did the apartheid system, which totally contradicted the principles of the United Nations, benefit from such 'complacency' on the part of Western states, whether France (with its Rights of Man), the Swiss (with its Red Cross), Great Britain (with its great principles), the United States ... and Israel!

In the weeks that followed the election of the Afrikaner Party, the government outlawed sexual relations between 'whites and non-whites', categorized Africans by ethnicity and colour, and created separate urban zones for each racial group.

Facing this overwhelmingly repressive machinery, the ANC expanded its support base as much as possible. The organization asked 200 white, black, Indian, and mixed-race organizations opposed to apartheid to join it. The ANC transformed itself into a 'mass organization' whose main objective was to set a vast mobilization campaign in motion. It planned non-violent actions that flouted the law. The time for a law-abiding approach was over. Facing measures that trampled on the rights of human beings, the ANC called for civil disobedience and non-cooperation, for boycotts and strikes.

Deaf to these calls, the Afrikaner National Party responded with a new law outlawing all 'communist' activities and all group meetings. It made it clear that any form of protest against the state would be considered criminal.

A series of non-violent mass protests, called the Campaign of Defiance, began on 26 June 1952. Those involved brought an enthusiasm, courage and a sense of history that mirrored the protests organized by Martin Luther King during the same period. On the morning of 26 June, 32 militants entered a train station through the entrance reserved for whites. They were immediately arrested. While being transported to prison, they sang hymns of liberty. Massive solidarity protests followed immediately. This level of cohesion seriously worried the government that had just instituted apartheid in order to divide people of different colour. In total, 8,500 demonstrators were imprisoned, and the repression hardened.

Mandela was arrested on 30 July 1952 with 20 other members of the ANC. They were sentenced to nineteen months of forced labour, but the sentence was suspended for two years because the judges – though fastidious and legalistic – concluded that their strategy was 'calm and avoided all forms of violence'.

In 1955 the ANC prepared the composition of the Freedom Charter. Questionnaires were circulated throughout the country: 'If you could make the laws ... what would you do? How would you set about making South Africa a happy place for all the people who live in it?' Thousands of responses were discussed and summarized. On 26 June the Freedom Charter was approved with great enthusiasm and remained a beacon throughout the struggle for liberation. The Charter envisioned a radical change in the political and economic structures of the country. In particular, it insisted that only the destruction of apartheid, which was the 'incarnation of injustice', could lead to positive change.

The authors of these demands could not remain free for long. On 5 December 1956 Mandela and almost all of the leaders of the ANC were arrested once again, this time accused of 'high treason'. The prosecution planned to prove that, with the assistance of foreign countries, they had engaged 'in a treasonable conspiracy, inspired by international Communism, to overthrow the South African State by violent means'. Although unfounded, this accusation was useful as a way of putting a brake on the support other countries might provide to the ANC, since it was the middle of the Cold War and the West was neurotic about the threat of communism.

But after four years of working through the files, thousands of pages of reports, the prosecution gave up and the judges, still as legalistic as before, released 155 of the accused. This verdict enraged the government, which decided to harden its response. From then on, only judges who would follow orders were appointed, and there would be no more of the 'legal niceties' that had protected the opposition.

The rise in violence, and the disdain for the law demonstrated by the Afrikaner National Party, led to international criticism of the regime. A few months before the verdict that released the members of the ANC, there was the tragedy at Sharpeville, south of Johannesburg. On 21 March 1960, 69 protesters were killed and 400 women and children wounded when they were demonstrating peacefully. The police fired without provocation into the crowd. This provoked an international reaction and protests broke out across the world; the Johannesburg stock market tumbled, there was a flight of capital from the country.

A state of emergency was declared. The ANC was banned but it refused to submit and went underground.

Is it possible for us to understand what going underground meant for a black person who had suffered under apartheid since they were born? In a sense, their day-to-day lives had, since childhood, been lived underground, their actions constantly walking the line between legality and illegality. As soon as they learned to talk, they understood the rules of daily self-defence. They learned quickly that they would never 'belong'. They knew that theirs was a separate existence, a life that ensnared them. They were rejected by the world, forced to lie to hide their feelings, condemned to play the innocent, to stay quiet, always mute with rage, always obliged to control their impulses and their words. Never trusting anyone, always on the lookout... In other words, a life underground.

After it had been outlawed as a political movement, the ANC was limited in the forms of action available to it, and it was forced to abandon non-violence. The organization reacted by creating an armed network, *Umkhonto we Sizwe*, 'The Spear of the Nation'. On 16 December 1961 a new ANC manifesto explained the change in tactics to the population: 'The time comes in the life of any nation when there remain only two choices: submit or fight. That time has now come to South Africa. We shall not submit and we have no choice but to hit back by all means within our power in defence of our people, our future and our freedom.'

Of course, this decision gave the oppressive government a trump card: in 1962 Mandela was arrested for calling for strike action and for leaving South Africa without a passport. His trial took place across October and November 1962 in Pretoria. From the beginning he sought to challenge a court entirely composed of white people: 'Why is it that in this courtroom I face a white magistrate, am confronted by a white prosecutor, and escorted into the dock by a white orderly? Can anyone honestly and seriously suggest that in this type of atmosphere the scales of justice are evenly balanced? ... I am a black man in a white man's court. This should not be.'

No argument would have saved him, however: the outcome of the trial had been decided in advance. On 7 November 1962 the jury found him guilty and he was sentenced to five years of forced labour. Seven months later, on 11 June 1963, with Mandela in prison, the political police raided the underground headquarters of the ANC at Rivona. There was a new trial and Mandela found himself in the dock alongside his comrades. They were all charged with sabotage and revolutionary conspiracy.

Mandela acknowledged that he was one of the founders of the *Umkhonto*. He admitted that he had resorted to sabotage 'as a result of a calm and sober assessment of the political situation'; that he had recruited experts in explosives, whose first mission was to attack government buildings in Johannesburg on 16 December 1961; that he had toured African states in 1962 to solicit the use of facilities to train soldiers; that he had studied all the techniques of war and revolution, from Clausewitz to 'Che' Guevara; that he had been influenced by Marxist thought just as Gandhi, Nehru, Nkrumah, and Nasser had been before him; and that he had himself received military training 'to be able to stand and fight with my people'.

The reason that conflict between whites and non-whites in South Africa did not end in a bloodbath is because the ANC – let us remember – had a leader like Mandela, who did everything possible to avoid a civil war, which often seemed the most likely outcome.

In all, six black men – Nelson Mandela, Walter Sisulu, Govan Mbeki, Raymond Mhlaba, Elias Motsoaledi, and Andrew Mlangeni – one Indian man – Ahmed Mohamed Kathrada – and one white man – Dennis Goldberg – were given life sentences in May 1964. Without international protest, including a resolution adopted by the General Assembly of the United Nations, they would have been sentenced to death. They were sent to prison on Robben Island, off Cape Town, the harshest outpost of the South African penitential system.

During the twenty-eight years he spent in prison, as detainee number 46664, Mandela managed to hold on to, and even to strengthen, his convictions. He wrote in his autobiography, *A Long Walk to Freedom*: 'I was now on the sidelines, but I also knew that I would not give up the fight. I was in a different and smaller arena, an arena for whom the only audience was ourselves and our oppressors. We regarded the struggle in prison as a microcosm of the struggle as a whole. We would fight inside as we had fought outside. The racism and repression were the same; I would simply have to fight on different terms.'

He also kept his 'optimism'. He knew the struggle was intensifying. In 1984 the anti-apartheid Archbishop Desmond Tutu received the Nobel Peace Prize; the South African government was subject to increasing international pressure, and little by little a number of nations began to impose economic sanctions on Pretoria.

It was thanks to international support that, after ten thousand days of forced labour, Mandela was freed on 11 February 1990 by order of Frederik De Klerk, who had replaced P. W. Botha as South African president in August 1989. As soon as this famous prisoner was released there was a global outpouring of enthusiasm. For the first six months, Mandela spent his time abroad. In Dar es Salaam, Tanzania, a crowd of half a million people welcomed him; in Cairo, the security services could not hold back the cheering crowds...

But Mandela didn't consider himself truly free: the struggle was not yet over, for violent atrocities were still a daily fact of life. While he continued to support armed struggle, he asked for the opening of negotiations; he repeated to the press that, as soon as the state ceased its use of violence the ANC would respond with peace.

When asked about the 'fear of the white minority', in the face of the new situation, he replied that in prison his anger towards whites had softened even as his hatred of the apartheid system grew. He insisted on the fact that he didn't want to destroy the country, and that his movement sought a middle ground between the fear of the whites and the hopes of the blacks.

Very quickly he clashed with President De Klerk, who made sure the negotiations dragged on, hoping that the euphoria surrounding Mandela's release would die down. The police opened fire on an ANC protest, killing 12, and De Klerk stoked the rivalry between partisans of opposing parties, inciting hatred between the Inkatha Party, a Zulu movement, and the ANC. In fact, a real war broke out between the two groups. Villages were burned, dozens killed, hundreds wounded, and there were thousands of refugees.

In reality, the negotiations between the National Party and the ANC had run aground on the democratic principle of 'one man, one vote'. The white authorities feared that the five million white South Africans would lose out to the 25 million 'non-whites'. So they attempted to dress up apartheid in a new guise: South Africa would no longer be divided between whites and 'non-whites' but between a multitude of communities: Xhosa, Zulu, Ndebele, Afrikaner, Anglophone... In the long term, they hoped to prevail over the black majority by attracting the Indians and mixed-race people to their camp.

But the economic sanctions imposed by the European Community and the United States were now devastating the economy. In addition, a tide of violence threatened to 'throw the whites into the ocean'. Finally, De Klerk gave in. After four years of negotiations, the first free elections in South African history finally took place. On 27 April 1994 Nelson Mandela was elected president of South Africa with 62.65 per cent of the vote. This date is now a holiday in South Africa: the 'Day of Liberty'. True to the promise he made during the negotiations, Mandela created a government of national unity comprising the ANC, the National Party, and the Inkhata Party. His two vice-presidents were Thabo Mbeki, of the ANC, and Frederik De Klerk, of the National Party.

In the final pages of his autobiography, Mandela writes: 'the oppressed and the oppressor alike are robbed of their humanity'. This profession of faith led him to create the Truth and Reconciliation Commission (TRC), whose mission was to investigate the crimes committed during apartheid. Monsignor Desmond Tutu was named president of the TRC. The goal was not to wipe the slate clean, but to offer amnesty to individuals in return for complete confessions. Essentially, this meant liberty in exchange for truth! On the judicial level, the results were mixed. As always, the small players, ordinary people – police, soldiers, citizens – confessed their crimes, but few higher-ups, least of all former president P. W. Botha, did the same. Botha was given a suspended sentence of one year in prison but, even then, he won his appeal.

Nevertheless this Truth and Reconciliation Commission saved South Africa from the risk of bloody confrontation and set an example for Africa. Mandela became a 'global icon of reconciliation'.

Forgiveness is important. But what about reparations for blacks who were despoiled from the beginning of colonization? Maybe I'm terribly naïve, but if someone steals from you and gets caught they have to give you back what they have taken. Is this simple kind of justice possible on the international stage? There is a worrying trend in world history. When slavery was abolished in the Antilles, the plantation owners were compensated by the state in return for the liberation of their slaves, but the slaves received nothing! What would have happened if Mandela had decided to take the land from the whites? Would Europe and the United States, which had accepted white domination over South Africa for so long, have accepted this? In 2009 Africans represented 79 per cent of the population, mixed-race people 8.9 per cent, Indians and Asians 2.5 per cent, and whites 9.6 per cent. The white minority, which enriched itself through the shameless exploitation of the blacks, own almost all of the economic riches of the country.

Is that justice?

Interplanetary Voyager

Cheick Modibo Diarra

Born 21 April 1952

> There are so many missed opportunities. Take that young girl sitting on the banks of the Niger River. She isn't going to school because, as chance would have it, she was born in a poor village. But she might also be the only one among the seven billion people on this planet with a mind capable of penetrating the secrets of H.I.V. or cancer.
>
> Cheick Modibo Diarra

At school, one of my sons was having trouble solving a geometry problem. He asked one of his friends to help him.

'It's no surprise that it's harder for you', the friend said.

'Why?'

'Because you're black!'

He was confused and upset when he came home and told me what had happened.

As luck would have it, my friend Cheick Modibo Diarra was due to come over for dinner that very evening. Recalling all of his achievements would be no easy task. Researcher at NASA, president of Microsoft in Africa and the Middle East, he has been in charge of several space missions, realising the dreams of many earthlings: the Magellan mission to Venus; the Ulysses spacecraft that embarked on a 17-year mission to study the sun; the Galileo spacecraft sent to Jupiter; and a whole series of missions to examine Mars: Mars Observer, Mars Pathfinder...

When my son told him about the exchange with his classmate, my friend, Cheick Modibo, explained to him that in all times, in all places, people of all backgrounds have contributed to humanity's achievements. He cited the names of many black scientists and researchers and added a few examples: the pyramids of Egypt, the gas mask, blood transfusions, the first open-heart surgery, the fastest calculator in the world, traffic lights, and the pencil sharpener...

My son's eyes opened wide.

Cheick Modibo Diarra's journey began in 1952, in Mali, in the small town of Nioro, eight years before the country's independence. His father was a clerk in the colonial administration. Many Westerners would describe Cheick Modibo's childhood as a very difficult one. But he experienced it as a very happy one: though his parents were poor, they were emotionally rich. Most importantly, they had solid values that helped make their son rock-like in his moral strength: you don't lie, you behave with righteousness and honesty, you give the best of yourself in your work.

Cheick Modibo was lucky to be raised by Binta, his father's second wife, who had a boundless love for him, and let him gain experience, putting no brakes on his sense of adventure. As a result, Cheick Modibo grew up without fear and with a desire to create. Throughout his life, he has always thrown himself into new adventures. And this woman who couldn't read or write gave him the gift of a kind of knowledge, the most important perhaps, which you can't learn at school. One day when he came home from school, proud of having received a very good grade, she congratulated him but then added:

'Did your classmates understand the lesson as well as you did? How much did you help them?'

Binta had never been to school, but she knew that individual success is a dead end. Malcolm X said that every time an individual proclaims he is the only one to have done this or that it means he hasn't done his work properly. You should never be alone at the summit. When you are alone, you are fragile.

At first, Binta's remark disturbed the young boy, but then it opened up a new path for him: that of collaboration, without which people cannot transmit anything, without which there would be no space mission exploring the stars. He got into the habit of explaining to his friends what they hadn't understood in class. Later on, working at NASA, he would learn how to collaborate with others, how to overcome the spirit of rivalry that drives all of us, to move beyond competition in order to sustain a collective project. What you gain from working in a context of rivalry, you lose a thousand times over in terms of effectiveness. 'Not to mention', he says, 'the risk of finding oneself marginalized.'

Though he knows how to share, Cheick Modibo is also used to taking responsibility. When he was 17 he became the head of his family. A tragedy turned his life and the lives of his kin upside down. There were two opposing political parties in Mali: that of the Marxist Modibo Keita, and another led by Fily Dabo Sissoko. Cheick Modibo's father was close to Sissoko. Having won power in many regions, Modibo Keita decided to reassign his adversaries to state jobs in locations hundreds of kilometres away. Cheick Modibo's father, who knew the relevant laws inside out, refused. Retaliation was not long in coming.

On 2 February 1959 Cheick Modibo Diarra heard shouting in the street. From the roof of a nearby farm hangar, where his family had just placed the harvest of millet, rice, and green beans, gasoline was dripping. The smell almost caused him to choke. Everything went up in flames. The family rushed out into the courtyard to escape the fire and smoke surrounding them, but stones were thrown at them to prevent them from fleeing. They were all trapped in the hangar that was about to become their funeral pyre when their attackers, turning their attention to the next target, took their eyes off them. That was their salvation. Moments later, the arsonists returned with policemen who put his father in handcuffs. Along with his brother, he was sentenced to ten years in prison for 'crimes against the State'.

Cheick Modibo's world collapsed. For the next ten years, he was never happy. Nor was his country. Basic goods were lacking, and the black market flourished. The Malian franc was devalued by 50 per cent.

His older brother, Sidi, had already left to study in France, so it was now his job to look after the family. During his school holidays, starting early in the morning, he not only cultivated the millet and rice fields with what was left of their seeds, but also used his intellectual abilities to allow him to make plans. He measured the length and breadth of the land he had to work and calculated its surface. Based on the size of the furrows, he calculated how many he had to dig with his ploughshare. He calculated how many hours he needed to complete his work, based on the time it took him to dig a single furrow.

How did a Malian turn out to be a born mathematician? Cheick Modibo told me: 'In France, when you are in love you don't count. In Mali, and in all poor countries, when you are in love you count, count again, and do a final tally, from dawn till dusk!'

Cheick Modibo Diarra wasn't satisfied with counting. His country was in ruins, his family decimated. He dreamed of transforming his environment, of leading his country out of poverty, of making life better, of building immensely complicated and modern machines! He discovered his vocation one day in high school when a teacher taught a lesson on electricity.

The teacher behaved oddly: as he was giving his lesson, he kept bouncing a lemon against the wall. Then he pierced the lemon with a copper rod and a zinc rod. He attached a small bulb to them, which immediately lit up! The 'lemon battery' fascinated Cheick Modibo: if he could understand the reactions of different elements, then he too would be able to create light, or achieve similar miracles.

From then on he had only one thing on his mind: he wanted to understand the workings of the world around him, and eventually the whole universe. He dismantled everything he could get his hands on: alarm clocks, radios, cameras, irons, motors, scooters, and then struggled to rebuild them...

In July 1969, the year he sat his final high school exams, Neil Armstrong and Buzz Aldrin walked on the moon. His teachers brought pictures of them to class. Cheick Modibo tried to understand the motives of these explorers: what had driven them to travel into the unknown?

He also identified with Galileo who, after having overturned the science of his era, ended up hounded by the Inquisition, forced to defend himself and to repeat: 'But it does move!' Yes, the Earth moves around the sun, the sun doesn't move around the Earth. Yes, every era has its inquisitors: they persecuted Galileo, and they locked up Cheick Modibo's father. His father, who taught him political and civic integrity. Cheick Modibo adopted his father's philosophy and extended it to his work as a scientist.

Having passed his baccalaureate, he hesitated between studying Classics in order to become a journalist or taking the preparatory classes for engineering school. In the end, it was the minister of education in Mali who made the decision: the country needed scientists more than men of letters.

After arriving in Paris in 1972, he studied mathematics, physics, and analytical mechanics at the Pierre and Marie Curie University, where he led the typically difficult life of African students. A young man used to the desert, to hills and woods, he suffocated in the constrained and cold space of the French capital. The rumbling of the metro replaced the sound of the cockerel. He had a hard time dealing with screeching brakes, the blandness of the unspiced food, and the mindset of professors who thought the identity of all foreigners could be reduced to something simple and transparent.

Analytical mechanics, which covers the basic principles of mechanics, bored him profoundly; as for the other subjects, he found them too theoretical. What was the point of solving Laplace's equations when Laplace had solved them in the eighteenth century? What he wanted to do was build machines. To discover unknown lands, open a path to the future.

In 1979 he pooled all his savings and left Paris for Howard University in Washington. He discovered a paradise. The university had been founded in 1866 to educate black pastors to tend to the four million slaves who had been freed from their chains the year before. Today, it welcomes 15,000 students from countries around the world. It attracts top-quality teaching staff and most importantly – this is its major asset – systems are studied in all their complexity and all of their possible applications are explored.

From January 1980 to May 1982, as he took courses in spatial mechanics, he wrote his Master's thesis on aerospace engineering, examining how to guide a satellite linked to a shuttle with a cable. He began the doctoral programme in mechanical engineering and wrote a thesis on the theory of space platforms. Having successfully completed his doctorate, he got the opportunity to apply his theoretical knowledge on the job when he was recruited by a headhunter from NASA. Cheick Modibo Diarra had earned the title of 'interplanetary navigator'.

He tells me: 'I build a probe, I put motors on it, I make it fly along the required trajectory, I position it where they ask me to … [W]hile I am flying the craft, astrophysicists ask me "Cheick Modibo, can you turn the probe so the camera can look in the right direction and take pictures?" And they observe what the stars are doing over here and over there…' He has the modesty of great researchers who know how much they still have to learn. An 'interplanetary navigator' is expected to have studied not only mechanical engineering but also spatial mechanics, astronomy, physics – among other fields – and to be able to combine all of them. You can count the number of people capable of doing this on two hands.

His first mission was on 4 May 1989: the destination was Venus, thanks to the Magellan space probe. But other planets were in their sights: Ulysses left for the sun, and Galileo – which travelled across space for 14 years – towards Jupiter. Sometimes the unexpected occurs: the Mars Observer never achieved its goal, which was to make an inventory of Mars. Contact with the probe was lost. It was the Mars Pathfinder which, a year later, after a journey of 497 million kilometres, landed on the red planet in 1997.

For Cheick Modibo Diarra, the key aim is to add to the sum of human knowledge, to bring the spark of humanity into space, and to know what distant worlds are made of. He is not interested in recognition for his personal achievements. He has his feet firmly on the ground and never forgets about the tragedy and injustice of our world. In 1999 he created the Pathfinder Foundation for Development and Education in Africa. In 2000 he organized the Forum on Education in Dakar. In 2002 he founded a research laboratory on solar energy in Bamako. He knows that energy, like education, is life, and the future. He founded the African Summit on Science and New Technology (SASNET), which has held several meetings in Africa (in Gabon and Mauritania) and supported various projects by African students.

In 2005 he was involved in the creation of the Global Francophone Digital University in order to offer real education where it is sorely lacking. On 20 February 2006 he was named head of Microsoft in Africa and the Middle East. Finally, he is a goodwill ambassador for UNESCO for Science and Technology.

'The greatest problem for Africa', says Cheick Modibo, 'is a lack of self-confidence. When we face a problem, we Africans always have a tendency to look for solutions outside of Africa rather than using our own creativity and ingenuity. Those solutions are costly and don't work. We have to move beyond "Afro-pessimism", give confidence back to all blacks, whether from Africa, the United States, the Caribbean, or Canada … We are equal to other peoples.'

The demographic explosion in Africa means that 60 per cent of the population is under 25. There are challenges to be confronted in the fields of energy, health, and infrastructure. People must be educated. 'Science is within everyone's reach', says Cheick Modibo. 'So many opportunities can be missed!'

The Voyager space probe, launched in 1976, has travelled through space for over forty years at a speed of 11 kilometres a second. About a decade ago, the technicians ordered it to turn around in order to take a 'family portrait' of the solar system. The photo speaks volumes: you can see the sun, Venus, Jupiter, Saturn, Uranus, and Neptune. But, at that distance, the Earth is insignificant.

'Look at the size of our minuscule solar system!' says Cheick Modibo. 'The galaxy has 200 billion suns like ours, and the planet Earth represents less than a grain of sand compared to the size of the cosmos. And yet human beings think they occupy a central position within the universe, and some even imagine that they alone constitute the universe.'

The Voice of the Voiceless

Mumia Abu-Jamal
Born 24 April 1954

> [I]t is possible for a single individual to defy
> the whole might of an unjust empire to save his
> honour, his religion, his soul.
>
> Mahatma Gandhi

The year was 1968. Thousands of young people demonstrated across the United States to demand the end of the war in Vietnam.

The same year, the young Mumia Abu-Jamal was 14 years old. He went to the stadium in Philadelphia along with three friends to protest against a rally held by George Wallace, a supporter of white supremacy and candidate for the presidency of the United States. They immediately found themselves drowning in a sea of white people; their Afros caused them to stand out even more. Spectators turned on them and, accompanied by a chorus of boos, they were pushed pushed towards the exit. Once outside, they were showered with blows. Mumia fell to the ground, and as he scrambled to his feet he cried out: 'Police! Help!' The sole response to his cries for help was a kick in the face from a man in uniform.

'I have been thankful to that faceless cop ever since, for he kicked me straight into the Black Panther Party.'

It is often said that this was the founding moment in the resistance of Mumia Abu-Jamal, the most famous death row prisoner in the United States.

In fact, Mumia had discovered the Black Panthers a few months earlier when a friend had shown him an issue of the newspaper, *The Black Panther*. He looked at the pictures of these armed black people, determined to defend themselves, to fight or die for the revolution. He was overwhelmed. Then he discovered Robin's bookstore, the first headquarters of the Black Panthers, where the books of Frantz Fanon, Malcolm X, Richard Wright, and many others were on display. He steeped himself in the writings of Harriet Tubman and Frederick Douglass. And those of Huey P. Newton: '[W]e have such a strong desire to live with hope and human dignity that existence without them is impossible.' But he also loved Nietzsche's philosophy, and would never repudiate it, despite decades of imprisonment on death row in SCI-Greene prison in Pennsylvania: 'He who fights with monsters should look to it that he himself does not become a monster. And when you gaze long into an abyss the abyss also gazes into you.'

What were the terrible events that led him to death row, and kept him there for thirty years, as in the days of the French monarchy and the *lettres de cachet*? What terrible crime could he have committed to deserve this kind of punishment in a 'democratic' country? First of all, it was down to the colour of his skin, and then also to his love of justice and truth. That resistance is written in his flesh. For many black people, the past is as present to them as their reflection in a mirror.

From the age of 14, even before being beaten up at the George Wallace rally, he had an FBI file because he had asked that his high school be renamed after Malcolm X. Then the Black Panthers put him in charge of their information section in Philadelphia. His political involvement meant that this very young man was considered a person 'to be arrested in a national emergency'. At that time, 40 per cent of the FBI's activity was devoted to spying on political militants, and only 1 per cent to organized crime.

The same year, he found work at a radio station where he denounced the corruption of the local police and politicians, as well as extreme poverty and lynching. The majority of those sentenced to death in America were African Americans, who only represented 15 per cent of the US population. When the murder victim was a white person the death penalty was applied 81 per cent of the time, but only 19 per cent of the time when the murder victim was black, Hispanic, Latino, or Asian.

Nicknamed the 'Voice of the Voiceless', he became a commentator on several radio stations and the news director for WHAT, a black radio station in Philadelphia. But Mumia was making waves, and too many people were getting wet. The politicians and the police grew to hate him. The exposure that he gave to the MOVE affair was, for them, the straw that broke the camel's back.

MOVE was a black community that believed that self-education would free them from the tawdry materialism of American society. They lived in great solidarity and they looked to Africa for inspiration: some considered the group to be a little bit nuts, while others described them as idealists. Founded by John Africa in the early 1970s, their objective was to oppose all injustices committed against humans, animals, and plants. But this existential attitude exasperated the authorities. These people refused to behave like 'good Negroes': they didn't shut up when you told them to; on the contrary, they defended their ideas and bombarded the authorities with their critiques.

The mayor of Philadelphia, an ex-policeman who used the slogan 'Vote white' in his election campaign, decided to beat them into submission. In 1977 his police increasingly used violence against the group. They didn't hesitate to beat a pregnant woman and put her in prison, or to throw another mother to the ground. Her three-year-old child died, his skull crushed.

Inevitably, Mumia Abu-Jamal interviewed those who witnessed these scenes, broadcast their statements on the radio, and wrote vitriolic commentaries denouncing violence and injustice.

The mayor of Philadelphia hardened his stance. On 16 March 1978 the community's main base and the four blocks around it were surrounded. It was now impossible to get food or supplies to the MOVE members. They were given 90 days to leave the premises. On 8 August, after officials determined the order had not been obeyed, bulldozers knocked down the fences, cranes smashed the windows, and 45 policemen entered the house. Men, women, and children were violently beaten, sometimes with the butts of rifles, and some were shot.

Suddenly, shots were fired from the roof of a neighbouring house. Policeman James Ramp was killed. An investigation revealed that it was one of his colleagues who shot him but that changed nothing. Nine members of MOVE were convicted and sentenced to a hundred years in prison and thirty years without parole! Once again, Mumia denounced this crime that seemed to belong to a time that black people had left behind. He reported on the case numerous times. The police exerted so much pressure that he lost his job at the radio station and found himself forced to drive a taxi at night. That was when everything changed.

To understand what happened, I have looked at the documents compiled by groups supporting Mumia, and spoken to Julia Wright, daughter of the writer Richard Wright, Mumia Abu-Jamal's spokesperson in France. Julia Wright supported the movements for independence in Africa, interviewing many key figures: Amilcar

Cabral, the pro-independence leader of Guinea-Bissau and Cape Verde; Agostino Neto, the father of Angolan independence; and Malcolm X. She accompanied Frantz Fanon's widow to the front line during the Biafran War (1967–70) and acted as an essential contact for the international branch of the Black Panther Party in France and Algeria.

Here are the facts: on the night of 9 December 1981, Mumia was driving his taxi. Searching for a fare, he drove past the intersection of Locus Street and 13th Street, as the bars were about to close.

He had just dropped off a passenger in West Philadelphia and was filling out his log when he heard screaming. He looked in his rear-view mirror and saw the revolving light of a police car. Nothing out of the ordinary in that neighbourhood. So he kept filling out the log. Then he heard shots. He looked in his rear-view mirror again and saw people running in all directions. Suddenly, he thought he recognized his brother William, 'staggering in the street'. He immediately opened his door and got out.

As he was crossing the street to help his brother, a uniformed policeman pointed his gun at him: a shot, a flash, and he found himself on his knees on the asphalt, seriously wounded in the stomach.

He closed his eyes, tried to breathe and fell unconscious. When he woke up, he was surrounded by a circle of police officers shouting at him, insulting him, and hitting him. Beyond the police officers he could see his brother: blood was running from his neck. He also saw a police officer lying on his back.

He was beaten some more, then thrown into a police van. A few hours passed. An officer opened the door, smacked him in the forehead and racially abused him.

Finally he was brought to a hospital where his initial 'treatment' involved being thrown to the ground and badly beaten. With blood filling his lungs, he couldn't speak.

The policeman who was killed was named Daniel Faulkner, and he was a member of the Fraternal Order of Police, a right-wing police union close to the Ku Klux Klan. Mumia was almost immediately accused of murdering him. When a black man is in the wrong place at the wrong time, he is automatically presumed guilty. In the Western imagination, a black person is often considered more suspicious than others. Among the Philadelphia police a rumour was circulating: it was time to correct the perceived 'injustice' that no Black Panther had ever been officially found guilty and given the death sentence.

In France some politicians claim that it is the 'blacks and Arabs who create problems'. They are always the prime suspects. In Eduardo Galeano's book *Upside Down: A Primer for a Looking Glass World*, I found a superb response to the cliché of the aggressive black person, the black delinquent: 'In the Americas and Europe the police hunt stereotypes guilty of earning an unconcealed fate. Every nonwhite suspect confirms the rule written in invisible ink in the depth of our collective conscience: crime is black or brown, or at least yellow. This demonization ignores history. Over the past five centuries, white crimes aren't hard to find.'

When my sons are shocked by statements about the alleged violence of black people, I sometimes suggest that they ask their interlocutors to think about history. Who massacred millions of Amerindians? Who uprooted millions of Africans and cast them into slavery? Who was responsible for colonization? Who sent 64 million people to their deaths during the two world wars? Who tortured and exterminated millions of Jews and Roma? Were blacks responsible for all these crimes?

When word went round that Judge Albert Sabo would handle Mumia Abu-Jamal's case, it was reasonable to assume that it was game over, for he was a life member of the Fraternal Order of Police and 99 per cent of the death sentences he handed down were for black people.

The investigation was botched. There was no ballistic evidence, bullets were impossible to identify, no fingerprints were taken, not to mention tampering with witnesses and the 'death' of a prostitute, an unreliable prosecution witness.

The case went to trial in 1982. The jury was mostly composed of white people who were fervent supporters of the death penalty ... and a lone black juror. Before the verdict was announced, a court stenographer heard Judge Sabo exclaim in his antechamber, 'I'm going to help them fry that nigger.' These details tally with an investigation carried out in the United States which showed that 68 per cent of those given the death penalty did not have a fair trial.

It is also important to know that this kind of trial costs a fortune. The poor often have to content themselves with the worst state-appointed defenders. As the Muslim preacher Robert Muhammad puts it: 'across the United States it is better to be rich and guilty, than to be poor and innocent'. (Mumia's legal fees have cost more than a million dollars to the various committees set up to support him.)

On 3 July 1982 Mumia Abu-Jamal was sentenced to death.

Three years later, with Mumia on death row, the MOVE community suffered more misery. On 13 May 1985 the new 'first black mayor' of Philadelphia prepared a final attack to put an end to the demonstrations in support of the 'MOVE 9'. The assault was launched. 15,000 bullets were fired into the house. A military C4 explosive, illegally supplied by the FBI, was dropped from a helicopter on to the roof. The explosion started a fire that burned 60 surrounding houses. In the rubble were six adults, including John Africa, and five children.

Five years went by.

Some of the witnesses who had been coerced by the police retracted their statements. For example, a prostitute admitted to having lied; she had previous convictions and was facing a suspended sentence, so she was threatened with never being able to see her daughter again if she testified in favour of Mumia. His lawyer asked for a new trial. But the Philadelphia Supreme Court, rather than judging the affair anew, avoided the question, declaring that this proof had arrived 'too late'.

Since it was not possible to have a new trial based on the facts, was it at least possible to show that it had been 'stained by racism'? A year later, the Supreme Court of Philadelphia recognized that there had been elements of racism, but passed on the final decision to the Supreme Court of the United States. And it was the US Supreme Court that ultimately ruled out a new trial. A new law had just been introduced that sought to demonstrate the effectiveness of the death penalty and counterterrorism, and its provisions included various requirements regarding the nature of proof of innocence.

So, Mumia continued his life on death row, which was punctuated by successive judicial decisions that his execution should proceed; each time they were overturned as a result of the international wave of protest initiated in France by Julia Wright: she contacted groups that traditionally supported the struggle of African Americans such as the Movement Against Racism and for Friendship between Peoples (MRAP) and the League for the Rights of Man.

A federal court finally overturned Mumia's death sentence in 2011 but he remains in prison on a life sentence. Mumia identifies as black in a white America with a two-track system. His case is an indictment of the US justice system, revealing its dysfunction. He is its bad conscience. So the easiest thing is to leave him behind bars.

But he continues the mental struggle against his incarceration. All those who visit him are captivated. His spirit is totally free.

He is a very acute observer of the political situation, even though he only has access to the information the prison allows him to see. He reads, writes, works, and, each week, speaks on the radio via telephone.

While on death row, his living conditions were deplorable. 'Imagine living, eating, sleeping, relieving oneself, daydreaming, weeping – but mostly waiting, in a room about the size of your bathroom … Imagine waiting – waiting – waiting – to die.'

And imagine being locked up for thirty years in that tiny cell 23 hours during the week, and 24 hours a day at the weekend. Mumia calls this the 'American way of death'.

The Emotional Truth of Rap

Tupac Amaru Shakur

16 June 1971–13 September 1996

'Tupac the son of the Black Panther and Tupac the rider. Those are the two people inside of me. I was raised off those ideals.' This is what Tupac Amaru Shakur, also known as Pac or 2Pac, declared a few weeks before his death. For this man had two personalities: angel and demon. On the one hand, he studied classical dance and wrote moving songs like 'Dear Mama':

> There are no words that can express how I feel
> You never kept a secret, always stayed real
> And I appreciate, how you raised me
> And all the extra love that you gave me
> I wish I could take the pain away

On the other hand, he was also a hothead who wrote songs brimming with hate!

2Pac was born in New York. It was his mother, a member of the Black Panthers, who called him Tupac Amaru, after the Quechua Inca chief who rebelled against the Spanish in the sixteenth century. As a teenager he was always in the street and hung out with traffickers of all kinds. He lived in one of those neighbourhoods where at the age of 10 you were more likely to be in a gang than to go to school; and if you aren't dead by the age of 20 that means you are rotting in prison.

I spoke with Oliver Cachin, a specialist in urban music, who cited for me a few verses from 'Message', a rap by E. D. Fletcher:

> A child is born with no state of mind
> Blind to the ways of mankind

God is smilin' on you but he's frownin' too
Because only God knows what you'll go through
You'll grow in the ghetto livin' second-rate
And your eyes will sing a song called deep hate
The places you play and where you stay
Looks like one great big alleyway
You'll admire all the number-book takers
Thugs, pimps and pushers and the big money-makers
Drivin' big cars, spendin' twenties and tens
And you'll wanna grow up to be just like them, huh

2Pac's violence, and that of his music, is a reflection of the world in which he lived. We know what life in the ghetto is. It's hard to be a woman there, hard to be different, hard to be black. The black person in the ghetto has to measure up to the expectations of the black community and earn its respect, while also measuring oneself against the white community for whom black life is almost invisible. To be black, a woman, to be different is always hard, but here life offers even less hope. There is nothing over the rainbow, dreams seem to be outlawed:

Black is black, not blue or purple
Bein' black is like a circle...
Listen to me if you will...
Reality is what is real
Reality is black is black
('Jungle Brothers')

Rap puts this daily struggle into words, and it disturbs people. It shines a light on shadowy corners that people don't want to know about, on people society wishes were invisible and mute. Rap goes straight for the target, it has a 'photographic eye', and provides a raw portrait of reality. It tells the story of the ghetto first hand and with a primal intensity. It speaks about life in the projects, family, what's going on in the rapper's head...

My brother's doin' bad, stole my mother's TV
Says she watches too much, it's just not healthy...
Rats in the front room, roaches in the back
Junkies in the alley with a baseball bat...
Don't push me cause I'm close to the edge
I'm trying not to lose my head

What frightens people about rappers is that they are telling their own stories. Right-minded people don't like 'that type of person' getting the chance to speak.

In 1990 2Pac was 19. He met Shock-G, alias Humpty Hum, the leader of the group Digital Underground. This Oakland band hired him as a dancer and sound technician. In the spring of 1991 he released his first album, *2Pacalypse Now*. He had found the path he wanted to follow.

At the time music wasn't interested in social conditions for black people. It was as though there were no longer any problems in the ghetto. But 2Pac had been made politically aware by his parents. He had not forgotten the lessons he had learned from them, he knew instinctively that he would be the voice of rebellion, the defender of black consciousness. The Black Panthers had been decimated. But he would speak out.

Rap would allow this oppressed people to once again illustrate the famous statement uttered by Jesse Jackson in 1970: 'I am somebody.' They could lift up their heads and rediscover their pride:

I may be unemployed, but I am Somebody.
I may not be very educated, but I am Somebody.
I might be in prison, but I am Somebody.

We exist, the rappers say, not because you have allowed us to, or because you have given us a role as watermelon eaters; *we are somebody* because we have created our own 'black' thing.

In reaction to the cultural invisibility of black people, a ghetto identity was created that we now call hip-hop culture. Working entirely by themselves, the creators of hip-hop forged, not a counter-culture, but a parallel culture that gives their lives meaning, that proves to them that what they are thinking can be shared. They would make their own culture for themselves: that's hip-hop. All of the component parts are equal: dance, with break-dancing or *smurf* (from the Smurf hat that they wear pressed down on their heads); rap, with a DJ who creates sound by mixing existing records, and the MC (master of ceremonies) who takes the mic; graffiti and word battles, voice percussion, slam, Kangol hats, hoods, outsized jogging pants and high-top basketball shoes; a language, too, with its own expressions, new rhythms; a way of walking...

This all took shape little by little. The constant factor in rap is a rhythm that inspires the singer and carries the song; and it's the vocal presence of the song, the text. DJs saw that what drove people mad were 30-second sections followed by wicked breaks. They had the idea of putting the same record on two different turntables and, moving from one to the other, playing the break over and over again.

France is the second homeland for hip-hop. How is that possible? How did an entire generation of young people who really didn't speak English that well become so passionate about an art form built primarily around words? How did rap *made in black* come to fascinate the thirty different nationalities living in France's housing projects, a fascination that led to the creation of their own version of rap? How is it that, twenty years later, this music became even more firmly rooted despite its exclusion from radio and television channels?

Well, it's simple. In general, a young resident of France's housing projects, whose family had been in France for three generations, was as alienated and rejected as a black person in the United States in the 1990s. That young person would watch television, looking for himself. Where was he? Nowhere.

When you read and listen to the media you get the impression that all the problems come from the housing projects and that if they didn't exist we would all live in a paradise.

The adolescence of some young people in the projects is a nightmare in which they discover racism. And it is no longer just words or images on television, but rather real doors closing, being stopped and asked for their identity papers. When they are 14 or 15, whenever they pass a police car it slows down. The police stare at them. Every second time, they are stopped and asked for their identity papers. For kids who are the children or grandchildren of immigrants, their entry into adult life is marked by an encounter with the police. This is the welcome society gives them: 'Give me your papers!'

Many young people in the projects are even more tortured by issues of identity because they are disconnected from their origins. They don't fit into the 'immigrant' box but they aren't placed in the 'French' box either, just in the 'projects' box. Their demand is: 'Respect us!' Their obsession is to make some cash just so they can exist.

In this state of limbo, they feel closer to a young person in Harlem, Brooklyn, or South Los Angeles than they do to any of their neighbours in the centre of the city. Any sense of unity comes from the American culture of hip-hop, particularly rap.

Rap culture is clearly a war to assert one's existence. In contrast to the 'rock attitude' – with its revolt against the adult world – rap is a separate world. The point is not to make music or sing, but to shout out who you are: individuals who have nothing, a third world imported into the world of the rich, a third world whose parents weren't respected and still aren't, a third world whose colour disturbs, where the number 93 (in reference to the Seine-Saint Denis department, north-east of Paris) scares people, a world reduced to burned-out cars, drug trafficking, and gang rapes. A world seen as an 'internal enemy'.

Ultimately, it is words that rap offers to young people. Rappers are the news reporters of the projects. We must listen to them. Rap relieves the tension of the projects. An intelligent cultural policy would be open to rap music.

It is true that rap culture is experienced as aggressive and violent by the rest of society. But have people really listened to the lyrics? Those who live with injustice are best placed to restore order. We have to listen to them, even if their harsh questioning of society is disturbing.

This generation doesn't recognize itself in the image of the submissive immigrant of the 1960s. These young people are no longer immigrants. They are French, but no one wants to hear that. The first wave of rappers – NTM, MC Solaar, IAM, and then Lunatic Booba, Sefyu, among others – gave their neighbourhoods an identity. They are, as NTM put it, the 'loudspeakers' of an entire generation because behind any rap group there is a neighbourhood.

The first French rappers followed their predecessors from the ghettos of New York and rapped about their own reality. We're going to talk about what's happening in Sarcelles, Bobigny, Vitry, Lyon, Marseille, or Rouen. Each story is different because it's both always the same and never the same situation. In contrast to the United States where people of different origins are grouped into neighbourhoods and communities, in France they live side by side. This is a richness that we find in rap groups that bring together young people of Senegalese, Malagasy, Spanish, Italian, and Marseillais backgrounds. It is not a rap that emerges from a particular ghetto, but a rap that is created by a constellation of groups or networks. The words of the excluded who have decided they want to be heard.

The kid from the projects who discovers this world naturally recognizes himself in it. In order to rap you don't need to have studied music theory, you just need a way with words so as not lose face in a rap battle.

Some high-minded people, both secular and religious, have criticized rap lyrics. They have sought to censure them, claiming they incite people to all kinds of hatred. They should read the great foundational literary texts: Genesis, *The Odyssey*, Shakespeare's plays, which are often extremely violent. Do we really think that artists act on all of their poetic declarations in their real lives? Didn't the pacifist poet André Breton declare that 'the simplest surrealist act consists of dashing down the street, pistol in hand, and firing blindly, as fast as you can pull the trigger, into the crowd'? We need to understand the role of fiction and dramatization in rap. It is a music filled with symbols that illustrate lives filled with rage. A music marked by coded 'exploits'. Muhammad Ali was the king of the poetic tradition of the boast: 'Last night I cut the light off in my bedroom, hit the switch and was in the bed before the room was dark', he liked to say.

Rap is the culture of words. First off, in the dirty dozen, where teens insult one another over a predefined rhythm and where humour is king; then come the rap battles in which they compete with each other. The goal is to humiliate the other as a way of showing you exist. The experience of suffering incites a virile defensiveness. No one wants me, but I'm going to make my mark. That is why the language is always outrageous.

The charisma of 2Pac, his imagination, his flow, his carefully crafted words made him an icon when he was alive. He was obsessed with productivity, always in the studio writing track after track. He worked with a sense of urgency and never lingered over a song. The voices were recorded in one take. He couldn't stand technicians who spent hours on the sound of a drum. That is how he made six albums in five years (with 15 others appearing after his death).

But 2Pac was at war with the universe and soon he ran into problems with the law.

In 1992, at the age of 21, he was arrested after an altercation that led to an exchange of gunfire, but then released.

In 1993 he acted in the film *Menace II Society*. He attacked the director and was sentenced to fifteen days in prison. In October of the same year he was accused of having shot at two police officers. But the legal proceedings were dropped.

On 30 November 1994 two individuals shot at him as he was recording in a New York studio.

Three months later, on 7 February 1995, he was sentenced to four and a half years in prison for sexual assault. His third album, *Me Against the World*, was released while he was incarcerated. It went straight to the top of the charts. Still behind bars, he accused the Notorious B.I.G., who had become a deadly rival, along with Puffy

Combs, Andre Harrel, and his own friend Randy 'Stretch' Walker, of having arranged the attempt on his life in New York.

On 30 November 1995, exactly a year after the murder attempt, Walker was killed in Queens.

'I talk about my shooting in New York', 2Pac explained in an interview about his latest record *Makaveli*, 'I give the names of the niggers who shot at me, of those who betrayed me ... Everything I can't say, I say in my raps.'

> Busters shot me five times, real niggaz don't die, Can ya hear me?
> Laced with this game, I know you fear me
> Spit the secret to war, so cowards fear me
> My only fear of death is reincarnation
> Heart of a solider with a brain to teach your whole nation
> And feelin no more pain
>
> ('No More Pain')

The war was fought through the music, except that after the music came reality.

A Californian version of rap known as 'Gangsta Rap' began to emerge in the 1980s. 'For the first time in a long while', Olivier Cachin told me, 'artists led their audience into the fires of hell, the urban ghetto where violence reigned supreme.'

2Pac was released from prison after eight months, in October 1995, thanks to Marion 'Suge' Knight of Death Row Records, who posted a 1.4 million dollar bond! As in Brian de Palma's movie *Phantom in Paradise*, 2Pac had made a pact with the devil. Death Row Records had the worst reputation of any record label. One of the many slogans that made this song factory notorious was this one: 'No one leaves this label alive.' It was meant to be taken seriously.

Marion 'Suge' Knight was the stooge of Michael Harris, a gangster sentenced to twenty-eight years in prison. For three years, he somehow held together the utopia of this 'Gangsta Rap' label. He was the one who transformed 2Pac into an icon of West Coast rap, in a violent conflict against those of the East Coast. It was a role the rapper played to its tragic and logical conclusion. The 'Gangsta Rap' artist became a 'badman' who didn't fear any of the consequences of his violence. The album titles make this clear: *Me Against the World*, to which Notorious B.I.G. responded with *Ready to Die*. They left the symbolism of words behind and moved into the world of action. Reality overtook the imagination.

2Pac threw himself frenetically into recording a monumental work in the form of a double CD: *All Eyez on Me*. As if on a mission, more and more megalomaniacal and messianic, soaked in alcohol and weed, he wrote and produced dozens of tracks in a few months.

On 7 September 1996, returning from a boxing match between Mike Tyson and Bruce Seldon at the MGM Grand in Las Vegas in a car with Marion 'Suge' Knight, he was shot seven times in the chest, the pelvis, the arms, the thigh, and the lung.

Some said there had been a violent altercation with another guy during the boxing match. Others saw this as vengeance by the Notorious B.I.G. Still others floated the usual theory of a conspiracy by the FBI. But it is more likely that this settling of scores was a conflict within the circle of rappers, a world in which everything that was built up was then destroyed.

Everything was set for the creation of a legend.

2Pac stayed in a coma for six days and died on the seventh, Friday the 13th, at the age of 25. Eight weeks after his death his record *Makaveli* was released. It was called *Makaveli* because, when he was reading *The Prince* by Machiavelli, he came across the passage where the author writes that to trick one's enemy one should fake one's own death.

That is why some people think that 2Pac is still alive…

The Star of Hope

Barack Hussein Obama

Born 4 August 1961

On this day, we gather because we have chosen
hope over fear.

> Barack Obama, inaugural address,
> 20 January 2009

'Lilian, it's wonderful, I never would have thought it possible!' my
mother told me after having watched the inauguration of Barack
Obama to the presidency of the United States on 20 January 2009.
My sons, meanwhile, were just surprised that there had never been
a black president of the United States before then. As for me, I was
very happy and relieved. I told myself that his election would change
the way in which many people think about race, and would give
great encouragement to those seeking to use education to combat
racism.

Obama's first two stars were his parents. His mother, Anne Dunham,
had Irish, Scottish, and Cherokee ancestors. '[M]y mother was
white as milk', he writes in *Dreams from My Father*. She came from
a humble family in Kansas that sought a more forgiving way of life
by moving to Hawaii. A free spirit, a 'progressive humanist', she
fell in love with the handsome, tall, and intelligent Barack Hussein
Obama Sr. He belonged to the Luo ethnic group from Kenya.
After successfully completing his studies in Nairobi, he went to
study economics at the University of Hawaii, where he was the first
African student.

Barack Obama's parents were married in 1960. This was the
first miracle, since mixed marriage was still considered a crime in
half of the states in the US. 'In many parts of the South, my father
could have been strung up a tree for merely looking at my mother

the wrong way', writes Obama. Not long before, in 1958, a couple, Richard and Mildred Loving, had been sentenced to a year in prison by a judge in Virginia. The couple were undaunted, and they began a series of trials that led, in June 1967, to the overturning of the verdict by the Supreme Court. There is something magical about this story given that the husband was named Loving and that the judgment that ended the ban on mixed marriage in Virginia was poetically called *Loving* vs *Virginia*. But several decades later, attempts at discrimination continue. In October 2009, in Louisiana, a justice of the peace refused to marry an interracial couple on the pretext that he didn't want 'to put children in a situation they didn't bring on themselves'.

Barack Hussein Obama Jr was born in Honolulu in 1961. Two years later his parents separated. Having received his economics degree in August 1963 at the prestigious Harvard University, his father returned alone to Kenya where a government position was waiting for him. A while later, his mother remarried with an Indonesian student, Lolo Soetoro, and in 1967 moved to Djakarta. It was there that Maya, Obama's half-sister, was born. Little 'Barry' adapted quickly, learned Indonesian, had kite battles, tasted grilled snake and grasshopper, but also discovered the extreme poverty of the peasantry and the extent of the inequality between Americans and Indonesians.

When he was 10 he returned to Hawaii to get an American-style education. He was welcomed by his maternal grandparents, who sent him to the best school on the island. It was there that Barry discovered his colour. Even though Hawaii was the most racially mixed place in the United States, his classmates saw him as black and were sometimes hostile to him.

At Christmas 1971, for the first time in many years – and the last – he met his father, who later, after various misfortunes in Kenya, died in a car crash in 1982. Over the course of a few days, his father showed him some dance steps, took him to a jazz concert, gave him a basketball and two records of African music – all symbols of an African-American culture that he hoped his son would connect with.

But the young Barry had a difficult time finding his bearings, torn between the whiteness of his mother and the blackness of his father, between parents who had loved one another but then separated; lost in a society where white and black were locked in confrontation. Incapable of doing otherwise, he sought to assert his identity, and in the process became a nasty kid, a *bad Negro* – or at least a caricature of one. With Ray, his closest black friend, he constantly repeated the insults whites directed at them and talked about the need to revolt. But this talk did not make him feel more secure in his identity; instead it made Barack Obama feel more fragile. For he knew that his white mother had no colour prejudice, and he deeply loved his grandparents despite their 'ordinary racism'.

Searching for an identity, he sought to find himself in others: Frederick Douglass, who five years after the abolition of slavery had been a candidate for president of the United States; the pan-Africanists Marcus Garvey and W. E. B. DuBois, who exhorted blacks to show themselves proud of both their colour and the civilization of their ancestors. He read the works of modern African-American authors such as Richard Wright, who denounced racist America, Langston Hughes, the poet of black pride, and Ralph Ellison, who wrote: 'I am not ashamed of my grandparents for having been slaves. I am only ashamed of myself for having at one time been ashamed.'

He particularly identified with Malcolm X, embracing his sense of revolt and his search for identity. Like Malcolm, he tried to reconcile the two parts of himself, seeking to be as black and as American as Malcolm had been. And, of course, he revered the pastor Martin Luther King, Jr, for the sharpness of his mind and his pragmatism.

Without Douglass, DuBois, King, Malcolm X, the Harlem Renaissance led by writers and musicians, without the Civil Rights movement, black theology, the black feminist movement, postcolonial criticism, without all these predecessors, Obama would never have been able to develop his profound sense of self, never mind become president.

After high school he studied at Occidental College in California where he discovered grassroots politics thanks to feminist and Marxist friends, who were inspired by the Black Panthers. These women and men fought white racism through acts of solidarity, creating 'liberation schools', educating people about black culture, helping young people get to university, making sure black people in custody knew their rights... These activities contradicted the hypermilitarized images of black people in the media. They were, in fact, pacifists, although still ready to defend themselves. Obama came to see their social engagement as a star that would light his own path.

His militancy gave him renewed confidence in himself, enough that he abandoned the name 'Barry' his father had saddled him with 'because it would go down better in the United States'. He reclaimed his real first name, Barack, which is African and means 'blessed' in Swahili.

In the autumn of 1981 he went to Columbia University in New York, from which he graduated with a diploma in political science two years later. Rather than accepting a comfortable career in a private company, he decided to participate in the struggle for civil rights as a community organizer. 'There's nothing wrong with making money', he wrote, 'but focusing your life solely on making a buck shows a poverty of ambition.' For three years, in Chicago, he worked with residents in poor neighbourhoods blighted by unemployment, organizing meetings, fighting to prevent delinquency, and taking up countless other causes. But he realized that he could spend his entire life as a neighbourhood activist and never resolve Chicago's problems. He came to understand that if he wanted to be useful he needed to get a broader perspective and analyse how the system functioned. This led him to study for a diploma in constitutional law from Harvard. Then, taking after his mother's free spirit and her humanism, he worked in a law office that specialized in the defence of civil rights.

He did not lack ambition: what was to come would prove that. But would he have reached the heights he did if he had not met Michelle Robinson? Michelle was a lawyer from a working-class family. Like Barack, she had turned down a well-paid position in commercial law and instead committed herself to the struggle for civil rights. Their complementary personalities saw Barack Obama's career take off. In 1996 he was elected to the State Senate of Illinois, where he excelled. Following the example of Martin Luther King, he preferred accumulating small victories rather than wading into huge battles he could never win. He succeeded in amending several Republican legal projects, and passed 26 bills including medical coverage for the poorest, the right to education for young children, and requiring video recording of interrogations of individuals suspected of crimes.

Conviction and courage: he had plenty of both. In 2002 he refused to support the invasion of Iraq. It was 'a dumb war', he said, 'based not on reason but on passion'. In 2003 he announced his candidacy for the United States Senate. The House of Representatives and the Senate together form the organ of legislative power in the United States, known as Congress. Obama won the seat on 2 November 2004 with 70 per cent of the vote! It was the most resounding victory in the history of the US Senate, so much so that the cover of *Time* magazine called him 'The Next President'. He was one of the few black people to hold a senatorial seat, following on from Carol Moseley-Braun, the only black senator from 1992 to 1998. Taking advantage of his prominence, he wrote a book whose royalties allowed him to pay off his student debt, buy a house, and continue his irresistible rise.

On 10 February 2007 he announced he was running to become the Democratic presidential candidate. During the primaries he confronted the formidable Hillary Clinton. Feeling threatened, she resorted to gutter politics, which resulted in her losing support: suggesting that Obama identified with Martin Luther King, she denigrated the pastor's civil rights activism; she made remarks about the 'Muslim origins of Barack Hussein Obama'; and made allusions to his supposed links to the Islamist currents responsible for the 11 September attacks. As Obama has always said, his father was indeed of Muslim background, but an atheist; as for his mother, she believed in moral principles like honesty and respect for others, which are found in all well-established religions. In this vile campaign, the gloves were off. During the primary in Mississippi, Clinton's ally Geraldine Ferraro declared: 'If Obama was a white man, he would not be in this position. And if he was a woman of any color, he would not be in this position. He happens to be very lucky to be who he is.'

His adversaries were bound by their belief in the opposition between black and white and in their sexism. Obama didn't make the same mistake. Loyal to the spirit of Frantz Fanon – 'The Negro is not, any more than the White' – he refused to let himself be defined solely by his colour. 'You shouldn't vote for someone because they look like you', he told Americans during his campaign.

Most Western observers believed that the fact that Obama was of mixed background was an advantage for him. In reality he was always either too black or not black enough. As his father was Kenyan, he wasn't a descendant of slaves and certain African Americans didn't think of him as one of their own. To be a real African American, don't you need slave ancestors? Obama had to remind them that DuBois had a Haitian father, that Malcolm X was a first-generation immigrant, and that King's role model was Mahatma Gandhi.

Finally, after a tight race, Obama beat Clinton and, from then on, focused on his battle with the Republican candidate John McCain. His campaign was the most effective electoral machine in the history of the United States: the best financed, the best media plan, and probably the most intelligent.

Certainly the economic crisis helped him, but only because Obama understood its causes. When Hurricane Katrina hit in September 2005, killing more than 2,000 people and leaving the black population to fend for itself, many accused President Bush of a weak response because the victims were black. Obama declared, however, that the 'government was color-blind in its incompetence'. It was a remarkable response, which widened the debate to the general irresponsibility of the Republican administration, and showed that the deprived of all colours shared a similar fate.

His candidacy was focused on reconciliation. 'Contrary to the claims of some of my critics, black and white, I have never been so naïve as to believe that we can get beyond our racial divisions in a single election cycle, or with a single candidacy – particularly a candidacy as imperfect as my own', he declared in his famous Philadelphia speech on 18 March 2008. 'But I have asserted a firm conviction ... that working together we can move beyond some of our old racial wounds, and that in fact we have no choice if we are to continue on the path of a more perfect union. For the African-American community, that path means embracing the burdens of our past without becoming victims of our past. It means continuing to insist on a full measure of justice in every aspect of American life.'

Obama was an exceptional orator, but he never lapsed into clichéd gestures or the familiar intonations of the African-American Baptist pastors. But nor did he seek to hide the colour of his skin. He was a man cultivated enough to be humble and surround himself with good advisors.

In response to the 'country first' platform of John McCain – a former military pilot, hero of the Vietnam War – who accused him of being the 'foreigner's candidate', Obama replied that, thanks to his diverse origins, he incarnated the American dream. The America of 2009 was no longer that of John Wayne, but that of citizens of Korean or Indian origin. François Durpaire, the author of the 2007 book *Barack Obama's America* – a prophetic book that has influenced my ideas here – reminds us that Obama's mixed background reflected unfolding evolutions in American society more widely. Tiger Woods, the great golf champion, has a background that mixes white, black, Native American, and Asian. Christmas at the Obamas 'looked like the United Nations Assembly'. Maya, his Indonesian sister, might be mistaken for a Mexican, his brother-in-law and his niece are Chinese... But Obama didn't fall into the electoral trap of calling himself mixed race. Instead, he claimed himself as both totally white and totally black, a descendant of Kenya and a descendant of Kansas. He wasn't African American. He was African and American.

He wasn't so naïve as to advocate a 'colour blind' society, for it was the consciousness of being black that had led certain people to advance the cause of civil rights. Acknowledging colour makes it possible to measure the degree of integration in universities and companies. Martin Luther King knew that it was his struggle that had pushed President Lyndon Johnson to prioritize civil rights and to sign the 1964 Civil Rights Act that made all forms of discrimination illegal.

John McCain was decisively defeated in the presidential election on 4 November 2008 by 365 electoral college votes to 173. What King himself, or my mother Marianna for that matter, could never have imagined had happened: the United States had elected a black man to the presidency.

What then?

Obama arrived at a moment of deep crisis, not only economically but also morally. We are faced with an unacceptable level of inequality between peoples and with the destruction of the earth, which will soon 'no longer be able to endure us'.

Obama was conscious of all this. He entered into the struggle against the pollution of the planet. On 22 September 2009 he declared at the United Nations that future generations are heading towards an 'irreversible catastrophe' unless the international community acts 'boldly, swiftly, and together'; he worked for the elimination of nuclear weapons, began the withdrawal of US troops from Iraq, and sought solutions to the quagmire in Afghanistan.

He knew that he had to be both impatient and patient because the major companies didn't want to lose their profits. What was required was intellectual, social, and political courage. Real change requires genuine struggle. Obama insisted on this aspect of social change, particularly while he was working on the difficult reform of the health system in his country, where close to 50 million Americans didn't have access to healthcare.

Stéphane Hessel, a famous Resistance fighter, who helped to draft the 1948 Universal Declaration of Human Rights, once told me: 'We have to put people back at the heart of our politics, to accept the mixing of bodies, encounters, cultures, and religions [...] We need a new activism so that the twenty-first century fulfils the promises of the Rights of Man, of a just form of development, of sovereign states – promises that were made but not kept during the twentieth century. National interests are important, but if we continue to focus on them we'll spend our whole lives as firefighters.'

In an increasingly global context the interests of the entire human race are at stake, and that led to a new kind of ethical politics outlined by Obama. So it was that, in June 2009, he gave a speech in Egypt whose aim was to renew the dialogue between his country and the Muslim world. '[T]his cycle of suspicion and discord must end', he said after having saluted one and a half billion Muslims with these words: 'As-salamu alaykum' – 'May peace be upon you'.

For all these actions, and especially for his diplomacy, 'founded in the concept that those who are to lead the world must do so on the basis of values and attitudes that are shared by the majority of the world's population', he was awarded the Nobel Peace Prize on 9 October 2009, forty-six years after Martin Luther King. He was the third president of the United States to be awarded the prize while in office, after Theodore Roosevelt in 1906 and Woodrow Wilson in 1919.

Racism still exists in the United States, as Donald Trump's presidency has shown us. Obama himself was forced to confront it. T-shirts, photographs, and drawings represent him as a monkey eating a banana, decorated with a Hitler moustache, or repainting the White House in black; Silvio Berlusconi, then the Italian prime minister, joked on several occasions about Obama's 'tan'. But the progress of liberty cannot be held back forever, and Obama's presidency was a wonderful encouragement for the women and men who, throughout the world, were struggling against injustice. The road is still long because human equality is still a relatively new idea. The Declaration of the Rights of Man and the Citizen in 1789 and the Universal Declaration of Human Rights of 1948 were only concerned with the white man. Today, every human being demands the full application of these declarations.

No, this Map is not Upside Down

The maps that we usually use place Europe at the top and at the centre of the world. It looks larger than Latin America when in fact it is barely half its size: Europe is 9.7 million sq km whereas Latin America is 17.8 million sq km.

The map reproduced on the following pages questions our representations. In 1978 the Australian geographer Stuart McArthur placed his country high and in the centre of the world map, rather than low and to the side. The map was influenced by the work of the German Arno Peters, who in 1974 chose to respect the actual surface area of each continent. He showed, for instance, that Africa with its 30 million sq km is twice as large as Russia, with its 17.1 million sq km. But on traditional maps, it's quite the opposite.

Placing Europe at the top was a clever psychological move invented by those who believed they were higher up, in order to make others think they were lower down. It's like the story that Christopher Columbus 'discovered' America, or the classification of 'races' in the nineteenth century that put the white man at the top of the ladder and others below. On traditional maps, two-thirds of the surface is devoted to the 'North', a third to the 'South'. But in space there is neither South nor North. Putting the North at the top is an arbitrary practice, and we could easily to do the opposite.

Nothing is neutral when it comes to how we represent the world. When the South no longer sees itself as existing at the bottom, it will spell the end of such received ideas. It's all just a question of habit.

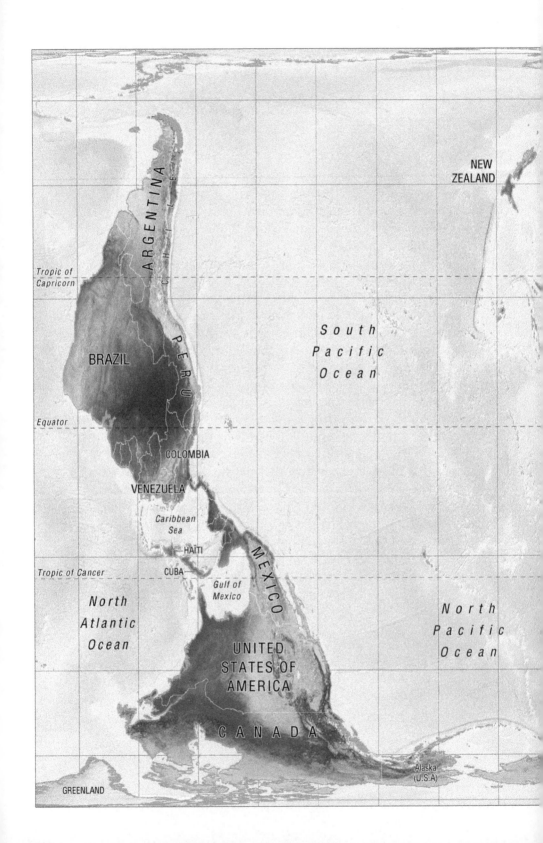

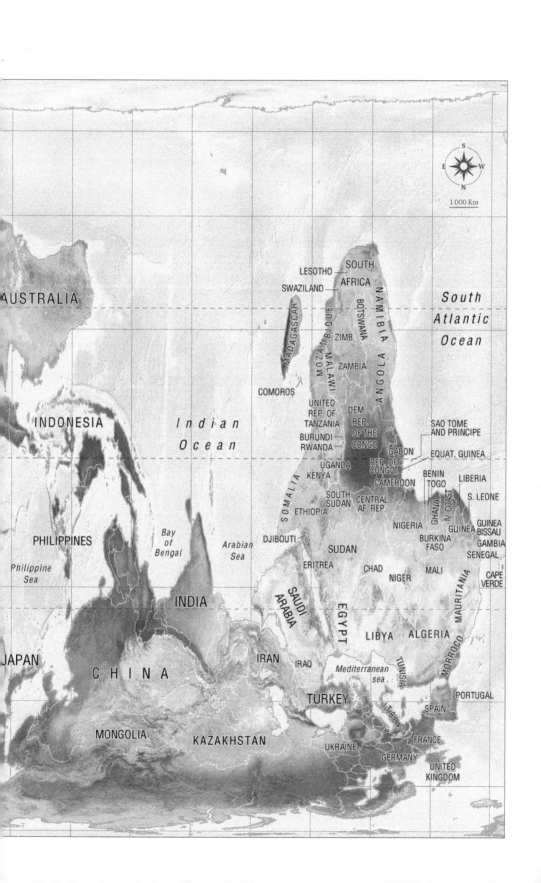

Words that Liberate the Future

A few years ago, a 13-year-old boy, Mathieu, came to my office. He had been expelled from several different schools and had spent twelve months in a boarding school with a reputation for dealing with 'problem' students. But nothing had managed to calm his violent tendencies or resolve his relationship problems. On the advice of a counsellor, his mother had agreed to take him for a psychiatric consultation with a paediatric specialist. In her view, Mathieu had always been unruly, but things got worse as adolescence began.

The child had grown up believing that his father had died when he was still a baby, though no one had told him how. The different versions he had heard hadn't allowed him to develop an idea of what his father was like. Around the age of 10, he became more aware of various contradictions, more aware of the inadvertent comments that suggested that his father was actually still alive and was in fact living not far from his house. He thus gradually came to understand that he had been abandoned by this man whom he imagined to be a monster.

Why had the family decided to keep the child in ignorance? To protect him from a difficult reality? Whatever the reason, he had more or less unconsciously experienced that which remained unspoken as the weight of a dreadful secret, creating a malaise that had found expression in his difficult behaviour.

To think that you are a child born from nothing, the child of God or the Devil, with all the dehumanization that this implies, makes it impossible to construct a sufficiently stable identity to enable you to face up to the world.

A few days ago, Lilian Thuram had me read his manuscript, *My Black Stars*. It seemed clear to me that a parallel can be made between children who don't know about their family origins and a people amputated from part of its history. There is the same need for recognition, the same more or less forceful demands, the same feeling of having been tricked or betrayed, which is linked to a similar risk of a retreat to an identity marked by the most reductive aspects of what one is (skin colour, gender, religious or philosophical beliefs...).

Malcolm X, Cassius X, and all those whom history forced to change their names remind me of these young patients born anonymously without any knowledge of their parents, for whom the impossibility of accessing even a tiny scrap of their history leaves them confused and unable to make sense of their lives.

What are the consequences when the truth about our origins is hidden from us?

The suffering is mostly related to our sense of identity.

Personal identity is built progressively in a complex process that brings together the feeling of being unique, that of belonging (to a family, group, or culture), and that of being worth something. These feelings develop in accordance with the child's experiences from a very young age, and they do so simultaneously in three areas: individual, group (family, friends, society), and cultural. These different contexts interact, and to be in harmony with oneself you have to feel both singular (different from others and with qualities that are unique to yourself) and recognized by others and accepted for these particularities, whether physical, behavioural, sexual. Liking the colour of your hair or eyes, knowing if you are a girl or a boy – these things contribute to the development of identity in the same way as being recognized as the son or daughter of your parents, perceived by others as being generous or bossy, loyal to certain values or considered a rebel. The knowledge of oneself, and appreciation of oneself – linked to the recognition of one's worth, in particular, to others – also help guarantee this equilibrium in one's identity.

Two complementary processes contribute to this: a mechanism of identifying with others and a mechanism of distinguishing oneself from them. Parents are the main pillars of this phenomenon of identification and rejection, then our ancestors (such as grandparents, known to us or about whom he have heard), close friends, and then social relationships (friends, enemies). Idols, heroes from the stories we hear as children, like the historical figures whose exploits or errors we learn about, also contribute to the creation of a pantheon that is both personal and passed on from those around us.

When one of the pillars of identity is missing, or the foundations are undermined by silence, the entire structure is weakened.

The same is true of any human society, which, like a child, needs to know who its ancestors are in order to develop an identity that is balanced and stable, that is in harmony with itself or, more precisely, with each part of itself. The stakes surrounding this knowledge are not just cultural or intellectual, but also psychological and educational. For such knowledge makes it possible to evolve calmly, to avoid a withdrawal into a closed identity that only draws on certain aspects of those who make up society. These aspects, which are presented as being characteristic – though they are often caricatural – encourage organization along ethnic, religious, or doctrinal lines and can lead to extremist positions.

This book reminds us about the men and women who have contributed to the history of humanity, but who have been forgotten by some or excluded from textbooks. It therefore restores a part of the collective memory of our society. I dare to hope that this necessary work of recognition, like that pursued in therapy, will contribute to the blossoming of our society.

In Mathieu's story it wasn't the absence of the father that was the cause of the difficulty, but the silence, the closing off of his access to his name and his personhood. No matter whether this man was good or bad, the silence prevented the child from identifying with him or distinguishing himself from him.

When I spoke to the mother she initially found it difficult to talk about the father of her child, who had shown himself incapable of taking on the responsibilities of a parent. This was due to the rancour she felt towards a man who had abandoned her while she was nursing an infant. But the memory of their first encounters were not buried that deeply. She recalled something of the man she had loved, what she had liked about him, and she sometimes saw it reflected in her son. She remembered the passion of the loving embrace of which Mathieu was the fruit. In the end, Mathieu was able to hear about that too.

A few weeks ago, I learned that Mathieu had met his father: they had nothing to say to one another and they didn't see each other again. But that vital encounter probably helped him to turn a corner, which might enable him to become a father in his turn.

Societies, too, have to face up to their history in order to move from ignorance to humanism, and to evolve harmoniously.

Dr Gilles-Marie Valet
Psychiatrist for Children and Adolescents

Bibliography

Abdelouahab, Farid, and Pascal Blanchard (eds), *Grand-Ouest: Mémoire des outre- mers*, Presses universitaires de Rennes, 2008.

Abu-Jamal, Mumia, *Live From Death Row*, Avon Books, 1995.

Abu-Jamal, Mumia, *Une Vie dans le parti des Black Panthers*, Le temps des cerises, 2006.

Adélaïde-Merlande, Jacques, *Delgrès ou la Guadeloupe en 1802*, Karthala, 1986.

Adélaïde-Merlande, Jacques, René Bélénus, and Frédéric Régent, *La Rébellion de la Guadeloupe 1801–1802*, Gourbeyre, 2002.

'Aimé Césaire refuse de recevoir Nicolas Sarkozy', *Le Monde*, 12 June 2005.

Antoine, Yves, *Inventeurs et Savants noirs*, L'Harmattan, 1998.

Bâ, Amadou Hampâté, *Amkoullel, l'enfant peul. Mémoires I*, Actes Sud, 1991.

Bâ, Amadou Hampâté, *Oui mon commandant! Mémoires II*, Actes Sud, 1994.

Bâ, Amadou Hampâté, *Contes initiatiques peuls*, Stock, 1994.

Bancel, Nicolas, Pascal Blanchard, Ahmed Boubeker, and Éric Deroo, (eds), *Frontière d'empire, du Nord à l'Est. Soldats coloniaux et immigrations des Suds*, La Découverte, 2008.

Bancel, Nicolas, et al. (eds), *Human Zoos: Science and Spectacle in the Age of Empire*, Liverpool University Press, 2002.

Bernal, Martin, *Black Athena: The Afro-Asiatic Roots of Classical Civilization*, Vintage, 1991.

Berthès, Colette, and Bernard Fillaire, *La Machine à tuer*, Les Arènes, 2000.

Béthune, Christian, *Le Rap, une esthétique hors la loi*, Autrement, 2003.

Beti, Mongo, *Main basse sur le Cameroun, autopsie d'une décolonisation*, Maspero, 1972.

Beti, Mongo, *La France contre l'Afrique. Retour au Cameroun*, La Découverte, 1993.

Beti, Mongo, and Odile Tobner, *Dictionnaire de la négritude*, L'Harmattan, 1989.

Blanchard, Pascal, Gilles Manceron, and Éric Deroo, *Le Paris noir*, Hazan, 2001.

Bonnet, Charles, and Dominique Valbelle, *Des Pharaons venus d'Afrique*, Citadelles & Mazenod, 2005.

Braeckman, Colette, *Lumumba, un crime d'État*, Aden, 2009.

Braflan-Trobo, Patricia, *Société post-esclavagiste et management endogène. Le cas de la Guadeloupe*, L'Harmattan, 2009.

Bretagne, Jean-Marie, *Battling Siki*, Philippe Rey, 2008.

Breton, André, *Martinique, charmeuse de serpents*, Pauvert, 1972.

Bulhan, Hussein Abdilahi, *Frantz Fanon and the Psychology of Oppression*, Plenum Press, 1985.

Cachin, Olivier, *Cent albums essentiels du rap*, Scali, 2006.

Césaire, Aimé, *Toussaint-Louverture. La Révolution française et le problème colonial*, Présence africaine, 1962.

Césaire, Aimé, *Non-Vicious Circle: Twenty Poems of Aimé Césaire*, trans. Gregson Davis, Stanford University Press, 1984.

Césaire, Aimé, 'What is Negritude to Me?', trans. Shawna Moore, in *African Presence in the Americas*, ed. Carlos Moore, Tanya R. Saunders, and Shawna Moore, Africa World Press, 1995.

Césaire, Aimé, *Discourse on Colonialism*, trans. Joan Pinkham, ed. Robin D. G. Kelly, Monthly Review Press, 2000; Présence africaine, 1955.

Césaire, Aimé, *Une Saison au Congo*, 'Points', 2001; Seuil, 1966.

Césaire, Aimé, *Nègre je suis, nègre je resterai* (interviews with Françoise Vergès), Albin Michel, 2005.

Césaire, Aimé, 'Négreries: Black Youth and Assimilation', trans. Dale Tomich, in *Black, Brown, and Beige: Surrealist Writings from Africa and the Diaspora*, ed. Franklin Rosemont and Robin D. G. Kelley, University of Texas Press, 2009.

Césaire, Aimé, 'Letter to Maurice Thorez', trans. Chike Jeffers, *Social Text*, 28.2 103 (2010): 145–52.

Césaire, Aimé, *The Original 1939 Notebook of a Return to the Native Land: Bilingual Edition*, trans. and ed. A. James Arnold and Clayton Eshleman, Wesleyan University Press, 2013.

Ceyrat, Antony, *Jamaïque. La Construction de l'identité noire depuis l'indépendance*, L'Harmattan, 2009.

Cherki, Alice, *Frantz Fanon, portrait*, Seuil, 2000.

Christy, Cuthbert, 'Liberia in 1930'. *The Geographical Journal*, 77.6 (June 1931).

Clark, Kenneth Bancroft, *The Negro Protest: James Baldwin, Malcolm X, Martin Luther King Talk with Kenneth B. Clark*, Beacon Press, 1963.

Coghlan, Benjamin, et al., *Mortality in the Democratic Republic of Congo: An Ongoing Crisis*, International Rescue Committee, 2007.

Condé, Maryse, *La Civilisation du bossale*, L'Harmattan, 1978.

Condé, Maryse, *An tan revolisyon*, Conseil régional de Guadeloupe, 1989.

Cone, James H., *Martin and Malcolm and America: A Dream or a Nightmare*, Orbis Books, 1992.

Conrad, Joseph. 'Geography and Some Explorers, 1924', in *The Cambridge Edition of the Works of Joseph Conrad: Last Essays*, vol. 7, ed. Harold Ray Stevens and J. H. Stape, Cambridge University Press, 2010.

Coppens, Yves, *Le Genou de Lucy*, Odile Jacob, 1999.

Coppens, Yves, Hubert Reeves, Joël de Rosnay, and Dominique Simonnet, *La Plus Belle Histoire du monde*, Seuil, 1996.

Cordier, Daniel, *Jean Moulin*. Vol. 2, *Le Choix d'un destin*, Lattès, 1989.

Cornelius, Steven H., *Music of the Civil War Era*, Greenwood, 2004.

Coubertin, Pierre de, 'France on the Wrong Track', *American Monthly Review of Reviews*, 23.4 (1901).

Damas, Léon-Gontran, *Pigments*, Présence africaine, 1962; Guy Lévy Mano, 1937.

Damas, Léon-Gontran, 'Whitewash' and 'Hiccups', in *The Negritude Poets: An Anthology of Translations from the French*, trans. and ed. Ellen Conroy Kennedy, Thunder's Mouth Press, 1989.

Damis, Christine, 'Le philosophe connu pour sa peau noire: Anton Wilhelm Amo', *Rue Descartes*, 36, 2002.

Davidson, Basil, *L'Afrique avant les Blancs*, PUF, 1962.

Davis, John H., *What Do White Americans Want to Know About Black Americans but Are Afraid to Ask*, Xlibris, 2007.

De Witte, Ludo, *L'Assassinat de Lumumba*, Karthala, 2000.

Degras, Jean-Claude, *Mortenol, le capitaine des vents*, New Legend, 2004.

Diarra, Cheick Modibo, *Navigateur interplanétaire*, Albin Michel, 2000.

Dibwe, Mutamba, et al., *Rapport 2009 du sénat sur le secteur minier*, Sénat Commission d'Enquête Secteur Minier, Kinshasa, 24 September 2009.

Diop, Boubacar Boris, *L'Afrique au-delà du miroir*, Philippe Rey, 2007.

Diop, Cheikh Anta, *Nations nègres et culture*, Présence africaine, 1954.

Diop, Cheikh Anta, *Civilisation ou barbarie*, Présence africaine, 1981.

Diop-Maes, Louise-Marie, *Afrique noire, démographie, sol et histoire*, Présence africaine, 1996.

Dorigny, Marcel, and Max-Jean Zins (eds), *Les Traites négrières coloniales. Histoire d'un crime*, Cercle d'Art, 2009.

Dubois, Laurent, *Les Vengeurs du Nouveau Monde. Histoire de la révolution haïtienne*, Les Perséides, 2005.

Durpaire, François, and Olivier Richomme, *L'Amérique de Barack Obama*, Demopolis, 2007.

Duval, Eugène-Jean, and Maurice Rives, *Pour une parcelle de gloire oubliée. Les tirailleurs sénégalais pendant les conflits du xxe siècle*, brochure deposited in BNF in 2006.

Equiano, Olaudah, *Ma véridique histoire*, Mercure de France, 2008.

Fabre, Michel, *Esclaves et Planteurs*, Julliard, 1970.

Fabre, Michel, *The Unfinished Quest of Richard Wright*, University of Illinois Press, 1993.

Fanon, Frantz, *Les Damnés de la terre*, Maspero, 1961.

Fanon, Frantz, *Black Skin, White Masks*, trans. Richard Philcox, Grove Press, 2007.

Farraudière, Sylvère, *L'École aux Antilles, Le rendez-vous manqué de la démocratie*, L'Harmattan, 2008.

Firmin, Anténor, *The Equality of the Human Races*, trans. Asselin Charles, University of Illinois Press, 2002.

Fisher-Blanchet, Inez, *Capitaine de vaisseau Mortenol: croisières et campagnes de guerre, 1882–1915*, L'Harmattan, 2001.

Fofana, Aboubakar (calligraphies), and Youssouf Tata Cissé (trans.), *La Charte du Mandé et autres traditions du Mali*, Albin Michel, 2003.

Galeano, Eduardo, *Upside Down: A Primer for the Looking-Glass World*, trans. Mark Fried, Metropolitan Books, 2000.

Gandhi, Mohandas, *Gandhi: Selected Writings*, ed. Ronald Duncan, Dover, 2005.

Garvey, Marcus, *Selected Writings and Speeches by Marcus Garvey*, ed. Bob Blaisdell, Dover, 2004.

Gassama, Mahkily (ed.), *L'Afrique répond à Sarkozy. Contre le discours de Dakar*, Philippe Rey, 2008.

Gautier, Arlette, *Les Sœurs de Solitude, la condition féminine dans l'esclavage aux Antilles du xviie au xixe siècle*, L'Harmattan, 1985.

Gendzier, Irène, *Frantz Fanon*, Seuil, 1973.

Gnammankou, Dieudonné, *Abraham Hanibal, l'aïeul noir de Pouchkine*, Présence africaine, 1998.

Gnammankou, Dieudonné, *Pouchkine et le Monde noir*, Présence africaine, 1999.

Gnammankou, Dieudonné, and Yao Modzinou (eds), *Les Africains et leurs descendants en Europe avant le xxe siècle*, MAT, 2006.

Goldman, Peter Louis, *The Death and Life of Malcolm X*, 2nd edn, University of Illinois Press, 1979.

Gould, Stephen Jay, *La Malmesure de l'homme*, Ramsay, 1983.

Grégoire, Abbé, *De la littérature des nègres, ou Recherches sur leurs facultés intellectuelles, leurs qualités morales et leur littérature*, Maradan, 1808.

Hale, Thomas Albert, 'Les écrits d'Aimé Césaire: Bibliographie commentée', *Études françaises*, 13–14, 1978.

Haley, Alex, *Racines*, J'ai lu, 1976.

Hauser, Thomas, *Muhammad Ali: His Life and Times*, Simon and Schuster, 1992.

Hector, Michel, and Marcel Dorigny (eds), 'Hommage à Gérard Barthélemy, un ami d'Haïti', *Revue de la société haïtienne d'histoire et de géographie*, 236 (2009).

Hochschild, Adam, *King Leopold's Ghost: A Story of Greed, Terror, and Heroism in Colonial Africa*, Houghton Mifflin, 1999.

Holiday, Billie, and William Dufty, *Lady Sings the Blues: The Searing Autobiography of an American Music Legend*. Penguin, 1984 (1956).

Hopquin, Benoît, *Ces Noirs qui ont fait la France*, Calmann-Lévy, 2009.

Jenson, Deborah, *Beyond the Slave Narrative: Politics, Sex and Manuscripts in the Haitian Revolution*, Liverpool University Press, 2011.

Jérémie, Joseph, *Haïti et Chicago, de Saint-Marc à Saint-Charles, Missouri*, Henri Deschamps, 1950.

Kesteloot, Lilyan, *Black Writers in French: A Literary History of Negritude*, trans. Ellen C. Kennedy, Temple University Press, 1974.

Kesteloot, Lilyan, *Histoire de la littérature négro-africaine*, Karthala, 2001.

Ki-Zerbo, Joseph, *Repères pour l'Afrique*, Panafrika/Silex/Nouvelles du Sud, 2007.

Ki-Zerbo, Joseph, and Djibril Tamsir Niane, *Histoire générale de l'Afrique*, vol. IV, Présence africaine/Edicef/Unesco, 1991.

Koechlin, Stephane, *Jazz Ladies*, Hors Collection, 2006.

Kom, Ambroise, *Mongo Beti parle*, Homnisphères, 2006.

Langaney, André, Ninian Hubert Van Blijenburgh, and Alicia Sanchez-Mazas, *Tous parents, tous différents*, Muséum national d'histoire naturelle, 1995.

Lara, Oruno D., *Mortenol ou les infortunés de la servitude*, L'Harmattan, 2001.

Louis, Patrice, *A, B, C... ésaire: Aimé Césaire de A à Z*, Ibis Rouge, 2003.

Lumumba, Patrice, 'Speech at the Ceremony of the Proclamation of the Congo's Independence', 30 June 1960', in *Patrice Lumumba, The Truth about a Monstrous Crime of the Colonialists*, Foreign Languages Publishing House, 1961.

Luther King, Jr, Martin, 'I Have a Dream' (speech, Washington, DC, 28 August 1963), US National Archives and Records Administration.

Luther King, Jr, Martin, *The Autobiography of Martin Luther King, Jr.*, ed. Clayborne Carson, Abacus, 2000.

Luther King, Jr, Martin, *The Papers of Martin Luther King, Jr: Volume V: Threshold of a New Decade: January 1959–December 1960*, University of California Press, 2005.

Macey, David, *Frantz Fanon: A Biography*, 2nd edn, Verso, 2012.

Malaurie, Jean, *Ultima Thulé*, Bordas, 1990.

Malcolm X, *Le Pouvoir noir*, La Découverte, 1965.

Malcolm X, *Malcolm X Speaks: Selected Speeches and Statements*, ed. George Breitman, Grove Press, 1965.

Malcolm X, *By Any Means Necessary*, ed. George Breitman, 2nd edn, Pathfinder Press, 1992.

Malcolm X and Alex Haley, *The Autobiography of Malcolm X: As Told to Alex Haley*, Ballantine Books, 1992.

Mandela, Nelson, *L'Apartheid*, Minuit, 1985 (1965).

Mandela, Nelson, *Un long chemin vers la liberté*, Fayard, 1995.

Maran, René, *Batouala*, trans. Adele Szold Seltzer, Thomas Seltzer, 1922.

Margolick, David, *Strange Fruit*, Allia, 2009.

Mason, Jr, Julian D., *The Poems of Phillis Wheatley*, 1966.

Michel, Marc, *Les Africains et la Grande Guerre. L'appel à l'Afrique (1914–1918)*, Karthala, 2003.

Moulin, Jean, *Premier Combat*, Minuit, 1965.

Muhammad, Elijah, *Message to the Blackman in America*, Secretarius MEMPS Ministries, 2009 (1973).

Niang, Mangoné, *La Charte du Kurkan Fuga. Aux sources d'une pensée politique en Afrique*, L'Harmattan, 2008.

Noël, Erick, *Être noir en France au XVIIIe siècle*, Tallandier, 2006.

Obama, Barack, *Dreams from My Father*, Canongate, 2016.

Obenga, Théophile, *L'Égypte, la Grèce et l'école d'Alexandrie. Histoire interculturelle dans l'Antiquité, aux sources égyptiennes de la philosophie grecque*, L'Harmattan, 2005.

Onana, Charles, *La France et ses tirailleurs*, Duboiris, 2003.

Parks, Rosa, and Jim Haskins, *Rosa Parks: My Story*, Dial Books, 1992.

Pastoureau, Michel, *Noir, histoire d'une couleur*, Seuil, 2008.

Peary, Robert E., *The North Pole, its Discovery in 1909 Under the Auspices of the Peary Arctic Club*, Frederick A. Stokes, 1910.

Philonenko, Alexis, *Histoire de la boxe*, Bartillat, 2002.

Pushkin, Alexander, *Eugene Onegin: A Novel in Verse*, trans. James E. Falen, Southern Illinois University Press, 1990.

Pushkin, Alexander, *The Complete Works of Alexander Pushkin: Lyric Poems: 1813–1820*, Milner, 2003.

Reynaud Paligot, Carole, *La République raciale, 1860–1930*, PUF, 2006.

Rives, Maurice, and Robert Dietrich, *Héros oubliés*, Frères d'armes, 1993.

Ross, Suzanne, 'A Brief History/Herstory to Free Mumia', in *Let Freedom Ring: A Collection of Documents from the Movements to Free U.S. Political Prisoners*, ed. Matt Meyer, Kersplebedeb, 2008.

Sala-Molins, Louis, *Le Code Noir ou le calvaire de Canaan*, PUF, 1987.

Salley, Columbus, 'Malcolm X, 1925–1965', in *The Black 100: A Ranking of the Most Influential African Americans, Past and Present*, Kensington Publishing, 1998.

Sartre, Jean-Paul, 'Black Orpheus', trans. John MacCombie, *The Massachusetts Review*, 6.1 (1964–65).

Schoelcher, Victor, *Esclavage et Colonisation* (introduction by Aimé Césaire), PUF, 1948.

Schoelcher, Victor, *Vie de Toussaint-Louverture*, Karthala, 1982.

Schwarz-Bart, André, *La Mulâtresse Solitude*, Seuil, 1972.

Senghor, Léopold Sédar, *Anthologie de la nouvelle poésie nègre et malgache de langue française*, précédé d'*Orphée noir*, PUF, 1948.

Serbin, Sylvia, *Reines d'Afrique et Héroïnes de la diaspora noire*, Sépia, 2006.

Simard, Éric, *Rosa Parks, la femme qui a changé l'Amérique*, Oskar, 2007.

Skouma, Freddy Saïd, *Le Corps du boxeur*, Pauvert, 2001.

Smeralda, Juliette, *Peau noire, cheveu crépu. L'histoire d'une aliénation*, Jasor, 2005.

Soudan, Royaumes sur le Nil, Flammarion, 1997.

Stiglitz, Joseph, *Globalization and its Discontents*, Norton, 2002.

Sullivan, Otha Richard, *African American Inventors*, John Wiley & Sons, 1998.

Sullivan, Otha Richard, *African American Women Scientists and Inventors*, John Wiley & Sons, 2001.

Taube, Michel, *L'Amérique qui tue. La peine de mort aux USA*, Michel Lafon, 2001.

Thuram, Lilian, *8 juillet 1998*, Anne Carrière, 2004.

Tobner, Odile, 'Espoir d'embellies', *Billets d'Afrique et d'ailleurs*, 166 (1 February 2008).

Toumson, Roger, and Simonne Henry-Valmore, *Aimé Césaire, le Nègre inconsolé*, Vent d'ailleurs, 2002.

Wallace, George C. 'The Inaugural Address of Governor George C. Wallace' (Montgomery, AL, 14 January 1963), Alabama Department of Archives & History.

Wright, Richard, *Un enfant du pays*, Gallimard, 1940.

Wright, Richard, *Black Boy*, Gallimard, 1945.

Wright, Richard, *Haiku: The Last Poems of an American Icon*, Arcade, 1998.

Wright, Roberta Hughes, *The Birth of the Montgomery Bus Boycott*, Charro Press, 1991.